Offending Identities
Sex offenders' perspectives of their treatment and management

Kirsty Hudson

WILLAN
PUBLISHING

Published by

Willan Publishing
Culmcott House
Mill Street, Uffculme
Cullompton, Devon
EX15 3AT, UK
Tel: +44(0)1884 840337
Fax: +44(0)1884 840251
e-mail: info@willanpublishing.co.uk
website: www.willanpublishing.co.uk

Published simultaneously in the USA and Canada by

Willan Publishing
c/o ISBS, 920 NE 58th Ave, Suite 300,
Portland, Oregon 97213-3786, USA
Tel: +001(0)503 287 3093
Fax: +001(0)503 280 8832
e-mail: info@isbs.com
website: www.isbs.com

ISBN 1-84392-115-4

British Library Cataloguing-in-Publication Data

A catalogue record for this book is available from the British Library

Project managed by Deer Park Productions, Tavistock, Devon
Typeset by TW Typesetting, Plymouth, Devon
Printed and bound by TJ International Ltd, Trecerus Industrial Estate, Padstow, Cornwall

Contents

Tables and extracts

Tables

Extracts

Acknowledgments

I wish to thank all the people who have provided guidance and support, both intellectual and emotional, from the start to finish of this book. Thanks must also go to the staff of the various prisons and probation services whose help was invaluable, and also to the National Society for the Prevention of Cruelty to Children (NSPCC). Particular thanks must go to the men who participated in the research, without whom this book could not have been completed.

Chapter 1

Introduction

Sexual abuse, and in particular sexual crimes perpetrated against women and children, has become widely acknowledged as a social problem in the United Kingdom. While it is important to acknowledge that sexual crimes are among the most under-reported (Grubin 1998; Scarce 2001; Myhill and Allen 2002; Fisher and Beech 2004; Walby and Allen 2004), they accounted for only 5 per cent of police recorded violent crime, and 0.9 per cent of all police recorded crime in 2003/04. In addition, research evidence generally reports lower reconviction rates for sexual offenders than for perpetrators of more routine crimes, such as theft and burglary (Hanson and Bussiere 1998). A study conducted by Hood *et al.* (2002) found that under 10 per cent of sex offenders were convicted of another sexual offence within six years. Nonetheless, public concern with the risks posed by sexual offenders is undisputed.

The public's highly emotive response to sexual offending has clearly been fuelled by media representations of sex crime and, in particular, the newsworthy value of the worst cases. The image of the sex offender that looms large in the press is that of an amoral, manipulative, predatory sociopath who preys on those persons in society, women and children in particular, who are considered most vulnerable (Greer 2003). Such powerful imagery succeeds in creating the inaccurate and misleading impression that sex offenders are somehow inherently different from the rest of society and are in need of treatment and management different from other types of offenders. This has led to growing pressure on the criminal justice system to protect communities from sexual offenders in their areas.

Current legislative responses have resulted in an increase in the number of sexual offenders receiving custodial sentences and for longer periods of time. However, the public's demand for draconian sentences is coupled with the expectation that something will be done to reduce the risk of future sexual offending. In the light of this, since the late 1980s there has been increasing recognition of the potential of reducing re-offending through treatment programmes. At the same time, in contrast to earlier more optimistic penal philosophies, where treatment programmes are undertaken they are no longer expected to 'cure' sex offenders but rather to help offenders control their behaviour in order to minimize the risk of them re-offending. To this end, stringent measures designed both to control and monitor sexual offenders in the community have also been introduced over the same period.

While a considerable amount of research and writing has been devoted to the treatment and management of sex offenders, one perspective notable by its virtual absence has been that of the offenders themselves. This book aims to fill that gap by exploring sex offenders' perspectives of initiatives designed both to control and manage their risk of re-offending. I followed and interviewed 32 male sex offenders between 2001 and 2003 over the course of their participation in a number of prison-based and community-based treatment programmes. Each participant was about to start one of three sex offender treatment programmes, namely the prison-based Sex Offender Treatment Programme (SOTP) and the Behaviour Assessment Programme (BAP), and the probation-led Community Sex Offender Groupwork Programme (C-SOGP).

While the book focuses on adult male sex offenders it is important to note that a third of all reported sexual offences are committed by the under-18 age group (see Richardson *et al.* 1997; Grubin 1998; Masson 2004 for a summary). Female sex offenders also make up approximately 0.5 per cent of all sex offenders in prison (28 females compared to 5,550 male sentenced prisoners in November 2003),[1] although the actual number of female offenders is considered to be much higher (Fergusson and Mullen 1999). Arguably, the true extent of female offending is difficult to determine given that in Western societies women are 'permitted greater freedom than men in their physical interactions with children' (Grubin 1998: 23). It is also perhaps too disconcerting to think that either women or children (precisely those members of society who are thought to be in need of protection from sexual abuse) are capable of committing such acts (Crawford and Conn 1997; Hetherton 1999; Kemshall 2004).

It should also be acknowledged that despite the growing preoccupation with the 'predatory paedophile' and 'stranger danger', sexual offending is not a homogenous act. There is of course a wide array of sexual offences ranging from what is commonly regarded as the less serious end of sexual offending, for example exposure, through to sexual murder (Fisher and Beech 2004). The men who participated in this research had committed the following types of crimes.

Child abuse

The majority (n = 22) of the men participating in this research had committed child abuse. Their offending behaviour ranged from non-contact offences to serious penetrative offences. Only one of these men had abused a child that was unknown to him.

Rape

Eight of the men who agreed to take part in this research had committed rape. Rape is defined here as a penetrative sexual act on an adult. Four of these men had raped a stranger; this applies to cases where the perpetrator had no contact with the victim prior to the abuse.

Sexual murder

Although there is no offence of sexual murder in the British legal system, offenders convicted of murder or manslaughter can participate in sex offender treatment programmes if there is an apparent or admitted sexual element to the crime (Fisher and Beech 2004). One participant had been convicted of murdering his victim. Although he was never charged with a sexual offence, forensic evidence suggested the possibility of a sexual assault. These details included a single matching pubic hair on the victim's cardigan, the fact that the victim's bra was ripped, and that her top was pulled over her head.

Internet offences

Finally, one research participant had been convicted of an internet offence. This involved downloading child pornography from the internet.

Table 1.1 presents a more detailed summary of the research participants' current offences, including information regarding their victims' sex and relationship to the perpetrator. Four categories have been used to describe each victim's relationship to the participant. The definition used to categorize offences committed against 'strangers' covers instances where the suspect had had no contact with the complainant prior to the abuse. 'Acquaintance' refers to cases where the victim was known to the participant. This might also include instances where the victim was 'groomed' over a period of time. The 'relation' category includes instances where the victim is a member of the participant's extended family. This includes stepchildren as well as nieces and nephews. Finally, the 'known' category includes cases where the offender abused multiple victims, where some of his victims were relatives and others were acquaintances.

Table 1.1 Research participants' profile

| Offence type | (n) | No. of victims | | | Victim information | | | | | | | | |
| | | | | | Sex of victims | | | | Relationship to victim | | | | |
		Single	Multiple	Information unavailable	Male	Female	Both	Information unavailable	Relation	Acquaintance	'Known'	Stranger	Information unavailable
Child abuse	22	13	9	—	5	14	3	—	8	11	2	1	—
Rape	8	7	1	—	3	5	—	—	1	3	—	4	—
Sexual murder	1	1	—	—	—	1	—	—	—	—	—	1	—
Internet offence	1	—	—	1	—	—	—	1	—	—	—	—	1
Total	**32**	**21**	**10**	**1**	**8**	**20**	**3**	**1**	**9**	**14**	**2**	**6**	**1**

As can be seen from the men participating in this research, sex offenders are not a homogenous group. These men also present different patterns of behaviour, different motivations for their behaviour and different levels of need. In addition, just as there are different types of sexual offences, men who commit such crimes have varying personalities and identities. This book is therefore interested in how the highly emotive and punitive social climate that surrounds the issue of sexual crime affects a sex offender's presentation of himself, and ultimately his ability to self-manage his risk of re-offending.

The structure of the book

The book is divided into three main parts. The first provides an overview of the measures in place both to manage and to treat sex offenders. Chapter 2 outlines the legislative response to sexual offending in England and Wales over the last two decades. In so doing, it outlines the continual trend of bifurcation and in particular the increasing, and overtly punitive, measures taken against sex offenders in sentencing. The chapter also starts to explain the current moral panic and obsession with sexual offenders by raising questions relating to the underlying debates that have shaped the new culture of crime control (Garland 2001).

Chapter 3 examines the role that rehabilitation plays in contemporary criminal justice policy. In particular, the chapter focuses on the new management styles and working practices that have been increasingly implemented in rehabilitative intervention with all offenders. The chapter then describes the current situation regarding sex offender treatment provision in prison and community settings. In doing so, it provides a brief overview of the three sex offender treatment programmes used in this research. Each programme is described in terms of eligibility criteria, programme content and style of delivery.

Part II provides an empirical account of the participants' perceptions of how they are 'treated' and 'managed'. Chapter 4 begins by exploring the participants' views of the ways in which the public perceive and react to sexual offending. Of special importance here is the effect that this has on the way they manage their identity. Drawing on Goffman's (1963) notion of impression management, the chapter explores how individuals with a conviction for a sexual offence construct their identity by differentiating themselves from negative attributes typically associated with sex offenders. In doing so, the chapter presents the subjective accounts of three groups of participants, who have been labelled as 'total deniers', 'justifiers' and 'acceptors', in order to highlight similarities and differences in the way they attempt to preserve a more acceptable image, unencumbered by the popular image of the sex offender.

Chapter 5 explores participants' decisions to start and complete treatment and the extent to which this is indicative of their state of denial. Consequently, the chapter concentrates on how personal, legal and temporal pressures might influence an individual's decision to take part in treatment. The chapter also goes some way in exploring the reasons given by participants for failing to complete their respective treatment programme, and the implications for their risk of future offending. This chapter is concerned with the participants who failed to complete treatment for reasons other than re-offending.

The next three chapters explore the participants' views regarding their involvement in treatment. Chapter 6 is divided into two main sections. The first explores the participants' perceptions of the group-work approach to treatment. In particular, it examines the relationship between the research participants, other group members, and the programme facilitators. In doing so, it examines the extent to which the group environment is conducive to the development of attitudinal and behavioural change. Following on from this, the second section explores whether the participants felt pressured to conform to the theories used within treatment to rationalize sexually abusive behaviour. This section traces the tensions and contradictions between programme content and the participants' construction of identity.

Chapter 7 then explores the participants' accounts of 'what works' in treatment, taking into consideration both the legal and formal obligations entailed in participating in treatment, and the demands of a process that is designed to reduce a person's offending. Within this context, the chapter examines how effective the main areas addressed in sex offender treatment programmes are at providing group members with the necessary skills to minimize their risk of future offending.

Chapter 8 traces the experiences of the two men taking part in this study who re-offended while participating in treatment. It begins by exploring the extent to which they felt they had benefited from treatment intervention. It also explores their fears of disclosing their risk of offending within a group setting. Having touched on this question in Chapter 6, Chapter 8 considers more fully the implications of conducting treatment in a group environment. In particular, the chapter explores the participants' desire to maintain an identity that is upheld and accepted by the group. To this end, the rest of this chapter explores all the participants' views on the measures designed to manage their risk of future offending in the community. Particular attention is paid to the sex offender register and the issue of full public access to the information contained in the register, in the light of the ability of such measures to prevent re-offending.

Finally, Part III sets out the conclusions of the book and offers some tentative suggestions on how best to deal with the threat posed by sexual offenders.

Lasting impressions

Scully (1990), in her study on convicted rapists, reported that curiosity about why and how her research was done was often greater than interest in the findings. Consequently, she was continually asked the same two questions whenever she presented her work: 'What motivated [her] to undertake the project, and what kind of experience was it for [her], a women, to be confined daily in prisons talking face to face with men convicted of rape, murder, and assorted other crimes against women' (Scully 1990: 1). Similar questions were repeatedly asked during this research study.

A quick answer to the first question is that as researchers we are similarly affected by moral panics. Thus, the main motivation for conducting this research was to determine how best to deal with sexual offenders in order to prevent future victimization. However, perhaps the most important thing I have learnt from conducting this study is that being a researcher does not provide you with any immunity from the intensely emotional issues that arise from research of this kind.

One of the biggest problems that I had to deal with was *my* need to justify repeatedly the reasons for undertaking this research. Returning to that first question then: What motivated me to undertake this study? I interpreted this question as a signal of disapproval and/or disbelief that someone would choose to sit in a room and talk face to face with convicted sex offenders. This feeling was accentuated by the fact that I came to like some of the men who participated in the research. On the one hand I could justify this safe in the knowledge that these men had multiple identities (see Chapter 4), and hence it was possible to like them while simultaneously maintaining a strong repulsion for what they had done in the past. But on the other hand it was hard to hold on to this balance when the popular view is to reject everything about them.

Another key problem was how to cope with listening to the participants' accounts of their offences repeatedly over the course of the research. The majority of participants were interviewed at three different stages of their treatment: before the treatment began, during the course of treatment and after the treatment programme had been completed. I felt that the best way to manage the emotional burden of their stories was to block it out when not engaged in this research. However, by not sharing how I felt about these accounts with others, my own thoughts and feelings were allowed to mount. Eventually this became too much to deal with alone. This caused great anxiety for myself, often resulting in emotional outbursts. On such occasions there was usually a trigger incident. For example, after conducting an entire week of interviews with participants attending the SOTP I found myself in a shopping centre crying. In front of me were two children of a similar age to one of the participants' victims. In his interview the participant had been both flippant and meticulous in the way he spoke about and described what he did to his victims. However, while the children I saw in the shopping centre reminded me of his victims, they were simply the catalyst for releasing the emotions that I had hidden away.

I also became aware of how the accounts that I had heard affected the way I perceived others and certain situations. For example, one of the participants had been a bus driver. He was convicted of murdering a woman who boarded his bus after it was no longer in public use. Over a year later I found myself aboard a bus in a location that I was unfamiliar with. I had asked the bus driver to tell me where to get off. Over the course of 20 minutes the bus gradually emptied of passengers until the point where I was alone on the bus with the driver. Immediately, my anxiety of the situation was heightened, made worse by my recollection of what I had been told in the interview with my participant. Although many people probably feel a little anxious about being alone on a bus, I became extremely frightened. As it turned out the bus driver had forgotten to remind me where to get off and promptly drove me to my required stop.

In some respects this particular example reflects a growing cynicism I have developed with regard to other peoples' sexual and sensual actions. In other words, I have begun to question the motives behind these actions. This can occur when I have physical (sensual and sexual) contact with other people. For example, since I have begun this research I have felt uncomfortable when my father has put his arm around me. This is not a peculiar occurrence between my father and me, but I had to withdraw quickly from this physical contact because I felt it could have sexually aroused him.

This cynicism has also occurred when as a bystander I have seen physical contact between children and adults, particularly adult males. I have also felt uncomfortable about my own feelings and thoughts when I have observed physical contact between adults and children. For example, I felt unnecessarily guilty once when I saw a father gently pat his son's bare bottom in front of me. Although this was simply playful contact between father and son, I felt that I was a voyeur in a sexual act.

One participant had a particular effect on the way I felt and behaved after the interviews were completed. He is called Clive for the purpose of this study. Clive had been convicted of raping a woman who was unknown to him. The rape had occurred only minutes away from where I was living at that time. Consequently, when he described his offence, I was able to visualize the exact location. This became even more vivid after I read Clive's prison record, including his victim's statement. While I had not disclosed where I was from to any of the participants, the prison where Clive was interviewed had forewarned the research participants, at the initial point of access, of my details. However, if anything, this made it easier for us to build up a relationship during the interviews. In fact, the interviews conducted with Clive were some of the most informative interviews that I undertook.

Throughout the interviews Clive would attempt to personalize the examples that he used to illustrate certain points to my own experiences. For example, perhaps one of the more bizarre instances was when he likened the Sex Offender Register to a woman's menstrual cycle, as the following quotation highlights:

> What I'm saying is that [the Register] it's part of your life now, you have to incorporate your life with it, the first day you get your period from then on until menopause you have to cope with your life with that in it, you have to. I've committed a sex offence now I have to incorporate my life with that in it, I know it's a stupid example but that's what it is, it's part of my life, I have to accept it. (Clive)

However, the sexual nature of this example was typical of the way Clive attempted to draw me into the discussion. Indeed, when discussing his sexual fantasies he suggested that my sexual preference might be to 'use whips' and to 'tie up [my] boyfriend', or that I might have had sexual fantasies 'about having sex on a double-decker bus'.

In the final interview, when we were discussing the issue of disclosing his offence to potential partners, Clive presented a hypothetical situation where we met up after he was released in a wine bar outside a known landmark in my area, and 'got to know each other and became friends'. In so doing, he sexualized a situation that I could easily relate to. Later in the same interview, Clive also asked me if I was planning to work in a prison, once I had finished the research. His concern was that I would get unwanted attention from the inmates. To emphasize this point, he asked me if I thought that he or other inmates could sit through 'the whole interview and not have sexual thoughts about [me]'. Apparently, he could not, although he had 'prevented himself from doing so', because in his mind he was respecting me. He also stated that there was nothing wrong with this 'as long as that person was not thinking of hurting [me]'. Although he claimed that he meant this to be taken as a compliment, it definitely made me feel uncomfortable about the familiarity he had shown throughout the course of the interviews.

This was not the only time that a participant had reflected on my sexuality. For example, once when I met David for an interview he had not been informed that he was coming to see me. He claimed that had he known '[he] would have shaved and put [his] aftershave on'.

However, Clive's comments became more threatening because he had an insight into parts of my life due to the fact that he had lived in the same area. Moreover, I later found out that Clive planned to return to the same area once he had been released. Indeed, Clive informed me of this just before he walked out of the interview room after his final interview. He told me not to be shocked if I saw him walking around as he was hoping to be released in the next couple of months. After a few weeks of constantly looking over my shoulder, or thinking that I had seen Clive, I contacted the local Probation Service and informed them of my concerns, asking them to let me know when Clive was released. They wrote back with an expected parole date and assured me they would let me know if anything changed. This meant I could regain some control over my fears and anxieties. However, when walking along a street I met Clive. I subsequently found out that our encounter was two days after he had been released. The probation officer had not informed me that his parole date had changed. The unexpected meeting instantly brought back all those thoughts about his offence and the possible threat he posed to me. However, several days later I began to rationalize our encounter and brief acknowledgement and conversation with each other. I realized that the anxiety was probably mutual and that the confidence and audacity he expressed in prison were the real cause of my fears, not the possibility that I would be his next victim.

Every researcher must be affected by their research. However, just as the risk posed by sexual offenders goes to the core of society's fears, then inevitably the nature of my research will have a lasting impression on me. But I have tried to ensure throughout this thesis that the arguments and narratives privilege the participants' own accounts, views and thoughts. Hence, I have attempted to avoid using the term 'sex offender' to define my participants. The words 'sex offender' appear in inverted commas in the titles of two chapters. Here the intention is to signal the constructed nature of the term. I hope I have presented and discussed 32 different personalities. Where I have categorized their actions and behaviour, this is based upon their own accounts and arguments. What follows is only a selection of stories that have dominated my analysis. There is, after all, no single way to portray the participants' views (Hammersley and Atkinson 1995). However, I have tried to provide lucid and transparent arguments that allow the reader to follow and understand the conclusions I have made.

Note

1 Monthly prison population brief November 2003, England and Wales, available from www.hmprisonservice.gov.uk

Part I
Setting the scene

Chapter 2

Managing the 'sex offender'

As in several other countries, in England and Wales the criminal justice system's attempts to combat sexual offending have resulted in what has been described as a 'criminal apartheid' (Soothill *et al*. 1998), with sexual crimes differentiated from other forms of offending. By the close of the 1990s, a variety of laws providing for increased sentences and extended monitoring and surveillance of sex offenders had been implemented ostensibly to protect the public, and children in particular, from the risks posed by this category of offender. Most of these laws have now been widened, strengthened and/or re-enacted through the Sexual Offences Act 2003.

This chapter explores the current legislative response to sexual offenders, including the most significant policies within the Sexual Offences Act 2003. The objective is to highlight a trend that has emerged in the response to sexual crimes (and, to a lesser extent, violent crime) in which the desire to protect the public takes clear priority over the rights of the individual offender. Of key interest here is why the sex offender and why now?

The 'dangerousness debate'

Despite the renewed interest in sexual crime, the main assumption behind the legislative focus on sexual offenders (the intention to protect the public and in particular children) is not new. The issue of how to protect the public from similarly 'dangerous offenders' was widely discussed in British policy and criminological circles during the 1970s 'dangerousness debate'. However, the differences in context between the 1970s and contemporary policy decision-making are recognizable in how the debates have been shaped.

The dangerousness debate was ignited by a highly publicized homicide case involving a diagnosed psychopath, Graham Young. Having been committed to a Special Hospital for poisoning members of his family, Young committed further offences in a similar manner following his release (Bottoms 1977; Floud and Young 1981; Radzinowicz and Hood 1981). Preventative measures were subsequently proposed that extended or made indeterminate prison sentences for offenders classified as dangerous (Butler Committee 1975; Floud and Young 1981; Bottoms 1995). The Butler Committee defined the dangerous offender as any individual that 'has a propensity to inflict serious physical or psychological harm upon others'. The proposed 'reviewable' sentence was therefore aimed at offenders judged to pose a risk of serious harm to the public (Butler Committee 1975). The length of sentence would be indefinite, with release dependent on judgements about risk.

Proposals for preventive imprisonment were resisted, not least because of strong and effective arguments by leading philosophers and criminologists (see, for example, Floud and Young 1981; Radzinowicz and Hood 1981; Bottoms and Brownsward 1983). It was widely argued that the concept of 'dangerousness' was vague and subjective, making the identification of 'dangerous' persons problematic. Concern was expressed that the term 'dangerous' could be applied to any number of cases and thus that any new powers would be open to abuse. Another key objection was that individuals should not be punished on the basis of crimes that they might commit in the future. This was argued to violate the presumption of innocence, and so punish a person on the basis of status alone (Floud and Young 1981). A contributing proposition was the concept of 'False Positives'; the extended incarceration of a person based on the false prediction that they will commit another offence (Bottoms 1977). The unreliability inherent in the science of prediction was seen by many as making imprisonment on the basis of it morally unacceptable (Bottoms 1977; Floud and Young 1981).

Current legislative response

The 1970s dangerousness debate was marked by the absence of any new legislation. In contrast, since the early 1990s England and Wales have witnessed a raft of new legislation and policy initiatives aimed primarily against sex offenders but also against 'dangerous' offenders in general. The legislation includes:

- The 1991 Criminal Justice Act, which initiated the move towards major incarceration of so-called dangerous offenders by permitting long protective sentences, well beyond the normal tariff, for sexual and violent crimes.

- The 1996 Sexual Offences (Conspiracy and Incitement) Act, which enabled Britons to be tried in this country for sexual offences committed abroad.

- The 1997 Criminal Evidence (Amendment) Act, which gave the police the power to obtain DNA tests from all convicted sex offenders serving a sentence.

- The Protection from Harassment Act 1997, which widened the definition of sexual crimes to include stalking cases.

- The Sexual Offences (Protected Marital) Act 1997, which regulated access to victims' statements in sex offence cases.

- The Crime (Sentences) Act 1997, which continued the trend of incapacitation by introducing a mandatory life sentence for serious sexual (and/or violent) offenders on a second conviction.[1]

- The Sex Offenders Act 1997, which introduced a requirement for sex offenders to register with the police their personal details and any subsequent changes to them. This requirement is commonly known as the 'sex offender register'.

- The Crime and Disorder Act 1998, which provided for the imposition of a civil Sex Offender Order (SOO) to restrict sex offenders' behaviour in the community. This was later amended in the Crime and Disorder Act 2002.

- The Sexual Offences (Amendment) Act 2000, which widened the definition of sexual crimes to include offences committed by a person in a position of trust.[2]

- The Criminal Justice and Court Services Act 2000, which made considerable changes to the sex offender register; introduced restraining and disqualification orders, to restrict the offender's movement and disqualify certain offenders from working with children; and placed greater emphasis on inter-agency partnership in the management of sexual (and violent) offenders in the community, commonly known as MAPPA (Multi-Agency Public Protection Arrangements).

Much of this legislation has been re-enacted in the Sexual Offences Act 2003. The next section explores in some detail the policies within the 2003 Act, as well as some of the key legislation that has gone before. Considered together, they emphasize further the striking difference in the political climate and cultural trends of the 1970s 'dangerousness debate' and today (see also Kemshall and Maguire 2002).

The Sexual Offences Act 2003

The Sexual Offences Act 2003 introduced further measures to detain sex offenders in custody for longer periods of time. This includes a discretionary life sentence for sexual or violent offenders assessed as 'dangerous'. The 2003 Act also unveiled a radical overhaul of what constitutes a sexual offence. Offences of buggery and indecency between men, which discriminated against male homosexual activity, have been abolished. In addition, the definition of rape[3] has been widened to include oral penetration so that it applies to both male and female victims. While rape can still only be committed by males (as it must involve penile penetration), the offence of 'assault by penetration' captures offences committed by both male and female perpetrators.[4]

The Sexual Offences Act 2003 focuses specifically on the issue of consent in sex between adults. Under the new legislation, defendants accused of rape have to be able to show that they took 'reasonable action'[5] to ensure that the other person consented to sex. In order to be able to consent to any sexual activity, a person must be given the choice and/or must have the capacity to make the choice. The 2003 Act therefore deals with offences where drugs have been administered with the intent to commit a sexual act, and introduces three new categories of offences to protect people with a mental disorder from sexual abuse and exploitation.

Increasing emphasis has also been placed on the protection of children. This includes removing a loophole in the law that allows individuals to claim that sex with children under the age of 13 was consensual. Under the 2003 Act anyone who abuses children under that age will always be charged with rape, rather than a lesser offence. It has also raised the age of those protected from familial child sexual abuse from 16 to 18, and extended the sexual exploitation legislation to include children aged 16 and 17. The controls surrounding the legislation concerning the 'Abuse of Position of Trust', which were introduced in the Sexual Offences (Amendment) Act 2000, have also been re-enacted and tightened through the 2003 Act. The Act also introduces a new set of offences specifically dealing with the exploitation of children up to the age of 18 through prostitution and pornography.

A final issue which merits some attention is the recognition within the 2003 Act that certain sex offences that do not involve physical contact with the victim still cause psychological distress. For example, the new legislation introduces gender neutral offences of indecent exposure, sexual behaviour in a public place and voyeurism. Similarly, a new offence of 'grooming' children for sexual abuse has been applied to adults who lure children for sex. Grooming can involve a process of gaining the trust of a child and/or setting up a situation where an adult is alone with a child, with the intention to commit a sexual act with that child. Grooming can occur in any aspect of life, although increasing attention has been given to the use of the internet. Laws tightening the controls over the internet were introduced under the Criminal Justice and Court Services Act 2000. This piece of legislation increased the maximum sentence for making and distributing indecent photographs and pseudo-photographs of children to ten years' imprisonment, and for possession to five years' imprisonment. Part two of the Sexual Offences Act 2003 provides for a new civil prevention order, the risk of sexual harm order (RSHO), which aims to restrict the activities of those involved in such activity.

The RSHO forms only part of the extensive measures contained in the Sexual Offences Act 2003 to deal with sex offenders in the community. However, it was the Sex Offences Act 1997 that gave special impetus to this process and paved the way for equally exclusive conditions for sex offenders in the community.

The Sex Offender Register

The Sex Offenders Act 1997 was a further development of the twin-track policies of the 1991 Criminal Justice Act. While the 1991 Act took steps to increase the number of sex offenders receiving custodial sentences (see above), it also made changes to the parole system, which meant that serious sex offenders would spend considerable periods under supervision in the community (Sampson 1994). An effective system to monitor the whereabouts of sex offenders was therefore believed to be paramount to public safety.

Following the lead of the United States (Hebenton and Thomas 1996, 1997), a 'sex offender register' was implemented under Part one of the Sex Offenders Act. This required sex offenders to notify the police of their personal details and any subsequent changes to them. While similar provisions had existed in several areas since the mid-1980s, the 1997 Act ensured nationwide compliance to the registration requirements. In addition, the emphasis was not simply for the police to hold a register, but to actively 'manage' the risk posed by offenders (Kemshall and Maguire 2002; Kemshall 2003a).

Significant amendments to the 1997 Act through the Criminal Justice and Court Services Act 2000 addressed some of the loopholes in the register (Thomas 2004). More recently, the registration provisions have been strengthened, and made easier to enforce, through Part two of the Sexual Offences Act 2003. As the law now stands, the initial registration must be done in person, and within three days of the date of their sentence. Offenders serving a custodial sentence must register, in person, within three days of their release from prison. The legislation necessitates that registered sex offenders confirm their details on an annual basis, as well as notifying the police of any change in their details within three days (reduced from 14), or if they spend more than seven days (reduced from 14) at an address other than their home address. Through the new amendments, the police also have the power to photograph and fingerprint offenders each time a notification is made, and require offenders to provide their National Insurance number when making a notification. The registration requirement is maintained for a period ranging from two years (for offenders who receive a caution for a 'relevant offence') to life, depending on the offence and sentence length.[6]

The categories of offender subject to the notification requirements of the 2003 Act do not differ substantially from the provisions contained in the original 1997 Act.[7] Through the 2003 Act, however, offenders who have received a conditional discharge for a 'relevant offence' are also made subject to the registration requirements. Although the main driving force behind the implementation of the register was public concern over paedophiles (Hebenton and Thomas 1996; Cobley 1997), the registration requirements apply to a wide range of sexual crimes.[8] Nonetheless, new civil orders have been implemented to counteract criticism that serious sex offenders are able to slip though loopholes in the law, even if they are manifestly still dangerous.

One particular aspect of the 1997 Act that caused concern was that the registration requirements only applied to offenders sentenced after 1991 (Plontikoff and Woolfson 2000). The Sex Offender Order (SOO) embodied within the Crime and Disorder Act 1998 (later amended in the Crime and Disorder Act 2002) was partly intended to counteract this criticism. The SOO was a civil order that courts could use to place sex offenders (including unregistered sex offenders) whose conduct indicated that they still posed a serious threat to the public under specific restrictions, breach of which was punishable by imprisonment (Knock et al. 2002). The main provision of the SOO included the use of what Kemshall and Maguire (2002: 14) have termed 'negative conditions' to restrict and control sex offenders' behaviour in the community. Similar restrictions on offenders' behaviour towards the general public were later introduced, from the point of sentence, through a Restraining Order embodied within the Criminal Justice and Court Services Act 2000.

Both pieces of legislation have now been replaced by Sexual Offences Prevention Orders (SOPO) under Part two of the Sexual Offences Act 2003. Like a SOO, the SOPO is a civil order intended to protect the public from the risks posed by sex offenders by placing restrictions on their behaviour, including imposing a requirement for offenders to register under the Sexual Offences Act 2003. A SOPO is maintained for a period ranging from five years to life and can be made at either the point of sentence (i.e. similar to the Restraining Order) or upon application by the police (i.e. similar to the SOO). Unregistered sex offenders who still pose a risk to the public can therefore be made subject to the registration requirements. In addition, SOPO may be made against violent offenders previously exempt from registration requirements. This includes offenders convicted of murder, manslaughter, kidnapping and abduction, as well as sexually motivated violent offences and intent to rape, if there is a risk of the offender committing a sexual offence.

The nature and type of offenders made subject to registration have also been widened through Notification Orders (contained in Part two of the Sexual Offences Act 2003). This order requires sex offenders who have received convictions for sexual offences abroad to comply fully with registration provisions. While the registration requirements of the 2003 Act enforce offenders to notify the police of their intention to travel abroad, they do not prohibit them from doing so. The Act has therefore implemented 'Foreign Travel Orders,[9] to prevent offenders with convictions against children from travelling overseas.

All of the initiatives contained in the Sexual Offences Act 2003 form part of broader public protection arrangements in England and Wales, commonly known as MAPPA (Multi-Agency Public Protection Arrangements), formalized through the Criminal Justice and Court Services Act 2000 (see Maguire and Kemshall 2004).

Multi-Agency Public Protection Arrangements (MAPPA)

Multi-Agency Public Protection arose 'out of a growing recognition that shared information, joint risk assessments and co-ordinated risk management plans across relevant agencies' would enhance the management of sex offenders in the community (Kemshall 2003a: 2). MAPPAs place a statutory responsibility on the police, probation and prison services to work jointly to establish arrangements for the assessment and management of the risk posed by both sexual and dangerous offenders in the community.

MAPPAs apply to registered sex offenders (including those required to register under the 2003 Act), violent offenders sentenced to a year or more in custody, and other offenders who, having served their sentence, still pose a risk to the public.[10] The level of risk an offender poses to the public determines the type of case management arrangements that can be used.[11] MAPPA has identified three separate levels at which risk is assessed and managed. Offenders that present a serious risk of re-offending (level 3), the 'critical few', are referred to Multi-Agency Public Protection Panels (MAPPPs), in which high priority is given to community safety.[12] Subsequent guidance (Home Office 2001b, 2002a, 2003) and reviews of the public protection arrangements (Kemshall 2001; Maguire *et al.* 2001; Kemshall 2003a; Maguire and Kemshall 2004) have outlined risk management procedures used in the classification of offenders, along with the overall management structure of MAPPA.

Key to the level at which a case is managed is the multi-agency representation and involvement. While a statutory duty is placed on the three services outlined above, if an offender is managed at level 2 or 3 a number of other agencies (including Young Offender Teams (YOTs), local health authorities, housing authorities and service departments, education authorities, social security and employment service departments, and social services) have an imposition to cooperate and contribute to these arrangements. In addition, MAPPPs provide for the disclosure of information to potential victims (whether a named individual or vulnerable groups) in exceptional circumstances.[13]

The exchange of information relating to an individual offender is determined by the level of risk an offender poses to the public; as the level of risk increases so does the level of representation, involvement and disclosure. However, despite the wider access to information on sex offenders, the Home Office has steadfastly refused to introduce a model of community notification, similar to that of the United States of America, whereby the local community would have a right to be informed of the names and addresses of people with convictions for sexual offences (Plontikoff and Woolfson 2000; Thomas 2003, 2004).

Megan's Law

In the USA, all 50 states are obligated to hold a sex offender register which the public have a right to access under 'Megan's Law'.[14] This legislation came about after the rape and murder of a seven-year-old girl called Megan Kanka in July 1994. The culprit was a twice-convicted sex offender who was living anonymously in a house on the same street with two other convicted paedophiles. It was argued that had the victim or her family known about the presence of a sex offender in the community, the crime could have been prevented. Megan's Law is thus 'not seen as an additional punishment, but as a form of regulation to achieve greater community safety and public protection' (Thomas 2003: 217).[15]

The notification provisions in the US work on a three-tier system of risk assessment (Brooks 1996; Tier and Coy 1997). Only offenders classified as 'high risk' (level 3) are subject to full community notification. While the manner of notifying communities varies between states, this has resulted in a requirement for a sex offender to wear identifiable clothing, or for placards or posters listing their crimes to be displayed. A number of states have also made such information available on the internet (Schopf 1995; Brooks 1996; Adams 1999; Cote 2000; Thomas 2003).

Demands to grant such access in the UK heightened with the unprecedented media coverage following the death of Sarah Payne in July 2000. Similar to the events in the US, the culprit, Roy Whiting, was on the sex offender register and known to the local MAPPP. However, in the UK, the general public, at present, are denied access to the details on the sex offender register.[16] Research conducted by Maguire and colleagues found an 'overwhelming view' among professionals working with sex offenders (including police and probation officers) that 'full disclosure to the community was almost invariably undesirable' (Maguire *et al.* 2001: 38). Similar attitudes were expressed by the police in research conducted by Plontikoff and Woolfson (2000). The government has concluded in accordance with the views of most practitioners (Home Office 2001a, 2003). However, a compromise package was sought. The Criminal Justice and Court Services Act 2000 placed a responsibility on the MAPPPs to complete and publish annual reports that disclose the number of MAPPA offenders living in a specified geographical area. 'Lay advisors' have also been appointed to take part in the strategic decision-making processes of the multi-agency arrangements in eight areas.[17] Both provisions are intended to increase public awareness and understanding of MAPPA, while avoiding the problems that would be created by full disclosure.

The main argument given by the Home Office against community notification is the fear that it would drive offenders 'underground' (Kemshall and Maguire 2002; Thomas 2003). This fear was exemplified after the controversial 'Name and Shame' campaign spearheaded by a Sunday tabloid, the *News of the World*, resulted in public disorder and vigilante action (some against wrongly identified people) in several areas. Granting public access to the register is thus believed to hinder rather than help measures to protect the public.

The evidence from evaluations of the US notification procedures also questions the effectiveness of such provisions in enhancing community awareness and self-protection. Research conducted by Edwards and Hensley (2001) has described the effects that community notification can have on the families of individuals who commit sexual crimes, and in particular the effect this might have on the occurrence and reporting of sexual abuse within the family. Preliminary findings presented from reports from New Jersey (where Megan's Law was first enacted) and Colorado suggest a decrease in the reporting of incest offences by victims and by non-offending family members due to the fact that they do not want to deal with the impact of public notification.

The fear that sex offenders are likely to re-offend in areas where there is no notification has also been raised in the US due to the 'likelihood to encounter' factor that determines who the information should be passed on to. New Jersey Supreme Court has defined this in terms of proximity: 'The term includes an entire immediate neighbourhood, not just the people next door, and takes into account schools and other institutions in the vicinity depending on their distance from the offender's residence, place of work or school' (Tier and Coy 1997: 58). The offender's proclivity for being at certain places that might not be 'in the vicinity' can also be taken into consideration. Even so, it has been argued that however widely the restrictions are drawn, the law will not remedy the problem of sexual offending but simply displace it somewhere else (Schopf 1995; Brooks 1996).

Unlike the widespread objections voiced against the introduction of a 'reviewable' sentence during the 'dangerousness debate' in the 1970s, current debates about community disclosure tend to pay little attention to moral and ethical concerns. Arguments against disclosure tend to be based not upon concerns about the intrusiveness of such disclosure, or an offender's right to privacy (once they have paid their debt to society), but upon fears that full public access to the sex offender register might impede rather than increase public protection. The government's refusal to grant such access should not therefore be viewed as evidence that the unjustness of such legislation has been recognized. Instead, it should be viewed as further indication that the desire to protect the public takes priority over the rights of the individual offender.

Despite political and professional (arguably one-sided) objections to full community disclosure, elements of the press and the wider public have continued to demand unlimited access to the sex offender register. For example, a MORI poll revealed that 58 per cent of adults surveyed thought that convicted paedophiles should be 'named and shamed' (MORI/*News of the World* 2000). A political party, 'The Community Awareness Party', has also been formed to back the *News of the World*'s campaign for full community notification, coined by the paper as 'Sarah's Law'. While the Home Office has been steadfast in its refusal to grant such demands, there would appear to be no ethical constraints on how members of the public believe sex offenders *should* be managed. As Petrunik (2002: 484) concludes, for such offenders there is 'zero tolerance'.

New risk penality

One explanation of society's preoccupation with sexual offenders draws on the new risk management philosophies and strategies that have come to dominate punishment rhetoric and practices in recent years. The growing prominence of the concept of risk in contemporary criminal justice and penal policy has been widely discussed (O'Malley 2000; Pratt

2000c; Rose 2000; Sparks 2000; O'Malley 2001; Hudson 2002; Kemshall 2003b). Drawing on wider risk theorizing[18] (Giddens 1990; Beck 1992), criminological debate focuses on the extent to which penal practices have been transformed by conditions of late or postmodernity.[19]

For Feeley and Simon (1992, 1994), the recent changes in crime control strategies reflect a significant shift from an old penology, responding to the needs of an individual offender, to a 'new penology', based upon risk and actuarial justice. Others have argued that their arguments are too dualistic and point to the continuities of the past and the present (Garland 1996; Ericson and Haggerty 1997; Pratt 2000a, 2000b, 2000c). However, what these accounts all have in common is that they recognize that society's heightened pursuit of security takes priority over the welfare and moral state of the offender.

Shifts have been recognized in the balances between:

> crime control and due process; between inclusionary (keeping offenders in the community) and exclusionary (banishing them, to other territories or to segregative institutions) penal techniques; between 'normalising' (making the deviant more like the normal citizen) and managing (not seeking to change the deviant, but restricting his/her possibilities of movement and action so as to minimise the threat to the normal population) strategies; between individualising (responding to the needs and circumstances of the individual offender) and aggregating (controlling groups or categories of offenders and potential offenders). (Hudson 2002: 41)

The current penal practices used to control the risk posed by sex offenders exemplify this transition.

To reiterate, since the 1990s clear trends have emerged in response to sexual crimes that prioritize provision for mandatory, indeterminate and preventative sentencing and surveillance. A variety of laws provide for increased sentences for both first-time and repeat sex offenders, elaborate risk assessments, and surveillance and restriction of movement or behaviour, in order to minimize the threat sex offenders pose to the normal population (Hudson 2002). Current sentencing practices clearly position the sex offender as the 'dangerous other', whose regulation and containment has become central to the risk-based approach to penality (Kemshall and Maguire 2001). For Feeley and Simon (1992) in particular, new penology is less concerned with working with individuals, and more 'concerned with techniques to identify, classify and manage groupings sorted by dangerousness' (Feeley and Simon 1992: 452). The term 'sex offender' thus becomes a managerial identifier for someone being a member of a risky group, in order to determine what should be done to control and manage them.

The risk-based approach to penality is also framed by an economic discourse of crime control, in which 'economic forms of reasoning and calculations' are translated into the criminological discourse (Garland 1997: 4). The increasing use of incarceration and zero tolerance initiatives towards sex offenders clearly exist outside this economic language (Garland 2001). As Chapter 1 identified, sexual offences constitute 0.9 per cent of all recorded crime, and reconviction rates of sexual offenders tend to be low (Hanson and Bussiere 1998; Hood et al. 2002). Laws aimed at addressing sex offenders are not therefore the result of actuarial prediction or careful risk management. Instead, penal expenditure is displaced in the interest of 'populist punitiveness' (Bottoms 1995) or by an 'expressive or symbolic rationality of punishment' (Kemshall and Maguire 2001).

Populist penal policy

One justification put forward to explain the government's punitive response to the threat posed by sexual offenders is that they are simply doing what the public want. Hence the emergence of what Bottoms (1995) has termed 'populist punitiveness'. The argument contends that with crime policies taking centre stage in electoral competition (Garland 2001), the government must be seen to respond to populist sentiment in order to gain political advantage. Within this penal context, public safety concerns are given absolute priority over the rights of offenders. Policy measures are thus constructed in ways that reflect the public's fear of sexual crime (Simon 1998; Garland 2001; Kemshall Maguire 2003). Longer prison terms and continued surveillance become the government's only rational response towards sexual offenders (Garland 2001). Any other attempt to deal with sex offenders becomes both 'politically and morally suspect' (West 2000a: 522). However, while the notion of populist punitiveness can be used to account for the scope of new legislation aimed at containing the threat posed by sexual offenders, it does not explain the level of support for these laws.

Prejudice, obsession or threat?

The unequal treatment that sex offenders face can of course be explained as a result of their own actions. Sexual offending clearly has a damaging impact on the victims of sexual abuse and on society, which evokes an emotive response. This emotion is evidently reinforced when sex offenders target children (Garland 2001; Petrunik 2002). Societal indignation is therefore understandable. However, as this chapter has identified, public opinion is subject to change. During the 1970s 'dangerousness debate', proposals for preventive detention were seen to be morally unacceptable. In the current moral climate, such laws are liked precisely because of their punitive nature. It is also easy to identify activities which, over time, have been effectively decriminalized or slipped down the law and order agenda. Certain homosexual activities were decriminalized in England and Wales in 1976. The age of consent for homosexual acts has also been lowered from 21 to 18.[20] In contrast, the age of consent for heterosexual activities has been raised from 10 in 1283, to 13 in 1875 and to 16 in 1885, where it still stands (Thomas 2000). Furthermore, the driving force behind the initial rise in the age of consent was to ensure the 'virginity of the daughters of the properties and politically powerful' rather than for issues of child protection (Gittens 1998: 177).

Perspectives of what is considered to be right and wrong (and how seriously wrong certain forms of sexual behaviour are) also vary between cultures and from place to place. The recent Pitcairn trials, in which seven male islanders[21] faced charges of rape or indecent assault, offers a pertinent example. Despite being a British territory (thereby under British law), some islanders (predominantly women) have contested that underage sex is a traditional part of island life. This was taken into account in the relatively lenient sentences proposed. The social and cultural process though which different types of activity become problematic must therefore be explored.

In the same way as risk society analysis has been drawn upon to understand recent developments in penality and social control, risk theorizing has also been linked to a growing penal populism. Risk society theorists (Giddens 1990; Beck 1992; Beck et al. 1994) claim that the risks associated with modernization, in particular industrialization and globalization, have become an integral part of contemporary life. According to Beck and Giddens, the social transformation associated with late or postmodernity has produced risks, or 'manufactured uncertainties' (Giddens 1998: 30), which exceed the tools and technologies used to assess and control them (Kemshall 2003b). Such risks are seen to be endemic to life in late-modern societies, and as a consequence have undermined traditional social and cultural roles and ideals.

Young (2001, 2002, 2003, 2004) claims that the economic and ontological upheavals associated with late modernity have created a shift from a society with strong inclusionary tendencies to one with 'pronounced exclusionary tendencies' (Young 2004: 551). According to Young (2004), this has generated a desire to secure identity by constructing an 'other'. Although Young places increasing emphasis on economic boundaries, he also describes a parallel process of inclusion based on a shared morality (Young 2004). Within this 'community' the question that remains is who

25

is to be included, and who is the 'community' going to defend itself against.

Arguably, shifts in the nature of public toleration are fuelled in part by the media, and in particular the tabloid press (Soothill and Walby 1991; Kitzinger 1997; Howe 1998, Kitzinger 1999; Cobley 2000; Farrell and Soothill 2001; Reiner 2002; Greer 2003; Kitzinger 2004a, 2004b). While research has shown that there has been some improvement in media coverage of sexual crimes, for example an increase in the reporting of rape cases (Kitzinger 1999) and greater prominence in documentaries, television drama, and soap operas (Soothill and Walby 1991; Mills 1997), the media clearly contribute to the 'othering' of sex offenders.

The media's representation of the sex offender conveys stereotypical descriptions that are designed to shock rather than educate (Greer 2003). For example, the media, and in particular the print media, have incorrectly magnified the public's perception of the nature and extent of sexual offending. Unusual cases are made to appear 'all-too-typical' (Garland 2001: 135). Attacks by pathological strangers still receive disproportionate attention even though the majority of women and/or children are sexually abused and/or killed by someone they know (Levi and Maguire 2002; Kitzinger 2004b). 'Stranger' rapes accounted for only 8 per cent of all reported rapes to the British Crime Survey conducted in the first half of 2000 (Myhill and Allen 2002). In addition, results from the British Crime Survey's self-completion module on interpersonal violence, sexual assault and stalking, showed that only 17 per cent of women sexually abused since the age of 16 were assaulted by 'strangers'. Fifty-four per cent were sexually abused by an 'intimate' (this category includes both former and current husbands or partners) and 29 per cent were abused by someone they knew (Walby and Allen 2004). Kitzinger (2004b: 27) describes this declining interest in routine abuse as 'symbolic expulsion', whereby the emphasis on stranger danger removes sexual violence from mainstream society. The language and tone used to portray sexual offenders, and particularly paedophiles, in print media adds to the inaccurate and misleading impression that sex offenders are somehow inherently different from the rest of society. At best, sex offenders are described as 'evil', 'wicked', 'beasts', 'monsters' and 'sex fiends', conveying characteristics that are barely human (Kitzinger 1997; West 2000b; Garland 2001).

The media's portrayal of the 'sex offender' has clearly heightened sex offenders' position as 'other'. However, media reporting cannot be blamed for the public's repulsion and disgust towards sex offenders. This would suggest that individuals are passive recipients of everything they are told. While the media has clearly tapped into community fears, it has not created them (Kitzinger 1999). This is not to say that the media's representation of sex crime and sexual offenders is blameless, rather it is 'at the very least counterproductive, if not blatantly irresponsible' (Kitzinger 1999: 212).

The portrayal of sex offenders in the media, coupled with shifts in public toleration, clearly problematizes the notion of popular punitiveness. The media response to the death of Sarah Payne is a case in point. Playing on the fears of 'stranger danger', the images conjured up by the media in the months that succeeded the death of Sarah Payne evoked stereotypical depictions of the 'mobile and anonymous sex offender' waiting to prey on children, giving the impression that such people were both large in number and typical among offenders (Hebenton and Thomas 1996: 249). What the print media fails to report is that most sex offenders are living in communities undetected and probably well integrated.

The media's institutional focus on negative news ensures that public perception, or 'mis-perception', will continue to be pushed in a 'pessimistic and vindictive' direction (Young 2004: 41). In addition, government initiatives aimed at reducing risk and gaining public support, inadvertently heighten public fear and anxiety, thus triggering what Kemshall and Maguire (2003: 111) have termed a 'spiral of action and reaction that has become difficult to control'.

An overreliance on popular punitiveness also suggests that there is consensus among the population (Hancock and Matthews 2001). While it is safe to assume that most of society agrees that sexual crime should not be tolerated, individuals are less likely to agree on the forms, or levels, of punishment. Hancock and Matthews (2001: 104) also point to the methodological problems associated with public attitude surveys, concluding that 'at best [they] provide a "snapshot" of public opinion and at worst [they] provide a distorted one-dimensional picture of what members of the public actually think'.

The media's seemingly unrestrained vilification of child sex offenders, at a time when the sexualization of children has reached unprecedented levels, also raises a number of questions. The widespread use of child models (especially girls) in the advertising of children's clothes and adult products, and the tendency of children's clothes to resemble adult fashions, have been used to convey a sense that the boundaries of a healthy sexuality are being blurred (Postman 1982; West 2000a; Silverman and Wilson 2002). Burman (1995) has illustrated this through the term 'woman-child', conveying images of 'childish women' and 'womanly girls' that focus on children's presumed innocence as a source of sexuality.

Writers who lament the loss of children's innocence call for a return of the 'innocent child' in order to protect children from paedophiles (Postman 1982; Silverman and Wilson 2002). Others, however, argue that the romanticized notions of the sexually innocent child endanger children (Gittens 1998; Kincaid 1998; Kitzinger 1999, 2004a). This argument suggests that childhood innocence (or sexual innocence) is something that 'adults wish upon children, not a natural feature of childhood itself' (Epstein and Johnson 1998: 97). Jenny Kitzinger, for example, describes how the idea that childhood innocence is stolen or lost by sexual abuse succeeds only to 'stigmatise and exclude the knowing child' (Kitzinger 1997: 166). Children who respond sexually, or who are sexually knowledgeable, are labelled as 'damaged goods' who no longer justify or warrant protection (Kitzinger 1997). Defining innocence as 'asexual' also enables abusers to defend themselves when abusing certain types of children. Kitzinger (1999) and others,[22] thus highlight the need to question the social construction of childhood itself, as our perception of childhood as an institution makes children more vulnerable.

The psychoanalytical literature has also looked beyond the 'sex offender' as 'other', and observed ways in which adults (usually men) both sexualize children and draw upon the discourse of childhood sexual innocence ultimately to protect themselves from their sexual feelings towards children (Kitzinger 1997; Walkerdine 1997; Kincaid 1998; West 2000a). Within this literature, the increasing sexual ambiguity of children at a time when there is growing awareness of sexual abuse and greater protectiveness towards children is not considered accidental (Kitzinger 1997; Walkerdine 1997; Kincaid 1998).

This argument points to the fact that the notion of childhood innocence is a source of sexual titillation. Research conducted by Freund and Blanchard (1989) found that 'normal' males showed some arousal to images of pubertal children. Similarly, in a self-report study of American college students, 22 per cent of men and 3 per cent of women reported having felt some sexual attraction to children (Smiljanich and Briere 1996). In addition, Renolds (2005) demonstrates how women make great efforts to become more child-like, and how child-like symbols such as school uniforms, sweets and toys have become sexually charged and used increasingly in 'salacious' humour. Paradoxically, the research highlights that the only option available when discussing children and sexuality is within the context of abuse and exploitation (Piper 2000). The psychoanalytical literature therefore claims that the confusion between adults' attitudes to children as sexual or nonsexual beings and the horror this evokes when brought into the public realm, feeds a stronger imperative to protect the child from adult sexuality. Society's extreme antipathy towards sex offenders, and particularly paedophiles, thus to some extent represents our own vulnerabilities, by displacing the fact that many adults find children disturbingly erotic (Walkerdine 1997; Piper 2000; West 2000a).

Research has also found that nonconvicted, 'normal' members of society hold many of the same beliefs as individuals convicted of rape.

This includes an acceptance of 'rape myths' and the use of violence towards women (Burt 1980, 1983). In addition, research conducted by Malamuth (1981) found that 35 per cent of a sample of US college males reported that they would be willing to rape if they were assured of not being punished. One explanation put forward to explain this is the role of pornography in reducing women in men's minds to the status of sex objects. However, for whatever reason, similar to the debates surrounding the sexualization of children, it would appear that 'sex offenders' are 'a good deal more like other people than most people would like to think' (Marshall 2000).

Conclusion

Criminals who perpetrate sexual crimes are, for a range of reasons, 'hated and despised more than almost any other offender' (Sampson 1994: x). Invariably, their 'sub-human' status has had an effect on their treatment in the criminal justice system. To recapitulate, the 1990s saw a toughening of sentences for sex offenders, culminating in the Sex Offender Act 1997 and the implementation of the sex offender register. The Criminal Justice and Court Services Act 2000 and the Sexual Offences Act 2003 both rectified problems that arose with earlier legislation and introduced further measures to control the perceived threat posed by sexual offenders.

The introduction of the Sexual Offences Act 2003 has also meant that more people will become subject to the extraordinary measures implemented to contain and control sexual offenders.[23] For example, intrusive community provisions penalize individuals for crimes that they might commit in the future. Similar legislation was rejected during the 1970s 'dangerousness debate' due to the unreliability of the concept of false negatives. In today's penal climate, sex offenders have little opportunity to demonstrate the inaccuracy of prediction (Hudson 2002). Sex offenders have thus become increasingly demonized, to the extent that there appears to be no ethical constraints on the ways in which they are managed (Sampson 1994). This has been borne out through the muted objection to the number and severity of measures against 'dangerous', and predominantly sexual, offenders.

The increasing use of exclusionary penal techniques has also contributed to the 'othering' of sex offenders in contemporary society. Garland (2000: 350) describes this type of sentencing as 'penal marking', whereby the offender is rendered 'more and more abstract, more and more stereotypical, more and more a projected image rather than a projected person' (Garland 2001: 179). In addition, the media and public perception of sex offenders has strengthened the categorization of the sex offender. Both succeed in obscuring important aspects of sexual offending, and hamper law-enforcement efforts by focusing attention on the wrong areas of danger and risk (Kitzinger 1999; Lynch 2002; Greer 2003).

Within this context, individuals who commit a sexual offence take on a 'social identity' (Breakwell 2001; Brewer 2001). This can be likened to what Goffman (1963) defines as a 'stigma'. The term stigma is used to refer to an attribute that is deeply discrediting. However, this perhaps oversimplifies the heightened moral panic about sexual offending. As this chapter has identified, it would appear that it is no longer the sex offenders' crimes that are unacceptable, but the sex offenders themselves. The representation of sex offenders as 'other' creates the impression that individuals who commit such acts are entirely different from us (Hudson 2002). However, Hudson (2002: 204) argues that to accept this is to 'deny the normal in those we label as monsters'.

Notes

1 The Home Secretary has the power to extend this by proposing detention until death, and has already used it on several occasions for sexual offenders.
2 This offence applies to a person over the age of 18 in a position of trust, i.e. a teacher or carer, who engages in any sexual activity with someone under that age.
3 The offence of rape was initially defined in section 1 of the Sexual Offences Act 1956. It was first substituted by section 142 of the Criminal Justice and Public Order Act 1994, in which the legal definition of rape was altered to include penile penetration of the anus and rape within marriage. A provision in the Sexual Offences Act 1993 also meant that boys under 14 could be convicted of rape.
4 This offence applies to a person who penetrates another individual with any part of the body (i.e. finger) or with an object (i.e. bottle), where the act is not consensual.
5 Reasonable action is judged by what an objective third party would think in the circumstances.
6 The notification periods are halved for offenders under the age of 18.
7 This includes offenders who have been convicted or cautioned for a 'relevant offence'; offenders found to be under a disability and to have done the act charged; and persons found not guilty by reason of insanity.
8 See section 80 of the Sex Offences Act 2003 for a list of 'relevant offences'.
9 See section four of Part two of the Sexual Offences Act 2003.
10 This group of offenders must have a previous conviction (committed anywhere) which indicates that they are capable of causing serious harm. See Section 67(2) (b) of the Criminal Justice and Court Services Act 2000.
11 Risk is assessed using risk assessment tools such as the Offender Assessment System (OASys), Risk Matrix 2000 and, in the case of young offenders, ASSET.

12 This might include routine home visits, covert police surveillance, and/or an issue of a SOPO.

13 MAPPA activity at level 2 involves more than one agency. However, unlike level 3, multi-agency cooperation is not at a senior level. MAPPA activity at level 1 involves a single agency, most commonly the probation service (for offenders on licence) or the police.

14 The Federal Violent Crime Control and Law Enforcement Act 1994

15 Thomas (2004) also provides a discussion on registration provisions in Europe.

16 Similarly, the public will be refused access to information contained on the Violent and Sex Offender Register (ViSOR), a single database for all offenders under MAPPA, which is under development.

17 These areas are Dorset, Hampshire, Surrey, West Midlands, Durham, Cumbria, Greater Manchester and the South-West.

18 Risk theory analysis will be discussed in more detail later in this chapter.

19 Postmodernity is used to signify a radical transformation in social forms and relations from modernity to the contemporary era (the period from the late 1970s onwards), whereas late modernity is used to describe the transformation as a gradual one.

20 The age of consent for homosexual acts was fixed at 21 for England and Wales by the Sexual Offences Act 1976 and lowered to 18 through the Criminal Justice and Public Order Act 1994. This legislation covers all parts of the UK.

21 Pitcairn has a resident population of 47.

22 See Petersen (2004) for a discussion on the appropriate levels of protection and freedom in child legislation.

23 See Bainham and Brooks-Gordon (2004) for a critical review of the social and legal debates surrounding the Sexual Offences Act 2003.

Chapter 3

Treating the 'sex offender'

Chapter 2 outlined a much more punitive response to sexual crime compared to the arrangements of the past. This clearly reflects the overarching ideology of the criminal justice system today. As many commentators have noted, contemporary crime policy is predominantly concerned with retribution, incapacitation and the management of groups of offenders, rather than the treatment of individuals (see, for example, Bottoms 1995; Garland 2001). The categorization of the sex offender as 'other' strengthens the belief that sex offenders are irredeemable and incurable. It seems that the reasons why people offend and what makes them stop are no longer important to the public, the media or the government.

Despite the punitive rhetoric of recent governments, the criminal justice system has not completely rejected rehabilitative intervention with offenders. In particular, since the mid-1980s the UK has witnessed a growth in the number of sex offender treatment programmes, both in prison and the community (Beech and Fisher 2004). This chapter explores this apparent contradiction. In doing so, it examines the role of sex offender treatment within contemporary criminal justice policy, including any indication of its effectiveness.

Rehabilitation redefined

Although rehabilitation has become subordinate to more punitive goals, treatment programmes do continue to operate. However, where treatment programmes are undertaken today, they clearly reflect wider shifts in penal policy and social control.

Garland (2001) has argued that the overriding purpose of treatment has moved away from the penal welfare framework of the past. As with sentencing practices, the offenders' individual needs no longer take centre stage. Instead, treatment has become increasingly concerned with protecting the public from risky groups of offenders (Feeley and Simon 1995). Indeed, Garland (2001: 176) argues that it is 'future victims who are now being "rescued" by rehabilitative work, rather than offenders themselves'. As will be shown later, the main rationale of sex offender treatment programmes is to try to modify deviant sexual behaviour in order to protect the public from future offending.

As a consequence, treatment is no longer viewed as a 'general all-purpose prescription' (Garland 2001: 176). On the contrary, rehabilitative intervention is predominantly targeted at offenders who are considered to pose the most risk to the public, in particular sex offenders and violent offenders. The regulation of treatment in this way comes nearer to an ideal in which only offenders that are most likely to 'make cost-effective use of this expensive service' are targeted (Garland 2001: 176).

A contributing development is the establishment of accreditation panels to ensure that programmes have a measurable effect in reducing reconvictions and that the programmes are delivered in the most effective way. A Joint Prison and Probation Accreditation Panel, now renamed the Correctional Services Accreditation Panel (CSAP), was established in 1999 to build from the experience of the General Accreditation Panel (GAP) and the Sex Offender Treatment Accreditation Panel (SOTAP) in the prison service (which were set up in 1996). Within this process, programmes are judged on a range of criteria guided by 'What Works' evidence (see, for example, Brody 1976; Mair 1991; Player 1992; McGuire 1995; Travers 1998; Raynor 2000; Bottoms *et al.* 2001; McGuire 2002; Falshaw *et al.* 2003).

In addition, the CSAP requires that offenders undertake a number of risk assessments to determine their suitability for treatment (see Grubin 2004 for a summary). This ensures that treatment is matched to the criminogenic and noncriminogenic needs of the offender. Treatment facilitators are trained centrally, receive formal supervision and are subject to ongoing monitoring (Beech and Fisher 2004). A programme manager and a treatment manager are also assigned to guarantee programme integrity. The role of the programme manager is to secure practical arrangements, while the treatment manager is responsible for ensuring that the programme content is in accordance with the programme design. Finally, information is routinely collected to ensure that treatment programmes are consistently delivered to maximize the effect of treatment. Audits are also completed by the prison department's Offending Behaviour Programmes Unit (OBPU) and the What Works Unit of the National Probation Service, and overseen by the CSAP.

Findings from a recent evaluation of the CSAP showed that in just over two years 15 programmes were accredited, and that six of these were for sex offenders (Rex *et al.* 2003).

Treatment approach

Accredited sex offender treatment programmes, in both prison and community settings, have adapted a cognitive behavioural group-work approach to treatment.

Cognitive behavioural therapy (CBT)

Cognitive behavioural therapy seeks to change an individual's internal (cognitive and emotive) functioning as well as their overt behaviour (see, for example, McGuire 2000). The cognitive behavioural approach to treatment views the offender as a rational decision maker. Unlike the medical model of the past, which saw the offender as a victim of circumstances, factors outside the offender's control (biological, psychological and social) are no longer seen to be responsible for an individual's behaviour (Marshall *et al.* 1999a; Hollin 2001). Instead, cognitive behavioural therapy is based on the assumption that the way a person behaves is determined by the way they think (Ross *et al.* 1988). The main aim of cognitive behavioural programmes is therefore to increase an offender's self-control over their offending behaviour by focusing on the antecedents of their offending.

The idea is for the offender to recognize 'faulty thinking' (cognition) and patterns of behaviour that have led to criminal behaviour. Special attention is placed on challenging 'dynamic' risk factors[1] that are linked to offending. The rationale is that these dynamic risk factors, at least in principle, can be altered through the acquisition of new skills (Denvir 2000; Raynor 2000). Cognitive behavioural therapy recognizes that self-control – not cure – is the aim of treatment. This not only reduces treatment expectations, but also better reflects the managerial process of the criminal justice system in that the goals of treatment become far more achievable (Howard League 1985; Travers 1998).

The group-work approach

Group-work is the most favoured method of sex offender treatment programmes. Research has identified a number of ways in which group-work contributes to treatment intervention with sex offenders (Beech and Fordham 1997; Craissati 1998; Forsyth 1999; Marshall *et al.* 2004). Craissati (1998) claims that groups provide sex offenders with an alternative experience to the 'isolation, secretiveness and shame' they might feel as a result of their offending behaviour. Forsyth (1999) similarly argues that the opportunity to interact with other group members can 'reduce one's sense of uniqueness'. This may help the offender to be more open about their offending behaviour, so facilitating change.

Craissati (1998: 63) also argues that groups provide a context that facilitates 'generalised learning'. Group members are able to gain a better understanding of their problems through other group members' accounts and experiences. This interaction with others is considered to be more effective than challenges coming from a group tutor (Beech and Fordham 1997; Fisher and Beech 2004; Marshall *et al.* 2004). Group-work is also more cost-effective in terms of both time and money.

There are five main techniques used in group-work: group discussions and brainstorming; victim and offender material (which includes the presentation of written material about aspects of sexual abuse to be presented within treatment); the hot-seat technique (this involves a group member sitting centre stage and undertaking work that is related to their offending behaviour); role-plays; and homework (cell work) (Prison Service 2000; Allam 2001; Probation Service 2001; Fisher *et al.* unpublished).

Treatment targets

The treatment targets typically used by both the prison and the probation services within accredited sex offender treatment can be summarized under five headings:

i. Dysfunctional attitudes and beliefs

ii. Empathy

iii. Deviant sexual arousal

iv. Social functioning

v. Relapse prevention

The first four treatment targets have been shown to be contributory or characteristic factors in sexual abuse, whereas the fifth component introduces relapse prevention techniques. This can help offenders to apply constructs and skills that are central to preventing re-offending (see, for example, Fisher and Beech 2004, and Marshall *et al.* 2004).

Dysfunctional attitudes and beliefs

Individuals who commit sexual offences typically hold dysfunctional beliefs and attitudes, which are commonly referred to as 'cognitive distortions'. A number of researchers have examined the specificity of cognitive distortions in both child sexual abusers and rapists (Marshall and Barbaree 1990; Ward and Keenan 1999). The results show that child sex abusers hold specific beliefs about children and sexuality, including seeing sexual interactions with children as 'educational, or in other ways beneficial to a child' (Marshall and Barbaree 1990: 371). They also indicate that rapists hold negative views about women, endorse violence against women, and accept rape myths. For example, the belief that women who wear revealing clothes or accept lifts from strangers are effectively asking to be raped. However, the research has failed to identify significant differences in the beliefs held by rapists and those held by other groups of offenders and/or non-offenders (see, for example, Segal and Stermac 1984; Morolla and Scully 1986; Pithers 1994). This is not to say that there are no differences. Rather, the attitudes justifying and supporting rape are more widespread in society (Burt 1980, 1983; Blumenthal *et al.* 1999).[2]

An individual's cognitive distortions are believed to arise from an entrenched belief system, or core schemas, which have been shaped by early life experiences (Ward *et al.* 1997a). These distortions enable the offender to justify their offending behaviour and minimize any guilt they might feel (Ward *et al.* 1997a; Prison Service 2000; Ward 2000; Allam 2001; Marshall *et al.* 2004). Consequently, an individual's attitudes and underlying belief systems play a major role in both precipitating and maintaining sexual offending behaviour. The fundamental aim of sex offender treatment programmes is to help offenders to identify cognitions that contribute to their offending behaviour. Techniques such as 'disputing' and 'cognitive restructuring' are used to challenge an offender's distorted beliefs so that they cannot be used to justify offending in the future (Murphy 1990; Barbaree 1991; Murphy and Carich 2001; Beech and Fisher 2004).

Empathy

The cognitive distortions outlined above can also serve to diminish the harm caused to victims of sexual abuse (see, for example, Marshall *et al.* 2001a; Marshall and Mouldern 2001). The aim of victim empathy is to help the offender to understand the victim's perspective. Although not identified as a dynamic risk factor on its own, it is hoped that increased victim empathy can deter future offending (Beech and Fisher 2004).

A number of programmes aim to educate offenders about common psychological problems experienced by victims of sexual assault. One way is providing the offender with visual and written accounts of victims' experiences. This provides offenders with a 'more articulate account of sexual abuse and its impact, that either the perpetrator or victim may be willing or able to communicate' (Craissati 1998: 68). It is also believed to be less threatening than if the offender was confronted by their own victim.

Recent research by Fernandez and Marshall (Fernandez *et al.* 1990; Marshall *et al.* 1999a; Fernandez and Marshall 2003) concluded that while the rapists in their study suppressed empathy towards their own victims, they did not suffer from generalized empathy deficits. Consequently, further techniques are used within treatment to develop an offender's empathy for their own victim(s).

Offence role-plays, in which group members are given the opportunity to take on roles of different people involved in the offence, such as the victim, are intended to help offenders experience, at an emotional level, what their victim(s) would have felt (Prison Service 2000; Probation Service 2001; Mann *et al.* 2002). In addition, offenders write hypothetical letters to their victim(s). This method is believed to reveal the level of empathy the offender has for their victim(s) (Webster 2002).

Deviant sexual arousal

The third treatment component is based on the assumption that some sex offenders have deviant sexual interests (Freund 1991; Marshall and Fernandez 2003). A deviant sexual interest is defined as any inappropriate thoughts or feelings about adults and/or children; e.g. an adult becoming sexually aroused at thoughts of having sex with a child, or forcing an adult to have sex without their consent. Although recent research evidence suggests that only a small number of sex offenders display arousal to deviant themes (Marshall and Fernandez 2003), this has been found to be the strongest predictor of sexual re-offending (Hanson and Bussiere 1998).

The approach of treatment is to explore the use of deviant sexual fantasies, in order to help offenders to understand the links between fantasy and offending and to teach the offender how to control and modify their own arousal (Prison Service 2000; Probation Service 2001). The type of fantasy that the offender engages in might also reflect the way they view women and children. Consequently, many programmes incorporate an education approach, addressing all areas of human sexuality and gender stereotypes, when tackling deviant sexual interest.

Social functioning

Sex offenders are generally regarded as experiencing difficulties in relation to intimacy and loneliness (Ward *et al.* 1997b). Treatment programmes draw upon Bowlby's (1969, 1973, 1979) 'Attachment Theory' to provide a framework for understanding offenders' intimacy deficits.[3] Bowlby claims that a child's development is shaped by its early attachment experiences. For sex offenders, this might include early sexual abuse, physical and emotional violence in the home, traumatic disruptions during childhood, and chronic neglect (see Hudson and

Ward 1997; Marshall and Marshall 2000). Such insecure attachments are said to provide sex offenders with an inadequate template for future relationships.

Attachment theory also proposes that insecure childhood attachments can lead to a lack of interpersonal skills, poor self-confidence and low self-esteem (Marshall 1989; Marshall *et al.* 1997). Such characteristics are said to decrease an individual's ability to achieve intimacy in adolescence and adulthood, thereby increasing their risk of committing a sexual offence (Sawle and Kear-Cowell 2001; Smallbone and McCabe 2003).

How sex offenders feel about themselves is also related to how well they cope generally in life. According to Mann and Beech (2002), individuals with low self-esteem fail to regulate their own behaviour. This lack of responsibility stems from a perception that they are not in control of their lives. Research also suggests that sex offenders tend to employ 'sex' as a maladaptive coping response (Cortoni and Marshall 1998; Swaffer *et al.* 2000). This might include retreating into abusive sexual fantasies and/or actual abuse as a way of dealing with stress.

A range of features are addressed within treatment that relate to the efficacy of an individual's social functioning. Many treatment programmes directly explore an individual's life trajectories and early experiences that might have contributed to their sexually abusive behaviour. Offenders are helped to identify situations and feelings that they find hard to cope with, as well as being assisted in the development of techniques intended to relieve feelings of personal distress and negative emotions (Endler and Parker 1990; Prison Service 2000; Probation Service 2001). Treatment also attempts to increase offenders' feelings of self-worth by helping them to identify and reinforce their own strengths (Marshall *et al.* 2002). Delivering treatment within a group format (having the experience of being listened to and helping others) also helps to improve individuals' self-esteem and social functioning.

Relapse prevention

The overriding goal of cognitive behavioural treatment is to reduce the likelihood of further offences. While the areas of treatment outlined above provide a context within which an offender may offend, the relapse prevention component of treatment aims to teach offenders how to recognize, avoid and cope with these situations in the future. The assumption underlying relapse prevention is that re-offending, far from being a spontaneous act, results from a chain of events (Pithers 1990). Models of offending have therefore been incorporated into treatment to help offenders identify events and situations that either increased or contributed to their (re-)offending.

Programmes have typically drawn upon Finkelhor's 'Model of Preconditions to Abuse' (Finkelhor 1984) and the 'Cycle of Offending', initially developed by Wolf (1984, 1988) but later adapted by Eldridge (Wolf 1984, 1988; Eldridge 1998). Both presuppose that offenders experience a number of stages leading up to their offence. These stages generally include the use of cognitive distortions and deviant sexual fantasy, and the use of covert and overt planning in order to groom both the environment and the victim. For example, Finkelhor (1984) proposed the existence of four preconditions that offenders must overcome in order to abuse. The first is that an offender needs to be motivated to offend. Once an offender is motivated they then need to overcome internal inhibitors – the fact their behaviour is wrong (step 2). They then need to create the opportunity to offend by overcoming external inhibitors – any physical barriers (step 3). Finally, offenders have to overcome their victim's resistance (step 4).

Once these thoughts, feelings and/or behaviours have been recognized, the idea is for the offender to generate techniques to avoid or cope with these situations in the future. More recently, offenders have been encouraged to develop 'approach goals', which reflect a more positive approach to relapse prevention (Ward 2002). Approach goals are those which lead to a life of satisfaction and fulfilment. Here the emphasis is on achieving something positive, i.e. a healthy relationship, rather than avoiding situations. The assumption is that once offenders achieve this state they will have no reason to offend.

All the approaches examined above are used within current accredited sex offender treatment programmes in the UK. These will now be explored in more detail.

Treatment for sex offenders in prison

The accredited Sex Offender Treatment Programme (SOTP) was introduced into the prison system in 1991 (Mann and Thornton 1998; Mann 1999; Beech and Fisher 2004). A Home Office report written at the time, explained that the rationale behind the SOTP was to protect potential victims rather than simply to benefit the prisoner (Home Office 1991). This clearly supports the notion of the 'victim' as centre stage in criminal justice policy (Garland 2001).

There are currently five accredited SOTP courses: the SOTP Core 2000 Programme (revised version of the already accredited Core Programme); the SOTP Extended Programme (usually for high-deviance offenders that may have completed the Core Programme but still have significant problems to address); the SOTP Adapted Core Programme (for low-IQ offenders);[4] the SOTP Booster Programme (a pre-release course); and the

SOTP Rolling Programme (for lower-risk sex offenders). See Beech and Fisher (2004) for a summary.

In order for offenders to be deemed suitable for treatment, and to ensure that they are matched to the appropriate SOTP, offenders are required to undertake a number of psychometric tests in addition to structured risk and need assessments (Hanson and Thornton 2000; Thornton 2002; Grubin 2004). Prisoners are excluded if they cannot speak English, are mentally ill, or if they are appealing against their conviction (Prison Service 2000). Exclusions are also made if the prisoner is in total denial of the offence.

The prison-based SOTP is applicable to all types of sexual offenders regardless of whether they have committed offences against children or adults, of either sex. The SOTP is also offered to life-sentenced prisoners who have killed their victim where there is a suspicion, or knowledge, that there was a sexual component to the killing (even if this is not mentioned in their actual conviction). Similarly, prisoners not currently convicted of a sexual offence but with a history of previous sexual offending may participate in treatment.

Participation on the SOTP is voluntary. However, a great deal is at stake for an offender to start and complete treatment. If, for example, an offender refuses to participate or fails to complete a programme, they are likely to be subject to various regime consequences (these will be explored in more detail in Chapter 5). Nonetheless, Beech and Fisher (2004) estimate that around 1000 men complete a SOTP in the UK every year, of which 80 per cent have offended against children, 15 per cent have offended against adults, and 5 per cent have killed their victims (Beech and Fisher 2004: 140).

The majority of convicted sex offenders will participate in the Core 2000 Programme. The Core SOTP is usually run as morning or afternoon two-hour sessions (typically Monday to Thursday), with one session completed per day. It is therefore run over six months. The Core 2000 Programme is divided into 20 blocks that make up a total of 85 sessions (see Table 3.1). The first block is aimed at enhancing group motivation. Blocks 2 to 9 cover distorted thoughts, beliefs, emotions, behaviours and physiological arousal, which might be linked to an individual's offending behaviour. Blocks 10 to 13 look at victim empathy. The final seven blocks cover relapse prevention intervention. These sessions aim to assist offenders in developing realistic relapse prevention plans and the skills and strategies to put them into practice (Prison Service 2000).

Fourteen participants in this research participated in the Core 2000 SOTP. Seven offenders had been convicted of child abuse, with crimes ranging from indecent assault to penetrative offences; six men had been convicted of rape (rape is defined here as an assault upon an adult); and one offender had been convicted of murder.

Table 3.1 Twenty Core 2000 SOTP blocks

Block	Title	Number of sessions
1	Establishing the Group	3
2	Understanding Distorted Thinking	1
3	Coping Strategies	2
4	My History	4
5	Active Accounts	16
6	Fantasy	2
7	Patterns in my Offending	8
Review	Coping Strategies	1
8	Feedback and Goal Setting	1
9	Cost and Gains of Offending	1
10	Victim Empathy	3
11	Victim Perspective Narratives	4
12	Victim Perspective Role-plays	8
13	Victim Letters	1
Review	Coping Strategies	1
14	Old Me	3
15	Future Me	3
16	Future Me Alternatives to Offending	8
17	Getting to Future Me	3
18	Setbacks	2
19	Future Me Role-plays	8
20	Feedback and Goal Setting	2

Treatment for sex offenders in the community

Much of what has been developed within the prison system has been introduced in the community. There are currently three independently accredited programmes designed for sex offenders run by the probation service: the Thames Valley Programme (TV-SOGP); the Northumbrian Groupwork Programme; and the West Midlands Community Sex Offender Groupwork Programme (C-SOGP). All three programmes are intensive programmes designed to protect the public by ensuring that sex offenders are equipped with the appropriate tools to prevent future abuse.

The programmes' grounds for exclusion are similar to those of the SOTP. Total deniers are not excluded from treatment. However, no more than two offenders are included in any group. Furthermore, total deniers typically receive one-to-one intervention prior to participating in treatment. Unlike the SOTP, participation in community-based programmes is not voluntary. Instead, offenders enter treatment as a condition of a

Table 3.2 The C-SOGP

Phase	Module	Title	Duration
1	1	Induction Module	Closed group – 50 hours
2	2	Cycles and Cognitive Distortions	Rolling group – approx. 190 hours
	3	Relationships and Attachment Styles	
	4	Self-Management and Interpersonal Skills	
	5	The Role of Fantasy in Offending	
	6	Victim Empathy	
	7	Relapse Prevention and Lifestyle Change	
3		Relapse Prevention Programme	Rolling programme – 50 hours

Community Rehabilitation Order (CRO, formerly the Probation Order),[5] or as a condition of release. Community programmes therefore have to cater for a wide array of offences, ranging from indecent exposure and downloading child pornography from the internet (which are more likely to receive community sentences) to rape and child abuse (which invariably receive custodial sentences). Despite this, due to resource issues (see Beech and Fisher 2004) community programmes are unable to provide a range of programmes to cater for the different needs of offenders. Instead, they are typically run as rolling programmes, which offer a number of modules that offenders can attend according to their needs.

As an example, the C-SOGP is separated into three main parts (see Table 3.2). Part 1, the induction phase, consists of a 50-hour closed group. The aim is to establish a positive group environment and enhance the group members' motivation to change their offending behaviour. During the Induction Module, offenders begin to understand the links between thoughts, feelings and behaviour and their offending. It also introduces the key principles of relapse prevention. The Induction Module first meets every day for a week, then becomes weekly, with each session being two and a half hours.

The second phase of the C-SOGP is the rolling treatment programme. Phase 2 is run as weekly two-and-a-half-hour sessions. Depending on the size of the group, the weekly meetings are conducted as half-day sessions (in effect one session a day) or as full-day sessions (in effect two sessions a day). The programme is expected to take approximately 190 hours. The modules covered explore the five key treatment targets outlined above and are designed to allow offenders to repeat and omit modules according to need. Offenders required to attend the C-SOGP as a condition of their Community Rehabilitation Order enter the pro-gramme at the Induction Module. Offenders who have successfully completed the SOTP may enter the programme at any module apart from module 6, Victim Empathy. This is because research has indicated that working on victim issues too early can have an adverse effect on what is intended (Beckett *et al*. 1994).

A shorter (50 hours) Relapse Prevention Programme (phase 3) has also been designed to meet the needs of offenders assessed as low risk/low deviance[6] prior to the Induction Module. Run as a rolling programme, the programme condenses the work done in phase 2 of the C-SOGP, placing greater emphasis on developing relapse prevention plans. Offenders assessed as low risk/low deviance after the Induction Module would also complete the shorter Relapse Prevention Programme rather than phase 2 of the C-SOGP.

Seven participants in this research participated on the C-SOGP. Six offenders had committed child abuse, and one offender had committed an internet offence. It is important to note, however, that at the time this research was conducted, the C-SOGP was in the process of accreditation. This meant that the facilitators were not trained to deliver the C-SOGP until midway through the programme, nor did the programme benefit from having a programme or treatment manager to check the pro-gramme in action. In addition, it was, at this time, jointly run by the probation service and the National Society for the Prevention of Cruelty to Children (NSPCC). The Pathfinders partnership between the NSPCC and the probation service was dissolved in April 2003. Since the C-SOGP has become accredited it has been run exclusively by the National Probation Service.

Treatment effectiveness

The impact of sex offender treatment programmes, particularly on child sexual abusers, has been extensively researched (Beckett *et al*. 1994; Hedderman and Sugg 1996; Alexander 1999; Beech *et al*. 2001; Friendship *et al*. 2003; Kenworthy *et al*. 2004). The majority of these studies have found some treatment effect, using recidivism or re-offending as an outcome measure (i.e. government statistics). However, research in this area faces numerous methodological challenges. These will be discussed in relation to specific research studies.

An evaluation of community-based sex offender treatment found that only 5 per cent of sexual offenders who had undergone treatment had been reconvicted for a sexual offence after two years, compared to 9 per cent of sexual offenders who did not receive treatment. This included nine offenders who were assessed as being highly deviant before treatment (Hedderman and Sugg 1996). A follow-up study found that only 10 per cent of the men who were classified as 'benefiting from treatment' were reconvicted after six years, compared with 23 per cent of men who were classified as 'not having responded to treatment' (Beech et al. 2001).

A two-year reconviction study, in which a group of prisoners who completed the SOTP were compared with a retrospective sample of sexual offenders, also identified small treatment effects (measured by reconviction) in low- and medium-risk offenders. However, the research pointed to the difficulty in demonstrating that the slightly lower reconviction rates of the treatment group were due to their participation in the SOTP rather than 'chance factors' (Friendship et al. 2003: 3). The authors therefore expressed caution in the over-reliance on reconviction data as a measure of treatment success (see also Merrington and Stanley 2000; Falshaw et al. 2003; Brooks-Gordon et al. 2004).

In addition, caution has been raised regarding the uncritical interpretation of evidence-based research. Brooks-Gordon et al. (2004) report that only a small percentage of research carried out finds its way into publication, with those written in English and presenting positive treatment effect more likely to be published. This is perhaps understandable given the huge investment, both financially and publicly, made in sexual offender treatment programmes, including the consequent desire for sex offender treatment programmes to be seen as effective (Brooks-Gordon et al. 2004). Nonetheless, it raises growing concern relating to the efficacy of treatment intervention with all sex offenders.

It has been suggested that the inclusion of nonofficial data in evaluations of sex offender treatment programmes would more accurately describe the impact that treatment has on reducing sex offenders' risk of future offending. This might include self-report studies or police intelligence files, which can be used to help identify instances of 'sexual re-offending' and 'sexual recidivism', i.e. respectively the perpetration of another illegal sexual act, or behaviour where there was a clear sexual motivation,[7] whether the individual was caught or not (Falshaw et al. 2003; Friendship et al. 2003). In addition, it has been argued that researching the perspectives of those being treated would provide a greater understanding of the 'processes of treatment' (Brooks-Gordon et al. 2004: 413) and the interface between the criminal justice system and those it deals with (see Chapter 1).

Alternative treatment groups

The vast majority of research completed to date has focused on the effectiveness of treatment intervention with child abusers. This has been fed into the 'what works' literature, which in turn has led to a fundamental rethinking of treatment approaches with offenders. Consequently, in terms of treatment provision, sex offender treatment programmes are targeted more at child abusers than at other categories of offenders (Polaschek and King 2002).

Despite this, current treatment intervention in both prison and the community is applicable for all types of offenders regardless of the nature of their offence. As this chapter has shown, child abusers, rapists, sexual murderers, exhibitionists and internet sexual offenders undertake the same treatment programmes, often participating within the same group. However, research into the characteristics and motivations of these different groups clearly shows that sex offending is not a homogenous activity (see Fisher and Mair 1998 for a review of classification schemes). For example, men convicted of rape tend to be younger, more impulsive and more aggressive than child abusers. They are also more likely to have been in a long-term relationship, and have substance misuse problems (Hudson and Ward 1997). Polaschek and King (2002) argue that current programmes do not offer interventions that will deal sufficiently with these problems. Similarly, men who have committed sexual murder and noncontact offences might also have unique treatment needs over and above other sex offenders (see Fisher and Beech 2004 for a summary). This raises the problem of transferring general theories and models derived from research on child abuse to other groups of offenders (McNeil 2000; Merrington and Stanley 2000; Hollin 2001; Cameron and Telfer 2004).

Models of offending used within sex offender treatment have been criticized for conveying the idea that all sexual offending follows a formulaic pattern. In response, the cycle of offending (originally developed by Wolf 1984, 1988) has been adapted into three distinct cycles; the inhibited cycle, for offenders who need to be disinhibited before they sexually abuse; the short-circuit cycle, for offenders who are less inhibited to commit a sexual offence due to the fact that they have committed several offences; and the continuous cycle, for offenders who do not have internal inhibitors other than the fear of being caught (see Eldridge 1998 for a summary). In addition, Hudson and Ward (2000) now talk of 'offence pathways' instead of 'models' or 'cycles of offending' to indicate further the heterogeneous nature of sexual offending.

Treating deniers

Different treatment models have been applied to offenders in total denial. Here, total denial refers to the denial of a specified behaviour on a particular day. This type of denial has been defined by others as literal denial (Cohen 2001), primary denial (Furniss 1991), absolute denial (Kennedy and Grubin 1992), physical denial (Salter 1988) and total innocence (Matthews 1991). As outlined above, it is preferable for offenders in total denial to be worked with separately prior to participating in mainstream sex offender treatment programmes such as the SOTP and the C-SOGP.

Deniers' programmes have had the aim, either explicitly or implicitly, of encouraging offenders to admit their offences in preparation for treatment. However, more recently, the emphasis of deniers' programmes' has been shifted away from 'confession' and aimed instead at providing an educational curriculum for convicted sexual offenders. As such, the success of the programmes is no longer judged by the percentage of offenders who admit their crime and then go on to standard sex offender treatment. Instead, it is measured on the basis of attitudinal change, knowledge gain, personal growth, and reduced recidivism (Stevenson et al. 1989; Marshall et al. 2001b). Schlank and Shaw's (1997) review of treatment programmes designed specifically for deniers presents preliminary findings that such programmes can alter the group members' thoughts, feelings and behaviour that predisposed them to re-offend. However, deniers' programmes operating in either prison or the community remain unaccredited.

Eleven participants in this research participated in an unaccredited prison-based deniers' programme named the Behaviour Assessment Programme (BAP). This programme is adapted from the (unaccredited) Middlesex Probation Service's Sex Offenders Deniers' Programme to apply to sex offenders who deny all, or most, aspects of their offending and have received a custodial sentence.

The BAP is a much shorter programme than both the accredited SOTP and the C-SOGP, consisting of only 15 sessions (see Table 3.3). It runs two days a week, typically as morning two-hour sessions, for seven weeks, with one session completed per day. Like the SOTP and the C-SOGP, the BAP is based on cognitive behavioural therapy and covers the five treatment targets outlined above. The programme looks at pro-offending attitudes and beliefs (sessions 2 and 12); victim empathy (sessions 10 and 11); social adequacy problems and lifestyle management (sessions 2, 3, 7 and 8); and relapse prevention (sessions 5, 13 and 14). It also introduces Finkelhor's four precursors of offending (session 4), and incorporates an educational approach to deviant sexual arousal (session 9).

Given that the BAP is designed specifically for sex offenders in total denial, the main functions of denial (for example, self-preservation) are also explored in session 6 (see Rogers and Dickey 1991 'adaptational model' for a summary). As denial is not considered to be directly related to an offender's propensity to offend (Beckett et al. 1994, Hanson and Bussiere 1998), it is not a primary focus of either the SOTP or the

Table 3.3 Fifteen sessions of the BAP

Session	Title
1	Introduction: Establishing the Group
2	Relationships, Power, Control and Consent
3	Relationships and Communicating Emotions
4	Finkelhor: The Precursors of Offending
5	The Process of Change and Relapse Prevention
6	The Dynamics of Denial
7	Personal Roles and Personal Responsibility
8	Rules of Human Conduct
9	Human Sexuality Information
10	Victim Empathy and Awareness: Part I
11	Victim Empathy and Awareness: Part II
12	Attitudes to Women and Rape Myths
13	Relapse Prevention: Skill Practice
14	Relapse Prevention: Avoid, Control and Escape (ACE)
15	Revision Session

C-SOGP. Nevertheless, both programmes attempt to reduce group members' level of denial throughout treatment in order to encourage offenders to speak more openly about their thoughts, attitudes, feelings and behaviours.

Unlike more mainstream programmes, the BAP does not focus on the individual's offending behaviour. Instead it invites the offenders to make links with related material that is presented in a hypothetical manner. The aim is for offenders to apply their new knowledge and learning to their own situation. This in turn should increase their understanding of the damage caused by offending, and reduce their risk of further abuse. The programme is therefore based on the assumption that many of the men inwardly admit to their offending behaviour but are determined not to admit it outwardly to others. (The BAP observed in this study did however accept sex offenders that admit to having offended as well as those that are in total denial, as there were no other programmes available.)

Alternative treatment

This chapter has so far dealt with cognitive behavioural treatment offered by the prison and probation services. There are, however, a range of alternative treatments used to control and manage the risk posed by sex offenders

Antiandrogens, which decrease deviant sexual arousal, are offered by the health service, either in special hospitals or medium secure units (Bradford 1997; Prentky 1997; Adi *et al.* 2002; Marshall *et al.* 2004). Preliminary research has found that the use of antiandrogen treatment reduces the frequency of masturbation and the intensity of deviant fantasies (Adi *et al.* 2002). However, since offenders must eventually learn to manage their behaviour without the aid of medication, antiandrogens should only be used in conjunction with comprehensive cognitive behavioural programmes (Adi *et al.* 2002; Marshall *et al.* 2004).

The use of periodic polygraph testing, or lie detectors, is also being piloted in the UK to assist in the treatment and supervision of sex offenders (Grubin *et al.* 2004; Madsen *et al.* forthcoming). In principle, this should act as a deterrent. In addition, used alongside treatment, regular polygraph testing can measure whether offenders are making adjustments to their behaviour in line with treatment goals. Early findings indicate that offenders who have experienced a second examination are less likely to engage in high-risk behaviours. They are also more likely to disclose information to supervising probation officers or treatment providers. However, there is the danger that use of polygraph testing will heighten the prototypical image that all sex offenders are proficient and practised liars, thus strengthening their categorization as 'other'.

Circles of Support and Accountability

In contrast, Circles of Support and Accountability are being piloted in three projects in Britain to aid the integration of sex offenders in the community.[8] The 'Circle of Support' provides a community (usually between four and six individuals) to the otherwise isolated sex offender (Silverman and Wilson 2002; Kemshall and Maguire 2003; Quaker Peace and Social Witness 2003). Circles are aimed at sex offenders who have been assessed as having high risks and needs, and those who have little or no support from friends and/or family in the community. The offender is referred to as the 'core member' of the Circle, and can have offended against children or adults.

Unlike all the initiatives outlined above, Circles take into account that any successful reintegration of offenders depends on the active participation of the community. It therefore relies heavily on volunteers to give up their time to provide support and accountability to sex offenders upon their release. All volunteers are screened and receive training. Where possible, Circle members will meet the offender once prior to release. The Circle will then meet with the core member once a week. In between, at least one Circle member will be in touch with the core member daily. Here, contact ranges from telephone conversations to face-to-face meetings.

The premise behind Circles of Support and Accountability is that by 'forging relationships' the core member will be deterred from re-offending (Silverman and Wilson, 2002). The Circle also monitors core members through regular contact. Information can then be shared with professionals involved in the core member's resettlement, in order to prevent future abuse. Preliminary findings from Canada, where Circles of Support and Accountability were originally developed, indicate that Circles have reduced re-offending by over 60 per cent among high-risk released paedophiles.[9] Such findings clearly challenge some of the oversimplified views that contribute to the debate about what should be done with, and to, sexual offenders in the UK.

Conclusions

Rehabilitation is no longer claimed to be a leading purpose of the criminal justice system. Instead, the key concerns of treatment are now to 'protect the public, reduce the risk of future victims and to do so with minimum resources' (Garland 2001: 176). As such, Garland (2001) has argued that the 'what works' movement, which has led to the replace-ment of the pessimistic conclusions most associated with Martinson (1974), is far from a return to rehabilitative optimism.

This chapter has highlighted the current situation for sex offender treatment in prison and the community. In particular it has focused on the three programmes used in this research, namely the accredited prison-based Sex Offender Treatment Programme (SOTP) and the Community Sex Offender Groupwork Programme (C-SOGP), and the non-accredited deniers' programme, the Behaviour Assessment Pro-gramme (BAP). All three programmes have adapted a cognitive behav-ioural group-work approach to treatment.

Such treatment interventions face numerous challenges with regard to the way they are implemented and the level of support they receive. On the one hand these criticisms point to the need to describe more accurately the impact treatment intervention has with all sex offenders. On the other, they point to the growing pressure to use the media more constructively to help promote support and understanding of the goals of treatment. To reiterate conclusions presented in Chapter 2, the media's institutional focus on the failures of the criminal justice system, including treatment, will only continue to push for more punitive and 'popular' measures to control sex offenders. Instead, the public need to be made aware that some sex offenders can benefit from treatment and refrain from sexual offending.

Notes

1 Some risk factors are 'static', meaning they have already happened and cannot be changed. It is also important to note that not all dynamic risk factors are addressed within treatment, for example, practical issues such as accommodation, employment, etc.

2 These conclusions support arguments presented in Chapter 2.

3 Attachment theory also provides a framework for understanding an offender's core belief system.

4 The Adapted Core Programme has been designed for offenders with an IQ of 70–80.

5 This usually has to be three years in duration.

6 Psychometric tests are completed by the offender before and after the Induction Module. The assessment measures the offender's progress during the treatment process, which, combined with Thornton's Risk Matrix 2000, gives a risk/deviance rating (Hanson and Thornton 2000).

7 This might involve instances where a convicted child sexual offender is found loitering outside a school.

8 The pilot projects are the Thames Valley Project, Hampshire Probation Area, working closely with the Hampton Trust, and the Lucy Faith Foundation (see Quaker Peace and Social Witness 2003 for an overview).

9 Findings from the pilot studies in the UK are expected in 2005.

Part II
Sex offenders' perspectives

Chapter 4

Sex offenders' identities

Chapter 2 discussed how the media, and in particular the tabloid press, provide the major forum for constructing the 'popular' image of the sex offender. Sex offenders are regularly portrayed as compulsive recidivists whose behaviour often escalates to lethal violent crime, e.g. 'How can we protect our children if these monsters are allowed to live? There is no cure for them ... they MUST HANG' (*Sunday People*, 30 July 2000: 4–5 [original emphasis]); 'Their evil is incurable says crime expert' (*News of the World*, 23 July 2000: 5).[1] Sex offenders, and in particular child abusers, have been represented as modern-day folk devils (Soothill and Walby 1991; Sampson 1994; Farrell and Soothill 2001). Within this context, this chapter is predominantly concerned with how the enduring 'stigma' (Goffman 1963) of a criminal record for a sexual offence affects an individual's presentation and management of their identity.

Interpreting the 'popular image'

Although this research cannot determine whether the public at large accepts the 'popular image' of the sex offender, such definitions appear to be confirmed by the men participating in this study.

Each of the men interviewed was asked how they thought the public would define a 'sex offender'. The dominant profile was that of a child sexual abuser, supporting the argument that the paedophile represents the latest in a series of moral panics (Garland 2001). When a wider range of sexual offending was discussed, the 'worst' case scenarios were considered to be accepted as the 'norm' by the general public. For example, Clive, a convicted rapist, described the stranger attacker, who uses a weapon to gain his victim's compliance, whereas Finn, having

53

been convicted of an indecent assault against a child, argued that the public believe that all sex offenders kill their victims:

> It's been proved that sex offenders will kill children for their own sexual pleasure, so all sex offenders are tarred with this mortal behaviour. (Finn)

The men interviewed also agreed on certain physical and social characteristics that society regularly imputes to the sex offender (West 2000a, 2000b):

> He looks a bit dodgy he hasn't got a girlfriend, he keeps himself to himself [therefore] he could be seen as a wrong'un. (Wayne)

Russell felt the public would depict child sexual abusers in terms of the 'old man with a walking stick'. Similarly, Thomas described the inhibited and lonely old man (West 2000b) as the 'classic paedophile':

> They could turn around and say I'm the classic paedophile I'm little bit of a loner, I've not been in a long term relationship for the last 15 years, I'm shy, I don't think that I'm a particularly attractive person, I've got all the classical characteristics. (Thomas)

It was generally accepted that the popular image of the sex offender had become so embedded within society that any individual possessing these attributes would be under particular suspicion of being labelled a sex offender. For example, West's (2000a) research highlights the undeserved[2] reputation of homosexual men being prone to child molesting. Of the 32 sex offenders interviewed in this research, four men (Graham, Ivor, Thomas and Zack) disclosed that they were gay. Thomas and Graham clearly felt that the public perceived homosexuals as having paedophilic tendencies:

> They [the public] think if you're a homosexual you're a paedophile and that all homosexuals are after young boys. (Thomas)

The role of the media in focusing public opinion was accepted by the men interviewed. The interviewees agreed that the press provide a highly distorted picture of the nature of sexual offending. Consequently, it was widely accepted that 'they [the public] haven't got a clue who a sex offender is' (Vincent). This corroborates with a number of research studies in this area (see, for example, Cobley 2000; Wykes 2002). Wykes' (2002) research highlights how ordinary men – husbands, fathers, uncles and lovers – are curiously absent from news reporting, despite the fact that they represent the 'typical' perpetrators of such crimes. Clive expressed a similar opinion:

> They [the public] don't realise that a boyfriend can be a [sex offender], her boyfriend or a close friend, or someone that doesn't use force, or a husband can do it to the wife. (Clive)

He also felt that the media reporting of the death of Sarah Payne (see Chapter 2) was indicative of the type of sexual crime that makes the news:

> It doesn't make the news if it wasn't a stranger that came and killed the child ... they're not thinking of the person inside the house. (Clive)

The interviewees were, nonetheless, perceptive enough to realize that given the public's indiscriminate use of terms such as 'beast', 'paedophile' and 'stranger danger' (i.e. the predatory sex offender who uses sadistic brutality), anyone who had a conviction of a sexual offence would be 'tarred with the same brush':

> Outside according to anyone I'm a beast, I'm an animal, I'm a danger. (Vincent)

Recognition of the media's role in articulating these opinions left the participants with little doubt over societal indignation.

Stigma and identity

The current manner in which society perceives and reacts to sexual offenders clearly had an impact on the way the interviewees thought about themselves and interacted with others. Their conviction of a sexual offence can therefore be likened to what Goffman (1963) has defined as a stigma. The term 'stigma' is used here to refer to an attribute that is deeply discrediting. However, this perhaps oversimplifies the heightened moral panic surrounding sex offending. As Chapter 2 illustrated, it is no longer merely the offending act that is unacceptable but the sex offenders themselves. To speak of the individuals' 'extended social identity', rather than stigma, better captures this.

There are various working definitions of 'social identity' (see, for example, Jenkins 1996; Breakwell 2001; Brewer 2001; Duveen 2001). Within this research, social identity is used to refer to an identity that is constructed, attributed value (good and bad), and ascribed to individuals from outside sources. An 'extended social identity' is that which is then internalized by the individual (Breakwell 2001; Duveen 2001). It therefore becomes an extension of who they are.

The concept of the extended social identity therefore recognizes that individuals with a conviction of a sexual offence do not live in a vacuum but face constant daily reminders of society's indignation towards them. Indeed, the men interviewed in this research were fully aware of how the public perceived 'sex offenders'. However, unlike a social identity, which is ascribed from outside sources, an extended social identity shifts the attention back towards the individual. In doing so, it recognizes that individuals with a conviction of a sexual offence are unable to separate completely their criminal act from their overall sense of self. Instead, their social identity, shaped by the 'stigma' of having been convicted of a sexual offence, becomes an extension of who they are.

The notion of an extended social identity also takes into account the unique and idiosyncratic qualities that make up an individual's identity. It acknowledges that an individual with a sexual conviction has multiple identities and characteristics besides the label of sex offender. Moreover, it encapsulates the idea that the extended social identity has an existence independent of its presence in any one individual (Breakwell 2001). However, despite popular belief, the stigma of a criminal record for a sexual offence (or an individual's extended social identity) is not inherent in any individual's physical attributes. Consequently, you would not know, just by looking at somebody, whether they had committed a sexual offence. This information has to be disclosed in some form or another.

The men interviewed in this study expressed deep concern that any public identification as a 'sex offender' would make if difficult for them to establish an identity as anything other than a sex offender. This draws on Becker's (1963) concept of the 'Master Status'. Becker argued that once an individual has been labelled a particular kind of person, in this instance a sex offender, that label can become the most salient part of the individuals' character, at least in terms of how they are viewed by others. For the men in this research, finding ways to manage their identity therefore became a primary concern.

The interviewees clearly engaged in a process of self-preservation in order to present themselves in a more favourable light (Goffman 1959). Goffman (1959) has described this process in a dramaturgical way. For example, he makes a distinction between two main sites of interaction, the 'frontstage' features and the 'backstage' features. In doing so, he points to a process of information control, or 'stage management', in what an individual chooses to conceal backstage.

It was typical for the men participating in this research to conceal (backstage) their stigma to those unaware of their conviction. As concerns about privacy and public exposure are particularly acute for sex offenders residing in the community, this became increasingly important for the men participating in the Community Sex Offender Groupwork Programme (C-SOGP):

> I'm not going to go around bragging about it, I'm going to keep it not so much quiet . . . but I'm not going to go out of my way to tell people. (Keith)

While all the men in this subgroup concealed their offence from members of the general public, a number of men also concealed their offence from members of their immediate family and close friends. In addition, Matthew, the only group member in full-time employment, concealed his offence from his employer and work colleagues 'in fear that [he] would lose [his] job'.

It is arguably more difficult for men serving a custodial sentence to conceal completely their offence, given that they will either be segregated under Rule 45 or in a prison that has become a vulnerable prison unit (which are known to deal predominantly with sex offenders). Nonetheless, the men participating on a prison-based treatment programme did not generally disclose information about their offence outside treatment, in fear of being persecuted by other prisoners or prison staff.[3]

The men interviewed in this research also attached great importance to the perceived reaction of those who knew of their conviction. The participants' desire to preserve a more favourable image during the interviews became evident in the way they discussed their offending behaviour. Scully and Morolla (1984: 530) have defined these 'accounts' as 'manifestations of an underlying negotiation of identity'.

The negotiation of identities

On analysing the accounts of the research participants, a broad division emerged between 'admitters' and 'deniers'. However, the breadth and complexity of the interviewees' accounts meant that the men did not always fit neatly into these categories and there was often overlap between them. For example, denial is used here to include the range of individuals from those who refuse to acknowledge any part of the offence through to denying specific aspects of the offence. The latter assumes that individuals admit to one part of their actions but not to another. In addition, it was typical for a number of interviewees to admit to committing the act, but to deny that their behaviour had caused any harm.

To some extent all the men interviewed denied some aspect of their offence. It was, however, possible to identify two types of denial: denial of facts and behaviour, and denial of wrongdoing. In the latter case, the legal system has determined that their actions were wrong and abusive, although the men's accounts of their actions do not correspond to this judicial perspective. The former case is more problematic, as the legal system is fallible. However, the discussion that follows is based solely on the men's own accounts of their behaviour and actions. Where discrepancies emerge between their own perspective and that of the criminal justice system, this can be identified from their own accounts and argument.

While acknowledging that there may be crossover groups, the men interviewed in this research were placed into three categories, namely 'total deniers' (n = 6), 'justifiers' (n = 4) and 'acceptors' (n = 22). Whereas the first two categories have been defined as 'deniers', the third category refers to participants who both admit to committing a sexual offence and accept that their behaviour was abusive.

Albert provides a unique example of the difficulty of pigeonholing the men interviewed in this study into these three categories. Albert was serving a life sentence for murder. Although he was never charged with a sexual offence, forensic evidence suggested the possibility of a sexual assault. These details included a single matching pubic hair on the victim's cardigan, the fact that the victim's bra was ripped, and that her top was pulled over her head. Interestingly, Albert only commented upon the state of his victim's attire during the interviews, choosing to conceal (backstage) arguably more discreditable information:

> The pathologist report stated that the body was in a state of undress. I pushed her out of the bus and her skirt came up. (Albert)

> I mean, they were looking at it because her bra was ripped at the front, they were looking at in the sense was it sexually motivated. (Albert)

While Albert admitted to murdering his victim, he denied that there was any sexual element and/or motivation to his crime. He was, however, willing to participate on the SOTP and to undertake work concerning the sexual elements of his crime. For this reason, Albert has been defined as an 'acceptor'.

The categories outlined above thus simply represent an individual's perception of their conviction, i.e. the way they speak about the offence of which they have been convicted. (In Albert's case, this refers to the way in which he spoke about his murder conviction.) This of course is subject to change over time and therefore represents a model for analysis focusing on a distinction between different levels of denial or self-admission. Consequently, the three categories used here simply represent dominant states of denial among these men at the time of the study.

The language of denial

The accounts of the men in denial exhibit two similarities. The first, and perhaps the most obvious, characteristic is that they do not define themselves as sex offenders. They did, however, acknowledge that they had been labelled as such by the criminal justice system, thus assuming their social identity:

> Well they obviously class me as a paedophile. I'm not but I'm classed as one. (Stuart)

The second comparison looks at the feelings of shame and guilt exhibited by the deniers. As these participants believed that they had been falsely convicted, the majority did not feel guilty about the offence. Similar to Salter's (1988) findings, the shame conveyed by these men was usually over some secondary effect of the abuse, for example their 'punishment', or the negative status that is assigned to the popular image of a sex offender:

> I think that it's just having to come here, the fact that they're trying to control my life. I think that's got as much to do with that than anything. (Jack)

> I think the biggest part of the problem, is the stigma and the shame I feel of being put on this charge. (Wayne)

Distinctions can, however, be identified in the accounts presented by the men defined as 'total deniers' and 'justifiers'.

Total deniers

Total denial refers to the denial of a specified behaviour on a particular day. The participants in total denial (n=6) denied the offence based on the assertion that it simply did not happen. They therefore asserted, at least outwardly, their innocence. On analysing these men's accounts, similarities can be seen with regard to the information that they chose to disclose about their 'alleged offence'. For example, this group of participants insisted either that their so-called victims were out to get them (i.e. that they were in fact the real victims) and/or that they were not the kind of person that could do that sort of thing.

A number of men questioned whether their victim(s) had made up the accusations to get compensation:

> They're doing it for the money they are, that's what it is ... the ex-wife the kids, money, money, money. (Stuart)

I've looked at compo, did they want compensation, that's the biggest part now why everyone is doing it to get a couple of thousand pounds. (Wayne)

Conversely, both Xandy and Vincent claimed that they had been accused of sexually abusive behaviour because they had refused to give in to bribes:

I know why it came about, because people thought I had money that I didn't have. They blatantly demanded money out of me and I told them to fuck off and then the next thing I knew there were these accusations against me. (Xandy)

Others claimed that their victims had accused them of sexual abuse as a way of 'getting back at them' for not giving them enough attention. Thomas, convicted of indecently assaulting his stepson's partner's two young girls, believed that the 'problems started' after the birth of their new baby. According to Thomas, his 'victims' became jealous of the amount of attention the new baby received, especially from him. Similarly, Paul felt that his children had made up the allegations because they were jealous of the time that he had been spending with his new partner's children:

Like I say, from what I can work out, there was a lot of jealousy between them, and she [his daughter and 'victim'] was trying somehow, well so hard to bloody get back at me, but where she got this story from I don't know. (Paul)

All the arguments presented above were substantiated by 'evidence' to suggest that their victims had lied. Stuart repeatedly maintained that he had alibis for two of the four occasions when the 'victims' said that the abuse took place. He also stated that his 'victims' had previously accused three men of similar offences in order to reinforce their deceitfulness.

Thomas and Wayne both used their sexuality to 'prove' that the offence could not have occurred:

I'm homosexual and the offence is against young girls. (Thomas)

Similarly, Wayne stated that he had been diagnosed as a 'paranoid homophobic' and consequently would not have been able to commit the alleged offences as they were against his nephews.

In the cases where there was more than one victim, 'conflicting evidence' was presented to 'prove' that their so-called victims had lied:

I'm here because of their lies. They gave conflicting evidence, this is what I can't understand, my niece said when she went out to go to the toilet, that when she came back I was in the back with the other girl. The other young girl said that I was in the front trying to touch her over her trousers and my niece reckons that she had her trousers round her ankles and I was in the back with her. Who's lying me or them? (Stuart)

She [his daughter and victim] says that I touched her between her legs without her clothes on, my other daughter said that I touched her between the legs when she had her trousers on, conflicting evidence all the way. (Vincent)[4]

Both Stuart and Vincent also pointed to the impracticalities of the accusations. For instance, Stuart claimed that it would have been impossible to have committed the abuse in the time that he was away with the 'victims':

Like I say I got suckered in dead easy and I didn't do nothing, just took them down to McDonalds, by their own admission quarter of an hour I was with them. You've got to drive two miles each way to McDonalds, cross four busy inter-junctions. I was only with them a quarter of an hour, if you see what I am supposed to have done; it would have taken you an hour and a half to do it. (Stuart)

Whereas Vincent argued that he would have needed extra limbs to carry out the abuse:

Now you tell me how I used two hands to hold her arms up against the wall, one hand on her chest, one hand opening her legs and one hand up between her legs, I'm not a miracle worker, but that's in her statement. (Vincent)

Medical evidence was also used by both men to substantiate their claim that their offence did not happen. Vincent argued that he was unable to commit the offence due to the fact that he had been diagnosed with 'Parkinson's disease, sciatica and asthma', whereas Stuart claimed that he had no need to commit a sexual offence as he was impotent:

I'm bloody useless, two and half bloody years I've been like this. From the waist down you can forget it. Bloody Samantha Fox could strip off in front of me and I'd sit there and read the paper, I can't do nothing, it's as simple as that. (Stuart)

All of the men in total denial expressed complete revulsion towards sexual offenders, highlighting the disparity between the prototypical 'sex offender' and themselves. Stuart used his position as a father to distance himself further from the image of the predatory stranger that looms large in the press:

> You know I'm a father myself, I've had children myself, so I don't like to be called [a paedophile] when you're not one. (Stuart)

Others drew upon their past behaviours to show that they had done nothing in their past to prerequisite sexual offending. Finally, five of the men who had previous convictions insisted that as they had admitted to things in the past they would have admitted to this, *if* they had done it:

> Yeah if I do something, if I've done something . . . then I'll say yep I done it. (Wayne)

> I will tell you one thing now, I will never admit to something I haven't done. If I'd done it I'd admit to it . . . If I done anything in the past and I've been caught I've admitted to it but I'm not going to admit to something that I didn't do, it's as simple as that, if I'd done it I'd admit to it but I didn't. (Stuart)

The information that the total deniers chose to reveal about the 'alleged offence' was (assuming of course that the men were guilty) used to reaffirm their innocence by displacing blame from their actions. Consequently, none of the total deniers in this study possessed any sense of victim empathy. Instead, they described themselves as the real victims:

> I hope that the little git [his victim] chokes herself to death. (Vincent)

> Speaking from myself I feel a victim. (Xandy)

Justifiers

Unlike the total deniers, the interviewees defined as justifiers (n=4) admitted that the act took place. However, they denied that their behaviour was abusive. Consequently, the accounts given by these men did not focus on whether the offence took place, but rather whether it could be justified (Scully and Morolla 1984; Barbaree 1991).

Similar to the findings presented by Scully and Morolla (1984), these men attempted to justify their behaviour by presenting the victim as culpable, regardless of their own actions. Three of the four justifiers described their 'victims as seductress' (Scully and Morolla 1984: 534). As an example, David presented his victim as a willing and enthusiastic partner:

I knew exactly what I was doing. I was led on for sex. If you're raping someone they don't undress themselves and they definitely don't undress you, they don't have orgasms. I was having a sexual relationship with my stepdaughter. (David).

Similarly, Keith and Yuval's accounts of the abuse clearly embellished the victim's actions above their own behaviour. Both men described their victims as a seductress who lured them into sexual action. Keith also suggested that he tried on a number of occasions to resist:

She was on the bed posing with a cigarette in her mouth and that, this neighbour of mine, a couple of doors down, in the meantime he's passed after being in the pub and seen the light on and knocked on the door, which he often did, well he was taking a couple of photos of her and they were asking me, and she was pulling me, 'go on, have your photo taken with me'. So after about twenty minutes I was fed up of her moaning I went in the photo and she had her top up and my hand was like [demonstrates how it was over her breast], more a sarcastic thing because I didn't want to be in the photo. (Keith)

The justifications used by Yuval can also be likened to another of the themes used by offenders to justify rape in Scully and Morolla's (1984) research. In their study, the deniers often used their victims' sexual reputation to evoke the stereotype that 'nice girls don't get raped' (Scully and Morolla 1984: 536). For example, discrediting statements about their sexuality and promiscuity were used by the rapists to substantiate their belief that their victim 'got what they deserved' (Scully and Morolla 1984: 537). In contrast, Yuval used 'discrediting statements' to imply that his victim 'was not the type of person that would get raped', but rather the type of woman that would 'cry rape':

I'm just saying she was the one in control like and that's the type of person she's like and people know what I'm like I've had girlfriends before and I've courted them for eight months and I've never even had sex with them like you know, so people know what I'm like and people know what she's like, and she's not the type of person that would get raped. (Yuval)

A clear distinction can be seen in the justifications used by Jack. Jack's offence related to photographic images and video clips of child por-nography, downloaded from the internet, found in his possession. Despite never denying the offence, Jack clearly disagreed with the law as the following extract from his statement given to the police highlights:

63

> I'm not denying that I downloaded pornography . . . I disagree with the law. They can't even prove that the images are real . . . the police and the courts are just trying to give me a bad name . . . Why is it a crime? It's in my head so what is the harm? (Jack)

Jack's justifications centred around two main points. The first draws on Goffman's (1963) work on stigma and identity. Goffman argued that stigmatized individuals hold the same belief about identity as 'normals'. Consequently, the way in which they define themselves is no different from any human being. The stigmatized individuals' deepest feelings of what they are, is their sense of being a normal person like everyone else. Jack therefore attempted to align himself with 'normals' by presenting his actions as something that 'most people do'. This enabled him to justify his actions as normal and thus to believe that he did nothing wrong:

> Sex is the most searched for word, I felt that I wasn't doing anything unusual, I thought it was perfectly normal to be doing this. (Jack)

As this chapter has already highlighted, the men in total denial used similar techniques. However, in these instances it was typical for the total deniers to claim that they were not the type of person that could do such a thing.

Jack's second justification was purely psychological. Jack clearly felt that he had not done anything wrong as he was not confronting a person but a machine. He therefore perceived his action to be completely impersonal and thus victimless:

> You dehumanize, well that's what I think any way, you dehumanize, you don't think of them as victims, they're just objects on the screen, it's as simple as that, and although deep down, to me it's just the entertainment, be it rather bad and it's just all acting, none of it is real, it's all staged, and they're all acting to a script. (Jack)

Some similarities can be noted between Jack's justifications and those used by the other justifiers in this study. For example, none of the men claimed that they were 'completely innocent' (Scully and Morolla 1984). For example, David acknowledged that he perhaps should not have had a 'relationship' with his stepdaughter, both Keith and Jack accepted that their behaviour may not have been completely proper, while Yuval recognized that he should not have been having an affair.[5] Nevertheless, despite their acceptance of 'some minor wrongdoings' (Scully and Morolla 1984), none of these men thought of themselves as sex offenders.

The vocabulary of motive

In contrast, the participants defined as acceptors (n = 22) both acknowledged that they had committed a sexual offence and blamed themselves rather than the victim for their actions. Consequently, nearly all of the men in this subgroup were more likely to regard their behaviour as wrong and beyond justification:

> I can't blame her for anything, it was me purely me, I took it, she had no choice in the matter. (Ben)

> I never blamed the victims like, no I pleaded guilty in court like, no one had to turn up or nothing like that you know, I took responsibility to it, I put my hands up. (Edmund)

> How could I blame my victim, no, I don't blame anybody apart from myself, I got myself into that position and I'm the one to be blamed me. (Greg)

However, despite admitting to the overall offence, the acceptors in this study denied aspects of their offensive behaviour:

> And there's one other thing my niece saying I really raped her, put my thing in her bottom, but I never done that I no I never, I feel like strangling her sometimes because I never done it. (Quinton)

> In the impact statement she said that she lost her bracelet in the process and that she thought she saw something shiny up to her face, the small bolt cutters were black metal, I've put it down to her imagination. She said that I kicked her in the bushes; I never I just picked her up and laid her down, she made it real aggressive. (Harry)

Similar to the men in denial, several of the acceptors suggested that the victim had contributed to the crime either by not resisting enough or by initiating the act:

> [We'd] gone up to her flat had a smoke and I raped her again, even though she consented to half, some of the things that happened. (Ben)

> Then they came over to me and they started putting socks down, down my trousers. Then they started putting stuff down their pants I think. Then they, I didn't tell them nothing then they started, my niece started taking her clothes off, she took her bottom half down you know knickers and, then she started sitting on me. (Quinton)

Clive also attempted to excuse his offending behaviour by alluding to the victim's sexual reputation (Scully and Morolla 1984):

> No way am I trying to blame this girl. When she offered me sex acts for money my thought process changed. I thought she was a tart, not a person, but someone that I could use to my advantage. I shouldn't have but I did. That was the turning point, I didn't see her as a person but as someone to use for sexual gratification. (Clive)

In addition, a number of acceptors aligned themselves with people that hadn't committed a sexual offence, or implied that these so-called 'normal' members of society had much more in common with them than they would care to admit:

> I mean I know I done wrong, I'm a sex offender, but I'm still human. (Ivor)

Although the deniers and acceptors in this study used similar techniques, they were used quite differently. For example, the acceptors can be seen to 'excuse' rather than justify their behaviour. For professionals working with sex offenders, these excuses have been defined as 'minimisations' (OBPU 2000; Allam 2001; Leyland and Baim 2001). The outcome is, however, the same. Denial and minimizations, or justifications and excuses, can be regarded as representing different stages of a cognitive process. Whereas denial and justifications signify a categorical statement, minimizations and excuses are concerned with the extent to which the offenders take responsibility for the offence. Deniers either totally denied or justified their behaviour in an attempt to 'dis-identify' themselves completely from the popular image of the sex offender. Unable to do this, the acceptors 'danced with denial' in order to distance themselves from their prototypical image of a sex offender (Happel and Auffrey 1995).

Distancing techniques

Nine distinct distancing techniques were used by the acceptors in this study to preserve a more acceptable identity both in the eyes of others, and to enhance their own sense of self-worth. These are:

i.   Distancing by category

ii. Distancing by degree of physical contact

iii. Distancing by consent

iv. Distancing by premeditation

v. Distancing by age of victim

vi. Distancing by relationship to victim

vii. Distancing by repeat offending

viii. Temporary aberration

ix. Shame

Similarities can be made with Sykes and Matza's (1957) 'Neutralisation Theory'.[6] The discussion will be explicit about where these overlaps occur.

Distancing by category

Mirroring the views of wider society, a hierarchy exists among offenders (particularly within a prison environment), with sex offenders regarded as the 'lowest of the low'. However, there also exists a hierarchy among those convicted of sexual crimes, as the following quotation from Colin illustrates:

> Sex offenders are of course the lowest of the low, but have their own hierarchy. Rapists are better than paedophiles. Paedophiles that have offended against teenagers are better than those who have offended against pubescent children, pubescent better than pre-pubescent, babies, toddlers. (Colin)

The rapists in this subgroup therefore distanced themselves from the paedophile, an offence generally considered to be 'worse' than theirs:

> I'm not trying to stereotype people on the group but there are some really bad, really, really, really bad I mean you know ... Yeah I mean, there with three-year-old kids like you know, and I don't like hearing anything like that. (Edmund)

> I would prefer to be called a sex offender to nonce. (Daniel)

The interviewees that had abused children often recognized their 'lower' status among other offenders. However, by distancing themselves from other types of crime they were also able to avoid feelings of shame and inadequacy:

> I can't stand drug offenders that have been out leeching on people to raid their moneybox to buy drugs with and things like that. (David)

All I can say is that some people, they do crimes for whatever reasons, the only one that I can think of worse is taking somebody's life. (Finn)

According to Neutralisation Theory (Sykes and Matza 1957; McCarthy and Stewart 1998), while offenders attempt to neutralize their own offence they will still show contempt for other types of offending behaviour.

The hierarchy of offences that this section has alluded to is by no means static. Each individual had their own dynamic principles that they believed would make their offence appear more acceptable or excusable to themselves and (many offenders believed) the outside world. These will now be discussed.

Distancing by degree of physical contact

A hierarchy emerged with regard to the amount of physical contact the perpetrator had with the victim. Euan, for example, unaware of a fellow group member's conviction, thought it would be something 'trivial' like indecent assault. In addition, all the men on the C-SOGP, at least initially, saw no reason for Jack, convicted of an internet offence, to be on the programme. Consequently, it was generally felt that the more physical contact the 'worse' the offence.

Such perceptions were used by Luke, convicted of indecently exposing himself and asking his victims to masturbate him, to distance himself from men who had physically abused their victims:

I would say theirs are worse offences, because mine was just verbal and theirs was a sexual assault, which is physical, so I would say it would be worse than my offence, because mine was verbal and theirs was physical. (Luke)

Similar findings were reported by the Respond Organisation (2000) in which a hierarchy emerged among a group of male sex offenders with learning difficulties, with those convicted of rape receiving all the hatred. Consequently, the group felt that it was far better to be guilty of indecent assault than rape.

Distancing by consent

As this chapter has already identified, a number of the acceptors denied aspects of their offending behaviour. In particular, a number of men denied that they used any force. For example, Harry denied that he used bolt cutters to ensure his victims' compliance, whereas Clive denied using a knife and referred to his victims' sexual reputation to excuse his behaviour. Typical of this type of denial is also the belief that the abuse was consensual, at least 'up to a point':

> I mean up to a point my offence wasn't an offence, up to a point, but then when we were having sex a point came when it became rape. (Clive)

Zack, convicted of sexually abusing children, also attempted to excuse his own behaviour by presenting his victims as both culpable and consenting:

> There was no force involved, and to be honest most of the time they would be undressed before I would, so it wasn't the case of me undressing them or anything like that, like if [one of my victims] was staying the night which some nights he would, he'd be in bed before I would, so I didn't sort of think well, yeah what have I done wrong. (Zack)

Children, of course, by definition are legally unable to give true consent. As such, rapists often used the issue of consent to distance themselves from child abusers. In contrast, offenders convicted of child abuse were quick to believe that the very fact their victims could not consent made their behaviour somehow better:

> The general attitude of rapists is that at least my victim is of a consenting age. If anything mine is better than theirs. I didn't force my victim . . . I'm not in for a violent rape, I had sexual relationships with children, it was something they enjoyed, a game they would come back and play. (Burt)

> I mean, if my victim turned round to me and said I don't want to do it what's the matter, I said it's all right go on then go on well go back to mammy . . . I mean my victims might say yes, I didn't throw them on a bed and say I'm going to do this, I'd say can I do this and can I do that and they'd say yes, to me, I know that it's wrong, and they're under the age of giving consent, but he took the victim, threw her on the floor and all that, to me that was the worst thing of all. (Ivor)

Distancing by premeditation

Research has shown that for at least some sex offenders, covert and overt planning takes place both before and after victims have been targeted (Marshall *et al.* 1999b). This might include grooming potential victims or engagement in deviant sexual fantasies (OBPU 2000; Swaffer *et al.* 2000;

Allam 2001). The majority of the men in this research identified premeditation with the popular image of the sex offender. As such they subsequently claimed that they acted spontaneously:

> There wasn't any fantasy in that even though it happened, suddenly it was just an act and that was it. (Ben)

> There was no violence involved, I never planned it, it started out like innocent and it just developed. (Harry)

> I didn't realize as such what was happening or why it was happening you know it was just happening. (Vincent)

> I wouldn't say I went out deliberately to do it, like I say mine was spontaneous over like a three- or four-week period. (Zack)

Distancing by age of victim

Generally within the same offence, the younger the victim is, the worse the offence is considered. Consequently, it was typical for the acceptors to compare themselves with offenders who had sexually abused a younger victim:

> My victims weren't that age, nowhere near, or nothing like that, there was one member on the group who had those younger thoughts and had been with a three-year-old. To be honest with you I just don't know, I don't understand them and even with the course I still don't understand how he got sexually aroused I really don't. (Edmund)

None of the interviewees in this study had abused an elderly victim. This was also true of the men who had decided not to take part in the interviews but had participated within the same treatment groups. This may have had a bearing on the research. Indeed, it can be assumed that the concepts that the offenders used as distancing techniques were dependent to some extent on the offences that were known to them.

Distancing by relationship to victim

Sex offenders are often classified according to their relationship with their victim (Fisher and Beech 2004). Similarly, the men interviewed in this research made distinctions between individuals who had abused victims that were known to them (including family members) and those who had abused strangers. Mirroring the perceptions of the wider public, acceptors who had abused 'known' victims typically regarded the stranger attacker as having committed 'worse' crimes. In contrast, the men that had targeted strangers were quick to excuse their own behaviour:

> My thinking was that [the people I knew] they had a life, while a stranger was just a face, nothing for me to connect with, there's nothing up here [pointing to his head] to trouble you with, yeah? (Edmund)

Distancing by repeat offending

Fifteen (68 per cent) of the 22 acceptors had no previous sexual convictions. All of these men attempted to distance themselves from the habitual sex offender:

> I suppose I am a paedophile, but I suppose a real paedophile is like repeat, repeat, repeat I suppose. (Matthew)

Even Oliver, who had a previous sexual conviction, tried to distance himself from the negative attributes of the repeat offender:

> I'm not a paedophile. As far as I'm concerned a paedophile is someone that keeps on re-offending all the time and I haven't done that, I have two offences but there's a big gap between the two of them, I don't re-offend, I don't go out targeting kids. (Oliver)

Temporary aberration

A number of acceptors also described their offending as a temporary aberration (Kennedy and Grubin 1992). This is consistent with the excuses used by the rapists in Scully and Morolla's (1984) research. For example, excuses were identified that permitted those rapists admitting to their offence to 'view their behaviour as idiosyncratic rather than typical, and thus, to believe they were not really rapists' (Scully and Morolla 1984: 538). Such excuses draw on external factors, for instance the use of alcohol and drugs, and emotional problems (Matthews 1991). The acceptors in this study frequently attributed their acts to similar external factors:

> Stuff had happened before this offence, like, marriage break-up, losing my father and stuff like that, which I don't talk about. Made me real aggressive. (Matthew)

> I think it was a combination of factors. One I had drunk, I did have quite a bit, not enough to make me stumble and when lifting heavy stuff my adrenaline was going. Drink and adrenaline plus being

aroused from seeing her, I thought she's a nice girl, chat her up and have sex you know. It got to the point where, you know, I wouldn't say I couldn't stop it but. (Harry)

If I wasn't drunk then nothing would have happened you know. (Russell)

Furthermore, Russell gave a typical example of an acceptor attempting to neutralize his crime in order to negotiate a 'nice guy image' (Scully and Morolla 1984; Kennedy and Grubin 1992):

I've grown up with an excellent family, I've worked all my life like and then suddenly this comes out of me when I'm you know off my head with drink and drugs like and I don't know why. (Russell)

Consequently, by describing his offence as a 'moment of madness' and himself as not a 'bad person', Russell attempted to convey his offence as not a representation of his true self.

The notion presented by some of the acceptors, that they had been 'made into' a sex offender, can be viewed as an extension of this concept. For example, a number of the acceptors who disclosed that they had been sexually abused, reflected on their abuse to excuse their behaviour, as the quotation from Oliver clearly shows:

I wasn't born a sex offender I was, this might be a stupid way of saying it, but anyway I was created to be by my uncle, I was created, but what I did to [my victim] was my fault [my uncle] wasn't there but to me I felt I was created to be a sex offender, I wasn't born to be one. (Oliver)

Shame

Evidently, the distancing techniques discussed so far have allowed the participants to enhance their self-image. In doing so, they also protect the individual from experiencing uncomfortable feelings of guilt and shame. Indeed, this was recognized as a technique that was used by others but not by themselves:

People like to think I'm not as bad as that person, my crime is not so bad, I robbed a bank so you burgled someone's house, then a shoplifter. He's got to find someone, maybe it will come down to a sex offender, a rapist. Rapists are then going to find somebody, so he finds a paedophile, and the paedophile he's got nobody else so he finds a child murderer and the child murderer has got nobody to go to because there's nobody below. It's just to make yourself feel better isn't it. (Clive)

However, 'shame' can also be seen as another way in which individuals manage their identity. Finn presents a perfect example. It was typical for Finn to present his offence as the 'lowest of the low'. He constantly referred to himself as 'unclean', 'a leper' or as 'evil'. He also expressed the view that his offence was unforgivable, and would often become tearful during the interviews. As such, Finn fully articulated the guilt and shame he carried with him. However, this shame became intrinsic to the way he coped with his negative self-image. Ironically, it became a vice that enabled him to distance himself from those evidently less repentant:

[I've] gradually come to the conclusion I may not like myself but at least I am doing something about it. (Finn)

There is part of me that hates myself but there is another part of me that's saying I'm doing OK, I've got to be slightly pleased with myself, I feel I shouldn't be pleased with myself but I am because I'm being honest. (Finn)

Similarly, acceptors who found it difficult to discuss their offence used this technique. This supports the argument presented by Pattison (2000). Speaking from a religious perspective, he has argued that while sacramental confession can provide a temporary relief, it can in itself be a shaming process. Consequently, this group of acceptors attempted to distance themselves from both offenders in denial and those who were considered too nonchalant in the way they spoke about their offence:

I'm not just saying this because I'm sat in front of you but I got regrets you know, I probably shouldn't say this but some, some would like spit it out like as if they were talking about being at a football match you know, and that surprised me a bit like you know, the way it rolled off the tongue type of thing like, and I don't know if that means anything like but I don't know, it just came out too easy. (Edmund)

Conclusions

The men interviewed in this research study generally accepted that the popular image of a sex offender implicitly incorporated many cultural stereotypes. They also recognized that if their conviction was revealed to others, then the 'popular image' of a sex offender, namely the predatory paedophile who rapes and murders young children, would become their master status regardless of their crime. The interviewees therefore engaged in a process of impression management in order to preserve a more acceptable social identity (Goffman 1959).

Total denial is perhaps the most obvious method that an offender can use to achieve this. For example, whereas the acceptors and the justifiers acknowledged that they had committed the act, in contrast, the total deniers denied participation in any sexual behaviour. However, only six interviewees contended that the offence simply did not happen. Arguably, this might have had more to do with the fact that this research took place within criminal justice settings. This will be discussed in more detail in the next chapter.

Of course, all the men in this study used denial to some extent to protect themselves from negative perceptions typically attributed to 'sex offenders'. In addition, the majority of men having both admitted to their offence and accepted that their behaviour had been abusive, engaged in distancing techniques to negotiate a more acceptable identity in the eyes of others. However, by drawing on discussion on identity, the chapter also examined the interviewees' sense of their own situation. In particular, it recognized that these men did not live in a vacuum and had access to the media. It therefore concluded that irrespective of their state of denial, the men interviewed in this research were unable to separate completely their criminal act from their overall sense of self.

The effect that this might have on the way in which individuals participate in and respond to treatment will be discussed in the following three chapters.

Notes

1 Both headlines occurred during the *News of the World*'s 'Name and Shame' campaign, following the abduction and subsequent murder of Sarah Payne in July 2000.
2 Research shows that sexual arousal to young children is more prevalent in heterosexual rather than homosexual males (West 2000).
3 The hierarchy that exists in prisons will be explored in more detail later in this chapter.
4 Vincent was accused of sexual abuse by only one of his daughters. However, the incident took place while both daughters were present.
5 Such assertions provide examples of how the interviews did not take place in a vacuum outside of the offenders' treatment. This will be discussed in more detail in Chapter 8.
6 Neutralisation Theory contends that sex offenders engage in pro-offending thinking in order to neutralize their offending behaviour. Similar to cognitive

distortions, techniques of neutralization therefore perform a major role in both precipitating and maintaining abusive behaviour (see Sykes and Matza 1957; McCarthy and Stewart 1998 for a summary).

Chapter 5

Motivation to change and treatment attendance

It is generally assumed that offenders who agree to participate in treatment are more motivated to change their offending behaviour than those who do not (Marshall 1993). Similarly, treatment completion is frequently used as an indicator of offenders' motivations to stop offending (Knopp 1984; Lee *et al.* 1996). However, these approaches overlook the significance of personal, legal and temporal pressures which might influence an individual's decisions to start and persist with treatment. The recognition of such factors raises questions about what is actually motivating an individual to participate on a programme. This chapter explores the motivating factors that influenced the men interviewed in this research to start and complete treatment and their subsequent motivations to change their sexually abusive behaviour.

Motivation to start treatment

The research identified 'intrinsic' and 'extrinsic' incentives influencing an individual's decision to participate in treatment. Intrinsic factors recognize an individual's internal desire to change their behaviour. In contrast, extrinsic factors are more symptomatic of the pressures on individuals with a conviction for a sexual offence to appear motivated.

Intrinsic incentives

It is perhaps not surprising that only the acceptors in this study (offenders who both admit to their offence and accept that their behaviour was abusive) expressed intrinsic reasons to account for their willingness to participate in treatment. The intrinsic factors included a desire to change aspects of their behaviour or character that might have contributed to their offending behaviour, and ultimately to reduce the chances of further offending:

> The more help I get with the problem I have the better, because it is a problem to do that on the outside, so you know I'm just trying everything. (Euan)

> I can't say I'm sorry in person to the victim so it's a way of me doing everything I can do to make sure that it doesn't happen again. Not to put someone in the same pain as the victim. (Ben)

> I realized I had a problem. I realized that I was creating damage and wanted to change my thoughts and my beliefs. (Colin)

> If anyone said to me why are you doing the course I would say I want to be there for myself, the first thing is I want to understand why I did it and I don't want to do it again, I won't do it anyway but, if anything happens in the future, I want some support or tools to help me so I won't offend again. I was quite happy to come on it to be honest. (Oliver)

From the outset, similarities can be drawn between the motivations expressed by the acceptors and the programme content, in particular victim empathy, cognitive restructuring and relapse prevention (see Chapter 3). However, there are methodological problems in reaching this conclusion. Not all the men in this research were interviewed prior to starting treatment. This raises questions about whether the intrinsic factors influencing the acceptors' willingness to participate in treatment arose primarily because programmes explore these areas. Alternatively, it could be argued that treatment intervention simply gave this group of participants the vocabulary to articulate their motives more clearly.

What is evident is that the intrinsic factors only accounted for a small proportion of all the motives presented by all the participants. While acceptors tended to prioritize intrinsic factors, their decision to attend a programme was also contingent upon extrinsic factors similar to those expressed by the men in denial. Consequently, the overwhelming majority of factors presented by the participants were extrinsic.

Extrinsic incentives

All of the men interviewed in this study expressed at least one extrinsic factor that influenced their decision to participate in treatment. In particular, the participants both totally denying their offending behaviour and those justifying their actions specified a combination of reasons other than motivation to change. These extrinsic factors fall into five general categories:

i.   A legal requirement

ii. Benefit to parole

iii. Privileges

iv. Coping strategies

v.   To facilitate offending

A legal requirement

An individual's crime and subsequent sentence will determine where they can attend a programme. This will then frame the extent to which they can choose to participate in treatment. As Chapter 3 highlighted, community-based treatment is primarily intended for adult males sentenced to a Community Rehabilitation Order (CRO, formerly the Probation Order) and for individuals released on licence from prison. In both instances, participation on the programme is compulsory – a formal condition of the CRO or licence. Community programmes have, in certain circumstances, been used in nonstatutory cases. In such cases, participation is voluntary.

For most of the men attending the C-SOGP, participation on an offending behaviour programme was a condition of their sentence. The compulsory nature of the C-SOGP was on the whole accepted:

> One reason is that I've got to do it. (Keith)

> I had to go on the course or they would take me back to court. (Jack)

> It was part of my court order for my first offence that I go on a pathways group . . . the judge said that I had to do it so it was either that or be banged up at the time. (Graham)

From this perspective it appears that this subgroup of participants were attending the C-SOGP primarily to avoid breach proceedings and their consequences. This raises questions about whether they would have volunteered if programme intervention had not been a legal require-ment. However, neither Oliver nor Nathanial were legally obliged to attend the C-SOGP, despite the fact that they are both convicted sex offenders.

Oliver was convicted of unlawful sexual intercourse in 1992 and received a community sentence. Then in 1998 he was convicted of three charges of incest, committed 16 years earlier, and sentenced to four months imprisonment. His time on licence had however ended prior to his participation in the C-SOGP. Similarly, Nathanial had served a two-year probation order for indecent assault on a 12-year-old girl. Substantial changes to both their personal circumstances led to the intervention from social services and ultimately their inclusion on the C-SOGP.

On release from prison, Oliver met and married his wife who had two children from a previous relationship. While both children were put on the child protection register, social services also requested that Oliver undertake the relevant risk assessments and participate in an offending behaviour programme. In the meantime, Oliver was denied the right to live with his new family. Consequently, while Oliver was not legally required to attend the C-SOGP, he was fully aware of the implications if he had decided not to participate on the programme:

> Because I married my wife and she's got two kids, they're only concerned about one at the moment, he's 14 and they think I may be a danger towards him, they want me to come on the course to get my danger level down. (Oliver)

Similarly, Nathanial requested to move back home to live with his parents, the legal guardians of his two children. Despite having already completed a community-based sex offender programme, Nathanial was assessed as at a high risk of re-offending. Social services agreed to fund Nathanial to repeat treatment in the hope that he would reduce his risk. Until this point Nathanial was only able to see his children while accompanied. He therefore viewed the C-SOGP as his last chance to become a full-time father again:

> Like I say this is my last chance, I've got to show that I'm making progress. (Nathanial)

While both men ultimately made the decision to participate on the C-SOGP, like the majority of offenders participating on the C-SOGP, they too faced an ultimatum in agreeing to participate in treatment. It is therefore difficult to ascertain the degree to which this subgroup of men chose to participate in the programme in order to address their sexual offending behaviour.

These findings are consistent with the reasons expressed by the men participating on a prison-based programme. The principle on which the prison service has based its approach in recent years is that engagement in treatment should be voluntary. However, evidence from the prisoners in this research suggests that it has proven difficult to turn such aspirations into reality.

Each of the men participating in prison-based treatment programmes (namely the SOTP and the BAP) was asked whether they thought their respective programme was voluntary. Only seven prisoners (28 per cent) felt that it was completely voluntary, while the remaining 18 (72 per cent) proposed that they felt pressured, or forced, to volunteer. This pressure was typically referred to as 'blackmail':

> I think they force you into it ... they blackmail you into doing it really. (David)

> It's blackmail. It's open deliberate blackmail. (Ivor)

> Although it's voluntary, they do use blackmail to try and make you do it. (Andrew)

The pressure experienced by the prisoners in this study corresponds to incentives offered within their respective penal establishments (Marshall et al. 1993):

> It will be like I've got to do this course, it's not a voluntary, even though these courses are actually voluntary, there's always that little bit of something hanging over your head, that carrot. (Ben)

The so-called 'carrot' or inducements offered to these men will be discussed in the next two sections.

Benefit to parole

Individuals sentenced to less than four years are released conditionally after serving one-half of their sentence. The position for those serving four years or more is considerably different. Under the system of Discretionary Conditional Release (DCR)[1] the parole board is empowered to grant a parole licence to such prisoners at any point between one-half and two-thirds of their sentence (Maguire and Raynor 1997). Similarly, life-sentenced prisoners are required to serve a 'tariff period'[2] of their sentence. Once this tariff period of detention ends, a life prisoner is able to challenge the ground for continued detention before an independent parole board or lifer panel (Ashworth 2000).

Risk to the public of a further offence being committed is the primary factor in deciding whether or not to recommend early release on licence (DCR). However, it is also deemed necessary to determine whether the prisoner has shown, by their attitude and behaviour, in custody that they are willing to address their offending behaviour through participation in appropriate programmes (Section 32(6) of the Criminal Justice Act 1991). The rehabilitative focus in the parole board's assessment of a prisoner's suitability for early release was evidently recognized by all the prisoners sentenced to four years or over participating in this research.[3] The general assumption was that release would not be granted unless the criteria of risk and addressing offending behaviour had been met:

> You're not going to get parole if you don't do SOTP. It's something you pick up, but it's more than likely true. You definitely would lose your parole, they say it's not parole based but when you get to parole they ask if you've done the SOTP. If you haven't they see you as a high risk and you won't get it. (Harry)

> I think it makes a difference at the later stage if you go on for parole, yes I've done this, yes I've done that, yes I'm trying to be a model prisoner, yes I'm sorry for what I've done, no I'm not going to re-offend. (Zack)

All of the prisoners eligible for DCR believed that completing the programme significantly enhanced their chances of early release. Four prisoners actually identified parole as their primary motive for taking part. Perhaps not surprisingly, all four men have been defined as deniers.[4] By definition, these men will see no reason to change their attitudes or their behaviour, as they deny any wrongdoing (Ingersoll and Patton 1990):

> Do you want to know my honest opinion? . . . I'm only doing this course to make my prison time easy like, I'm trying to get out of here as quick as I can like. (Xandy)

> The only reason I'm doing this programme is to help my parole. The system is arse upwards. If you tell them you're not guilty and don't do any courses then you won't get parole, if you tell them that you're guilty even if you don't believe it, do the courses you'll get parole . . . To get parole, to get out of here earlier. I'm here when I shouldn't be so I don't want to spend any longer than necessary. (David)

For Vincent, the only other denier eligible for early release, while parole was expressed as his main reason for volunteering to participate on the BAP, he failed to attend the first session. In a subsequent interview he admitted that as his chances of parole were greatly reduced given his state of denial, he had decided to withdraw from treatment.

Privileges

Additional extrinsic incentives also played a crucial role in persuading individuals to participate in treatment. For example, it was generally believed that programme participation would either increase a prisoner's chance of progressing to a lower grade of prison, or entitle them to more privileges:

> I have a 15-year tariff, 2007. Unless I address my problems I won't progress, just go from Cat B to Cat B with the same questions being thrown at you. So you may as well say OK and just do it, accept that that question needs to be addressed . . . You'd be cutting your nose off to spite your face if you didn't do it. (Albert)

> When I came into prison I wasn't physically forced, but if you don't do it you won't get things. (Clive)

A 'differential regime' operates in all prisons whereby inmates may earn certain privileges. The scheme operates on three levels – basic, standard and enhanced – each having its own different levels of privileges to be earned. For example, if you progress from standard level to enhanced level you will be allowed more personal belongings and private cash; those on basic level will receive less. Participation in treatment was believed to increase a prisoner's chance of progressing to enhanced level:

> If you don't do it you won't get enhancement and you'll stop on an inferior wing. I've got a telly, I'm on the best wing. If you don't do it you're not allowed to spend as much. (David)

However, it was generally demotion to a lower level and the subsequent loss of privileges that influenced the majority of prisoners' decision to participate on their respective programme:

> Yeah, because you have to sign a form, although there are implications with this. If you don't sign the form you're told that you will lose your enhancement, told that it will be taken away from you. I don't know whether it's true or not. (Greg)

> Well a lot of people have told me if you don't go on this course you get your television taken off you, get your enhanced taken off you, you get put back on A wing – you're sort of degraded. (Ivor)

While this reflects a much less ambitious motive for treatment participation, it is perhaps more realistic in relation to life in prison. As Albert stated, 'you don't get much in [prison], but what you do get you want to keep hold of.'

Coping strategies

Participants identified further factors, associated with the effects of incarceration, which influenced their decision to participate in treatment. Goffman's (1961: 14) work on asylums defined the prison system as a 'total institution'. His work stressed the transformation of the self that allegedly results from entering a people-processing institution. Consequently, he described institutionalization as a process of 'role dispossession' in which inmates are stripped of their identity and experience a 'civil death'. Similarly, Sykes (1958) contended that an inmate's personality is eventually destroyed by imprisonment, resulting in the inmate being defined as a non-person (Sarbin 1967). Research in this area has been subject to much criticism due to exaggerated claims (Walker 1987). Nevertheless, prisons are essentially punitive (Coker 1987). They are all designed, to some degree, to restrict individuality and personal freedom. It is therefore inevitable that inmates will be affected one way or another by their new environment.

A number of the prisoners interviewed in this research expressed problems adapting to the highly repetitive and monotonous prison regime. Within a prison environment inmates are denied autonomy in their personal movement and activities. Treatment participation therefore offered the inmates an ideal opportunity to break up their daily prison routine. It also presented them with an effective distraction from their remaining sentence:

> I'm doing an anger management course, I've asked the education officer to do maths exams, I'm doing this other course with you now and as I said I'm doing the Samaritans. I want to keep busy when I'm in here. (Stuart)

> It's something to do, I'm not wasting my time. (Wayne)

To facilitate offending

The possibility that individuals will volunteer for treatment to gather information to facilitate sexual abusing, either through attaining 'contacts for a paedophile ring' (Colin) or material to aid sexual fantasies, was also expressed by some of the individuals participating in this research. However, this motive was offered to explain why 'other' sex offenders might have agreed to participate in treatment and not to explain their own willingness to attend a programme:

> Some people go on for funny motivations; one I personally think was there to collect material for his own masturbation fantasies. He had offended against two pre-pubescent children. When someone

was giving an account of his offence he sat there all quiet and then asked, 'What kind of knickers did she wear?'. We also thought it was a bit suspect when he went to the toilet, we think it was to masturbate. (Colin)

Its absence from the motives expressed by the interviewees in this study is not surprising, especially when there is the perception that incentives can be gained from treatment participation. The complex relationship between denial and identity, outlined in Chapter 4, also highlights the difficulty an individual has in acknowledging themselves as a 'sex offender'. Clive alluded to this in a letter sent post-treatment. In it he implied that there was 'another side to prison, beside the party line, such as networking', which he was sure that no one spoke about. The extent to which this desire actually reflects an individual's decision to participate in treatment cannot therefore be underestimated.

In summary, the majority of reasons expressed by the men in this research for starting an offending behaviour programme were clearly linked to the degree of control the criminal justice system had over that person. For example, the majority of men on the C-SOGP were required by law to attend the programme. Even where participation was voluntary, individuals agreed to participate in treatment for a variety of reasons other than motivation to change. The extent to which extrinsic factors influenced the decision of the men serving a custodial sentence to participate in treatment related to the varying effects of imprisonment. For example, Albert commented on the additional constraints a life sentence entails:

When you're a fixed-termer they can't turn round and say they're not letting you out. With a lifer they can, they have you by the short and curlies. (Albert)

The assumption is, therefore, that as 'guilty men [they were] not in the position to say no' (Daniel). However, some of the participants interviewed in this research did not regard themselves as guilty.

Motivation of total deniers

Total denial is generally seen to reflect an individual's unwillingness to participate in treatment and often lack of motivation to change their behaviour. Upon first reflection, the evidence presented in this chapter would support such claims. Vincent's state of denial clearly contributed to his decision not to attend treatment. While the remaining total deniers all completed treatment, their decision to participate was influenced by the possibility of parole or increased privileges. However, it was typical for the total deniers to offer alternative reasons to account for their willingness to attend a programme to those already discussed. Total deniers' motives therefore present an interesting case study.

All of the men defined as total deniers participated on the Behaviour Assessment Programme (BAP). To reiterate, the BAP has been designed specifically for sex offenders who deny their offence. The aim of the programme is to motivate individuals to change their sexually offending behaviour without them having to outwardly admit to the offence. Nonetheless, one of the main reasons expressed by the men in total denial for participating on the BAP was that they assumed it was a 'general behaviour' programme:

> This is to do with the, like the SOTP is for sexual offenders and sexual offences and things like that, this one is for general behavioural. (Xandy)

> I assumed [the BAP] was to cover all crimes, the general, looking at my general behaviour. (Thomas)

This would explain why an individual who asserts his innocence would agree to participate in treatment. However, on closer examination of the data, the majority of men in total denial were aware of the sexual content of the BAP.

Firstly, total deniers (incorrectly) believed that the primary goal of the BAP was to make them admit to their offence, thereby accepting, to some degree, the label of a sex offender, and the programme's role in challenging their denial:

> [They will want me] to admit that I committed the offence. (Thomas)

> They probably think I'm in denial and they want to try and admit it, they think I'll come to terms with something that I've done which I haven't done. If I had done it by now I would have held my hands up but I didn't and I'm not going to. (Stuart)

Secondly, a number of the men identified reasons of how they could benefit from learning about sexual offending behaviour. For example, given that a number of the men in total denial claimed to have been 'set up' (see Chapter 4), they expressed a desire to learn how to avoid similar situations in the future:

> I went on this course to see what I can learn by it, more so for when I get out, to see the do's and don'ts because hopefully I'm not

coming back in here, I know there's no guarantee, you know I don't want to get myself into a situation that could put me back in here. (Paul)

It was felt that this information could then be passed on to others:

If I learn something in there maybe I can stop someone else being accused, you never know. (Stuart)

This was consistent with the reasons presented by Yuval, the only justifier participating on the BAP:

I think if this can happen to me it can happen to anyone and I got nephews and a son out there and you know it's something which I can make them aware of like the situations and that. (Yuval)

Wayne was the only total denier who acknowledged that the BAP was a sex offender programme. In contrast, Wayne offered two alternative reasons to account for his willingness to participate on the BAP. The first reason related to his own victimization. Wayne believed that treatment participation would help him deal with the sexual abuse he experienced as a child and ironically prevent him from ever committing a sexual offence himself:

When I come in I explained to one of the officers that I've been a victim of abuse myself and he suggested that the course would be some benefit, so anything that can help me to cope with that then well I'll look at. (Wayne)

They [a psychologist] said . . . the abused turn into the abuser, I've never dreamed of it but if that is a possibility and statistics support it then I've got to look at it, I don't want to turn into somebody like that so if I can do something about it now that will stop it then it's worthwhile. (Wayne)

Secondly, Wayne assumed that attending a treatment programme would give him the opportunity to put across his perspective:

Because maybe at the end of the day the people at this side of the counter are going to realize that I'm not [guilty]. (Wayne)

It was evident that the total deniers who started treatment acknowledged, at least inwardly, that the rationale behind the BAP was within the field of sexual offending. However, the title of the Behaviour

Assessment Programme (BAP) enabled these men to justify their attendance on the programme. This is consistent with their reasons for not wishing to participate in the prison-based Sex Offender Treatment Programme (SOTP). While many of the men in total denial were willing to participate in the BAP, they would not have volunteered for the SOTP. Evidently, the reasoning behind an offender's reluctance draws on semantics.

An offender's unwillingness to participate on the SOTP while agreeing to participate on the BAP related to the connotations of the term 'sex offender' in the accredited programme's title. Outwardly agreeing to participate on the SOTP meant that they would be stigmatized by association:

Interviewer   So if this programme were called the sex offender behaviour assessment programme would you go on it?

Stuart   I wouldn't do it, if it was for, to go on that you're actually admitting you're a sex offender right on that and that's, they're treating you then for your problems of that, well I wouldn't do it because I'm not a sex offender and I never will admit to being a sex offender, I didn't do it so I won't admit to it, if I'd had done it I would have admitted it by now but I haven't.

This assumption was corroborated by the men participating on the SOTP:

If someone does the SOTP they're a nonce, or a 'paedo', even though they may not be, might be a sex offender, but you're guilty, you're a paedophile because you've done the SOTP. I'll get more stick from inmates. (Clive)

By doing the SOTP it's a form of saying that you're guilty for what you've done. They'll definitely know what you've done because you've done the SOTP. (Harry)

A lot do ETS [Enhanced Thinking Skills] but a lot of them refuse to do the SOTP. It comes down to stigma. (Finn)

The BAP therefore enabled the men in total denial to seek help legitimately without facing the stigma of being identified as a sex offender. Based on this premise, it can be assumed that this group of individuals inwardly admitted to their offence.

Thomas presents an interesting case to support this conclusion. For example, Chapter 4 revealed how he recognized characteristics in himself that he ascribed to the 'classic paedophile'. He also claimed that he 'must have some sort of behavioural problem or [he] wouldn't be in [prison]'. Furthermore, one of his reasons for participating on the BAP was to see if he did do something wrong. Thomas's persistent questioning of whether it was possible for a child sexual abuser genuinely to love their victim is also evidence that he was not totally entrenched in denial:

> Perhaps they [paedophiles] think they're genuinely doing it because they think they love the children, because most people think of paedophiles as just doing it because of their own desire . . . It may have started out as a purely, just a, what I call a platonic friendship with a child and it's just sort of escalated, I don't know I'm not a psychologist I'm just an ordinary human being who's found himself in a rather unpleasant situation and I'm trying to understand how I've ended up in prison and it's been a very difficult process. (Thomas)

However, it was why he thought 'others' might refuse to do the BAP that is arguably indicative of his guilt:

> Perhaps they're genuinely innocent of the offence, that's the honest truth. (Thomas)

Similar opinions were expressed by the other men in total denial:

> Because I think they're frightened of what they might say or what would come out. (Paul)

> A lot of them are afraid to face the truth. (Wayne)

The evidence presented in this research therefore suggests that total deniers should be able to reduce their risk without openly admitting to their guilt. Consequently, willingness to participate in treatment, in this instance, may provide some indication of motivation to change.

Relating motivation to denial is therefore highly problematic. The danger is that such denial might exclude from treatment offenders who can benefit. This finding is consistent with broader literature in this area (Maletzky 1993; Schlank and Shaw 1997; Hanson and Bussiere 1998). Denial might therefore be better used to match the intervention required to the needs of the offender, rather than to determine the offender's suitability for treatment. All six of the men in total denial were correctly asked to participate on the BAP. However, only one of the four offenders defined as a justifier in this study (offenders who admit to committing a crime in the legal sense of the word, but deny that their behaviour was an offence) was eligible for the BAP. The SOTP was available to David, whereas Jack and Keith attended the C-SOGP. Both Keith and David failed to complete their respective programmes. (The reasons as to why they failed to complete treatment will be explored in the next section.) It might have been more beneficial for these men to participate on the BAP. It should also be noted that four of the men participating on the BAP admitted to their offence. It may also have been beneficial for these offenders to participate on standard sex offender treatment programmes (namely the SOTP and the C-SOTP) that focus on the individual's sexual offence. This will be explored further in Chapter 7.

Failure to complete treatment

Similar to an individual's reluctance to start treatment, an individual's decision to drop out of a programme has often been associated with lack of motivation to change their sexual offending behaviour. Six participants in this research failed to complete treatment. Of these, only two men voluntarily dropped out of treatment. David had been participating on the prison-based Sex Offender Treatment Programme (SOTP) and dropped out after block 4. Zack dropped out of the prison-based Behaviour Assessment Programme (BAP) at session 13. Participation on both programmes is 'voluntary'. In contrast, the remaining four men, Nathanial, Keith, Graham and Luke, failed to complete the Community Sex Offender Groupwork Programme (C-SOGP). Apart from Nathanial, their participation on the programme was compulsory. As this chapter has highlighted, for most of the men attending the C-SOGP, participation was a condition of their sentence. It must therefore be acknowledged that the remaining men might only have completed treatment to avoid breach proceedings.[5]

Of the four men who failed to complete the C-SOGP, Keith and Nathanial were both asked to leave the group by the programme facilitators. Both Graham and Luke committed further sexual crimes while participating on the C-SOGP, and were subsequently imprisoned. Graham and Luke's individual case studies will be explored in the next chapter. The rest of this chapter explores the reasons for dropping out of treatment other than re-offending. Factors that have already been explored include issues surrounding identity, the manner in which the programme is presented, and the conditions under which individuals enter treatment. This section identifies three further explanations to account for an individual's failure to complete treatment: the issue of confidentiality; stigma by association; and issues relating to the setting of treatment within the criminal justice system.

Confidentiality

As outlined in Chapter 4, it was unusual for the interviewees to have disclosed their offence to anyone outside the treatment group due to concerns about privacy and public exposure. Confidentiality was therefore considered to be an essential component to ensure all sex offenders' persistence in treatment:

> My main concern is confidentiality. I would leave the course if this happened. Any trust, even for the tutors, would go out the window. (Ben)

This was particularly acute for the men participating on the Community Sex Offender Groupwork Programme, who feared involuntary disclosure would lead to vigilante action and public disorder:

> Well, the tape[6] going missing, everything that is said, you're on film, if that tape gets into the wrong hands, it could create all hell. You know there are eight of us here; all it needs is for one of those tapes to go missing, and well you don't know what the outcome will be. I know your address wouldn't be on there as such but they got a picture of you and someone could say oh I know him, he lives up so and so and well you never know what's going to happen then do you? (Luke)

The men's anxieties were nonetheless sufficiently alleviated after the first session of their respective groups. This enabled groups to establish rules and regulations, including the importance of confidentiality:

> The first session we made up a contract, with a set of rules that we're all going to obey and everybody had to give a rule that they wanted putting on this contract, like you don't talk about anyone else when you get out of the room, you don't discuss anybody's case to anybody else, which you don't do. (David)

> In a group you sign, you write out a contract on the wall and everybody passes discussion on that contract, that's the first lesson of every course and that contract stands for every day you're in that group, even if you don't do the group, that contract stands. You do not talk about other people, you don't mention any other people's offences, what they've done, what they talk about in the group, it's trust, confidentiality and all that, non-prejudgemental, high esteem, appropriate sense of humour, timekeeping, teamwork. (Ben)

Consequently, the majority of men interviewed felt that the issue of confidentiality had been appropriately dealt with and saw no reason to leave the programme. This is perhaps more indicative of a shared fear of disclosure. Arguably, confidentiality is maintained simply because all the men are in the same situation. They can therefore be seen to comply with the 'I won't tell if you don't tell' scenario:

> All of us are in the same boat, I'm trusting him with mine as they're trusting me with theirs so it goes two ways I suppose. (Matthew)

Stigma by association

This chapter has demonstrated how total deniers attempt to preserve an acceptable public image by refusing to participate on the Sex Offender Treatment Programme (SOTP). Similarly, the concept of stigma by association was articulated by a number of interviewees as a factor that could influence their decision to drop out of treatment. Arguably this is another technique used by individuals to distance themselves from the popular image of a sex offender (see Chapter 4). For example, a number of participants expressed anxiety about being in a group with offenders who had committed an offence that they (and some believed the outside world) considered to be 'worse' than theirs:

> If I had to go on that group or if there was a group with say, six paedophiles on there then I would have drawn the line, I would have said just hang on a minute, all of these are in for kids, what similarities is my crime towards these, you know the sort of from my offence at this top of the scale to their offence down here at this level you know, what am I going to get out of it and I'd have felt like I wasn't getting anything out of that you know ... If I'm shut up with paedophiles I would walk out. (Albert)

In the case of David, being associated with child abusers was given as one of his reason for actually dropping out of the programme:[7]

> If I'm shut up with paedophiles I will walk out ... Another inmate starting the SOTP, when I saw him on recreation he said, 'I hope you're not on the same group as me', I said 'Why?', he said nothing. He may not want things coming out in front of me. Don't know what he's in for and if it's for fiddling with kids I don't want to know. There could be problems. I'll give it a try for so long but I'm not going to put myself under any stress because of them. (David)

> I just couldn't be bothered with it. For the simple reason I didn't think that it suited me for what I'm in for, there is a group of nine

different inmates who are in for all different types of things. And some of the things they're in for are totally disgusting. (David)

David's failure to complete treatment was also indicative of his state of denial. He was convicted of rape against his 16-year-old stepdaughter. Although he admitted to committing the act, he denied that his behaviour had been abusive. He has therefore been defined as a justifier. David's reasons for leaving the group therefore conveyed his interpretation of what a sex offender is, and by proxy what he was not.

Systemic issues

Systemic issues can also be seen to have had an impact on an individual's decision to drop of out treatment. For example, the threatened removal of incentives associated with treatment participation was identified as influencing a number of interviewees' decision to continue with treatment:

I had a worry the other week I almost jacked in the course . . . Social services got involved again, making contact saying you're not going to see your son even if you do the course, so that was nearly it, goodbye see you later . . . but it turned out not to be the case. (Ben)

Zack dropped out of treatment after having completed 12 of the 14 sessions of the BAP. His reason for failing to complete the programme had little to do with motivation to change his behaviour. Instead, it was as a result of friction between himself and his cellmate:

[I left] because of the cellmate I'm in with, he was just doing my head in I just completely flipped. I wasn't talking to anybody I wasn't doing anything in this jail. I just wanted to get out of this jail. I wasn't eating I wasn't coming out of my cell I wasn't doing nothing . . . it was nothing about the programme at all. (Zack)

In summary, an individual's decision to leave treatment is not necessarily indicative of their lack of motivation to change their sexually abusive behaviour. However, research has generally concluded that failing to complete treatment can be countertherapeutic, as many offenders will not have come to terms with the consequences of what they have done (Friendship *et al.* 2003). In fact, individuals that start treatment but drop out before the end are likely to become more defensive and engage in techniques that distract responsibility for their behaviour away from themselves and onto their victims. This will now be explored in more detail in relation to the participants who failed to complete treatment in this research.

Failure to complete treatment: An assessment of risk

Four participants failed to complete treatment for reasons other than re-offending. However, Zack only missed the last two sessions of the Behaviour Assessment Programme (BAP), one of which was a revision session. As such, Zack will not be included in the following discussion. Instead, his views on programme content will be explored in Chapter 7. This section is predominantly concerned with the accounts of David, Keith and Nathanial. To reiterate, whereas David voluntarily dropped out of the prison-led Sex Offender Treatment Programme (SOTP), both Keith and Nathanial were asked to leave the Community Sex Offender Groupwork Programme (C-SOGP).

David: A case study

As this chapter has already noted, David was convicted of rape against his 16-year-old stepdaughter.[8] He has been defined as a justifier in this research based on the fact that he admits to having a sexual relationship with his stepdaughter (see Chapter 4). He was nonetheless found guilty of rape and received an eight-year custodial sentence. David's primary motive for taking part in the SOTP was to increase his chances of getting parole. However, David dropped out of treatment after completing his Life Timeline exercise in the My History block of the SOTP (see Chapter 3).[9]

David's participation in the first four blocks of the SOTP reaffirmed his belief that he had not committed a sexual offence. Indeed, one of the reasons presented by David for dropping out of the SOTP was that he did not like listening to other group members' secrets and confidences. This was based on his belief that he had nothing to offer of his own. Consequently, while he acknowledged that others had offences to discuss, from his point of view he did not. This was evident in his presentation of his life history (during his last session). David's Life Timeline documented his refusal to take responsibility for his offending behaviour. His description of the offence outlined his belief that what happened between him and his stepdaughter was consensual and not rape:

> My stepdaughter . . . always fancied herself as a hairdresser and in the evenings, after I had been in the shower, she always used to like to blow dry my hair. . . . One night while she was busy with my hair, I could feel that she was rubbing her breast on my shoulders as I

was sat on a stool, I ignored it as I thought it might have been an accident, but the next night it started to happen again and instead of ignoring it this time, I reached behind myself and started to stroke the inside of her leg, to which she reacted by opening her legs more for an easier access for me. I found it quite easy to fancy her as she was fully developed . . . and was beautiful, like a young model of my wife. Anyway one thing led to another and we ended up having sex on the dining room table, but it wasn't me that started this as she had unzipped my trousers to get my penis out, and gave me oral sex before moving on to the table. . . . Anyway we had sex quite often after that, when we had the opportunity, and she always enjoyed it reaching orgasm on most occasions. (Extract from David's Life Timeline)

David showed no victim empathy, wanting instead to see his step-daughter get her comeuppance for what she had done:

As for my stepdaughter I would imagine that eventually something will come to her as God sees that you reap what you sow. I just hope that it is in my lifetime so that I can enjoy the revenge for what she's done to me. (Extract from David's Life Timeline)

Keith: A case study

Likewise, Keith failed to recognize the implications of his actions prior to being asked to leave the C-SOGP. Keith was convicted of indecent assault of a 14-year-old girl and of possessing obscene photographs of a child. The offence took place in his parents' home after he had invited his 15-year-old son and some of his son's friends back to the house. At some point in the evening one of Keith's (adult) friends also joined them. Keith's account of the incident was as follows:

They were messing around on the computer, I went to get cigarettes with [my son] and one of the other girls . . . when I came back from getting cigarettes I opened the door and they rushed to the door with my digital camera, the one girl lifted her top up and took photos of herself, so she asked me would I print it out. There were a few more photos being taken but I was trying to get the programme on the computer. (Keith)

Although Keith implied that he was hardly involved in the photographs, he did admit to being badgered into posing with one of the girls. This picture depicted Keith with his hands over the girl's breasts (see Chapter 4). Nonetheless, Keith did not regard his actions as abusive, based on the fact that his so-called victim 'persuaded [him] to have [his] photo taken with her': 'It certainly wasn't against her will.'

Keith was subsequently sentenced to a Community Rehabilitation Order with the condition that he attend a C-SOGP. Due to his lack of commitment to the programme (which was evident in his lack of attendance), Keith was asked to leave the group. In light of this, Keith was only interviewed once after having completed the induction module of the C-SOGP. However, it was evident from Keith's participation on C-SOGP that he failed to recognize the sexual element of his offence or the potential harm caused to his victims. For example, he was unable to see the inappropriateness of two adults (himself and his co-defendant) engaging in activities of a sexual nature with a number of young teenage girls. In addition, Keith did not recognize that he had responsibility as an adult, and as the occupier of the property, that was greater than his victims. Keith also found it difficult to accept that the young girls could have felt abused in any way at the time, or after the event.

Nathanial: A case study

Similar to Keith, Nathanial was asked to the leave the C-SOGP as the group tutors felt that his commitment and contribution to the group was negligible. Nathanial was convicted of the indecent assault of a 12-year-old girl with learning difficulties. Despite being defined in this study as an acceptor, throughout treatment Nathanial failed to accept full responsibility for his offending behaviour. For example, he failed to recognize he was responsible for the abuse and for preventing the victim from disclosing. In addition, in his description of his offence he also described how his victim used to 'wear short nighties' and liked to have 'play fights' that resulted in the two of them 'rolling around on the floor'. In doing so, he implied that his victim had 'led him on' (extracts taken from Nathanial's account of his offence). His account of the offence changed surprisingly little during the time he attended treatment. When in fact he did admit, or accept, responsibility for his behaviour, it was felt that this was more indicative of his desire to please the tutors rather than an indication of real change. This was acknowledged but contested by Nathanial, as the following quotation highlights:[10]

> Like I said I put the blame on myself but they [the tutors] didn't believe me after. The boys [the other group members] were even saying I was copying everyone else, but I was saying what I thought. (Nathanial)

Nonetheless, the facilitators overwhelmingly agreed that Nathanial lacked motivation to change his attitudes and behaviours that predisposed him to sexually abuse and therefore decided to withdraw him from the group. This was accentuated by the fact that Nathanial had already failed to complete a previous group.

All three men left treatment with no sense of guilt regarding their actions. Moreover, all three men showed characteristics that are typically exhibited by sex offenders, such as their patterns of denial and minimization, their deficits in victim empathy, and their use of distorted thinking. Arguably, without a clear understanding of their offending behaviour, there is nothing stopping these men from committing similar offences in the future. However, given that Keith's participation on the C-SOGP was compulsory, he was in breach of his conditions. As such he was required to attend another Community Sex Offender Groupwork Programme. It is thus possible that these problems might be resolved following completion of treatment. Conversely, both David and Keith have been defined as justifiers in this study. Their failure to complete their respective groups might have been more indicative of their reluctance to admit to the harm caused by their offending behaviour rather than a reflection of their lack of motivation to change. Arguably, both David and Keith might have benefited more from the educational approach used in the BAP. Indeed, in the case of David, this is corroborated by claims from family therapists that using hypothetical situations can be helpful in breaking through denial in incestuous families (Schlank and Shaw 1996). Consequently, Keith's participation on his next group might have the same results.

Nathanial's participation on the current C-SOGP was not a legal requirement. As this chapter has already highlighted, Nathanial agreed to participate on the C-SOGP at the request of social services. His primary motive for taking part in treatment was to secure better access with his children. However, having failed to complete treatment, all contact between him and his children remained under supervision. In addition, he continued to be regularly monitored by social services.

Conclusion

This chapter has identified a number of factors that influenced an individual's decision to participate in treatment. For example, it was more likely for the acceptors in this research to articulate motives that were directly related to the five main treatment targets of programmes designed specifically for sexual offenders (see Chapter 3). However, while the acceptors claimed that such intrinsic motives had influenced their decision to participate in treatment, they also identified a number of extrinsic factors that were consistent with reasons presented by the participants in denial. Indeed, all of the participants in this research claimed that either legal or temporal pressures had biased their decision to start treatment, albeit to different extents. Of course, it remains possible that once an individual starts treatment they may acquire more positive views, and their motives may change.

The chapter also identified how more portentous motives might have been omitted from the participants' accounts. This draws on Goffman's (1959) concept of stage management, which has been discussed in Chapter 4. To reiterate, Goffman described the use of defensive and protective techniques that individuals employ in order to manage their identity. Arguably, it might be the case that the participants in this research concealed 'backstage' (Goffman 1959) their desire to use treatment as a form of pornography. Instead, this was suggested as to why 'others' engaged in treatment. For example, a number of the participants implied that sex offenders might participate in treatment to talk about their fantasies and offending histories, and become aroused in doing so. Consequently, while they reaffirmed the social representation of the sex offender as irredeemable, they also protected themselves from this element of their extended social identity.

Similarly, the design of the Behavioural Assessment Programme (BAP), in particular the exclusion of the term 'sex offender' in the programme's name, enabled total deniers to acquire help in changing their sexually abusive behaviour while avoiding the stigma of being defined as a sex offender (assuming, of course, that they were really guilty). Consequently, there is clear evidence to suggest treatment intervention with these men could be worthwhile. Essentially the BAP offers a possible approach for dealing with total deniers other than simply excluding them from treatment and allowing them to be released without trying to modify their risk. Whether or not the BAP is successful in reducing a total denier's risk of future offending will be explored in Chapter 7.

This chapter has also identified a number of reasons as to why an individual might fail to complete their respective treatment programme. For example, the participants who failed to complete treatment (for reasons other than committing a sexual offence) in this research expressed issues surrounding identity, as well as more systemic factors. Of course, it could be argued that these men were simply unmotivated to change their sexual offending behaviour, and their reported concerns were merely excuses. Certainly, the accounts presented here suggest that these men left their respective treatment programmes with their risk unaltered. The findings also suggested that this might have been prevented if the individual's state of denial had been better matched to treatment intervention.

It is also important to bear in mind that although individuals may outwardly appear motivated to change their sexually abusive behaviour, they may not have intrinsically changed. Indeed, it was generally believed that Nathanial agreed with everything that the programme tutors said without making the internal cognitive shift. This will be explored in more detail in the following chapter.

Notes

1 DCR replaced the parole system in England and Wales in 1992 (Ashworth 2000).
2 The tariff period is the specified time that the offender should serve before the offender's case is considered by a parole board.
3 All 14 of the interviewees participating on the SOTP were eligible for DCR, as were four of the participants participating on the BAP. The seven remaining participants who received a custodial sentence were sentenced to less than four years and therefore eligible for conditional release after serving one-half of their sentence.
4 This includes both the participants defined as 'total deniers' and 'justifiers' in this research study (see Chapter 4).
5 This cannot be used to account for Oliver's reasons for completing treatment. Oliver, like Nathanial, was participating on the C-SOGP at the request of social services. His participation was therefore 'voluntary'.
6 Each treatment session was recorded to monitor the progress of treatment tutors.
7 For the majority of offenders this concern was overcome by actually participating in treatment. This will be discussed in more detail in Chapter 6.
8 David had also adopted his victim.
9 The Life Timeline exercise draws on Bowlby's (1969, 1973, 1979) 'Attachment Theory'.
10 This is typically referred to as 'talking the talk'. The implications of 'talking the talk' during treatment will be discussed in more detail in the following chapter.

Chapter 6

Honesty and conformity in a group setting

The remaining chapters are predominantly concerned with the participants' views regarding their respective treatment programmes. Chapter 7 examines their perceptions of programme content, as well as their accounts of their offending behaviour. In particular, it discusses the participants' perception of what they felt they had gained from participating in treatment. Similarly, Chapter 8 explores the accounts of the two men who re-offended while participating on the C-SOGP with regard to what (if anything) they felt they had gained from the programme. The purpose of this chapter is to explore the participants' observations about programme delivery. In doing so, it helps to identify under what social and institutional contexts effective treatments can be achieved. It also illustrates how the group environment can both enable and limit a group member's *performance* within treatment.

The group-work approach

To reiterate, all three treatment programmes used within this research were delivered in group format. These are the prison-based Sex Offender Treatment Programme (SOTP) and the Behaviour Assessment Programme (BAP), and the Community Sex Offender Groupwork Programme (C-SOGP). All three programmes draw on some, if not all, of the group-work methods outlined in Chapter 3. These are: group discussions and brainstorming; victim and offender material; the hot-seat technique; role-plays; and homework (cell work).

Similar to findings presented in previous research, the more active and participatory methods appeared to be more effective at engaging the offender with treatment (Vennard *et al.* 1997). For example, the group participants felt that the opportunity to take part in role-plays, and/or to present work they had undertaken in relation to their offending behaviour, was most effective at encouraging open expression and a sense of responsibility with regard to their current offence:

> The process of doing [a role-play] really made you think. If you take it seriously and do it properly it's a good exercise in empathy. (Andrew)

These techniques are typically used within treatment to enable individuals to offer constructive feedback to other group members. The men interviewed considered this to be more credible and less threatening than the treatment facilitator challenging the offender directly:

> If [the group] think it's bullshit then we'll say it's bullshit, whereas of course, the tutors they have got to be careful how they challenge somebody. They can't come out and call somebody a liar whereas we can. (Edmund)

In addition, offenders who were not actively taking part in these techniques felt that having the opportunity to hear differing perspectives had helped them to reappraise their own thoughts, feelings and behaviours, as well as being able to recognize the errors that other people make, and how others are affected by events. Craissati (1998: 63) has defined this process as 'generalised learning':

> I can now see where they are coming from, if you're harming people then it's wrong, I accept that now. (Jack)

The participants were overwhelmingly positive about the methods used within group-work. However, it became apparent that this was dependent on both the relationship between the group participants and their relationship with the group's facilitators (Yalom 1975).

Profile of facilitators

The men who took part in this research participated in one of six treatment groups. (Whereas all the men participating in the C-SOGP and the BAP attended the same group, the men who participated in the SOTP attended one of four treatment groups.) A different team of facilitators led each group. The SOTP was typically facilitated by two psychologists, balanced by the inclusion of one male and one female, and one uniformed member of staff (male), who would be used in the case of absentees. This is typical of most accredited treatment programmes. In addition, all the staff that facilitated on the four SOTP groups used in this study had undertaken the relevant programme training.

The BAP was co-facilitated by the head facilitator of the prison's Offending Behaviour Programmes Unit and a senior probation officer, male and female respectively. As the BAP is a much shorter programme than both the SOTP and the C-SOGP (consisting of only 15 sessions), it was not necessary to have a third treatment facilitator. However, due to the programme's unaccredited status, neither facilitator had been trained to facilitate the BAP. Nonetheless, both facilitators had experience of facilitating on accredited treatment programmes.

The C-SOGP was predominantly co-facilitated by two female probation officers. Unlike the SOTP, the C-SOGP did not benefit from having a dedicated member of staff who could facilitate the programme in the case of absentees. Instead, in such instances, one of five different tutors, including probation and social workers, of both sexes, would 'step in' to facilitate the programme. When this was not possible, the programme sessions would have to be cancelled. The staffing problems that the C-SOGP faced reflect the programme's unaccredited status at the time that the research was conducted (see Chapter 3). This also meant that the programme facilitators had not been trained in the accredited version of the C-SOGP prior to facilitating the group. However, the majority of tutors had facilitated on other accredited programmes. Furthermore, the principal facilitators received training on the accredited C-SOGP midway through the running of the programme.

Group members' perceptions of facilitators

Whereas Chapters 3 and 4 identified the different groupings of 'sex offenders', this chapter explores the interviewees' views regarding the different groupings of staff; most obviously, male and female, and in the prison setting, uniformed and specialist staff, such as psychologists.

The research found that the majority of offenders preferred there to be a gender mix of facilitators. Nonetheless, it was generally accepted that the female tutor offered an important perspective to the group process. For example, a number of offenders found it easier and more natural to talk to a woman:

I preferred her; I preferred talking to a female person than I would a male person. (Ivor)

Similarly, a number of group members believed that the female facilitators had a 'calming effect' on their respective group (Pietz and Mann 1989):

She would have a calm manner, say something to you and she would be able to defuse the whole thing. Whereas . . . a male has a male way of thinking. (Clive)

In contrast, research carried out as part of the Sex Offender Treatment and Evaluation Project (STEP) (Beech *et al.* 1999) observed in one programme that the lack of a female tutor resulted in the group developing a 'macho' group culture.

Finn, having committed an offence against a young girl, also claimed that having 'a female voice, quiet and very soft . . . almost child like' in the group helped him to 'slip into the [victim empathy] role-play very easily'. Of course, a more cynical reading of Finn's argument might question whether having a female tutor play the role of the victim enabled him to relive the offence in a sexual way.

The importance of tutor consistency was also advocated by programme participants, particularly those attending the C-SOGP. Indeed, Craissati (1998) has argued that consistent facilitators over a long period of time provide continuity and stability for clients. Within the current research this subgroup of men claimed that they had developed better relationships with the tutors that they had seen the most throughout their treatment. Conversely, they claimed that rotating facilitators meant that the tutors were not able to 'keep up to speed' with the group's progress:

> I find it easier with the two than changing all the time, because you get trust with them sort of thing and they're not going to bullshit you sort of thing. (Oliver)

Consequently, the C-SOGP's need to spread the workload across personnel had a negative impact on the cohesion of the group. In such instances, while consideration needs to be given to a gender mix, it is probable that consistency is more important in establishing effective treatment.

Similar to findings presented by Clarke *et al.* (2004), the occupational background of programme facilitators made very little difference to how they were perceived. However, where prison officers were used to facilitate the SOTP, a number of prisoners articulated some anxiety about having officers present in the group. This apprehension derived, in the majority of cases, from the officer's position and role within the prison:

> First of all I thought like watch this like because he's an officer isn't he, you know what I mean, perhaps . . . he'll come from here and go back to there maybe and say stuff. (Harry)

Although a prison officer's responsibilities vary according to the type of institution and the level of security, their duties essentially typify the inmate's controlled environment. For example, their duties include supervising and escorting prisoners, employing control and constraint procedures, carrying out security check and search procedures, and writing reports on prisoners. As such, it would appear that their position within the prison culture acted to contradict, discredit or otherwise throw doubt upon individual officers' ability to develop group cohesion:

> All I could see when he was sitting there was the uniform. To me now that's like everyday around the prison, he could trap me and things like that, that was going through my mind, might tell him something, who's he going to tell, he's an officer that sort of thing. (Ivor)

Furthermore, as the above quotation highlights, it appeared that the officer's uniform reinforced prison officers' authoritarian role within the prison establishment. This raises the obvious question as to whether this could be resolved by prison officers wearing civilian clothes (as the psychologists do) while facilitating treatment programmes. The following quotation from Edmund suggested that this could, at the very least, dispel inmates' first impressions of a prison officer's role within the treatment group:

> I wouldn't confide in him, I think it's because he's in uniform, [for] me I think it would be better if . . . he just came in his civvies and not the uniform, he still looks like that authority you know. (Edmund)

However, the remaining SOTP participants claimed that they overcame their initial anxieties and learnt to 'talk to the person and not the uniform' (Ivor). In such a way, prison officers can be seen to 'cross the line'. Goffman (1961: 90) has described this as a process of 'role release', where there is a release from the formalities that govern inmate–staff contacts and a softening of the usual chain of command. Again, this supports evidence presented by Clarke *et al.* (2004: 10), in which the programme participants insisted that 'personal qualities and individual characteristics' determined what made a good tutor.

To summarize, it would appear that the group-work approach, including the use of more practical and active methods and the use of consistent tutors of both sexes, helped to create a highly cohesive group environment. Similar to the findings presented by Craissati (1998), a number of the men participating in this research also claimed that the group dimension offered them an alternative experience to isolation.

However, whereas Craissati (1998) highlighted the importance of group-work when working with child sexual abusers (for whom isolation, secretiveness and shame are central to their offending), this study found it to be true of both child and adult sexual abusers.

The group process

Despite initial anxieties about participating in treatment within a group setting (see Chapter 5), the participants' recognition that they were not alone in their situation created an atmosphere of unity, respect and support within the group:

> I actually trust the people in the group, which was good. (Ben)

> I think they're working good. We're all pulling together, that's what I like about it as well. (Oliver)

As an example, Matthew – convicted of indecently abusing a child – felt more comfortable in the group, knowing that there were 'people in the room who were in the same situation'. In the same way, Albert, convicted of murdering a 20-year-old female, claimed that he benefited from being in an environment 'with a group of lads that to a degree have got the same problem as well'.

The support offered by other group members was also considered to help participants in discussing their offending behaviour openly within the group setting. For example, Finn recalled having to present his life history to the group for the first time. He described 'cringing inside', a feeling he claimed increased as the exercise went on. He also explained how, having completed his presentation, his initial response was to 'run away'. However, this anxiety was allayed by the support that he was shown from other group members. Finn, and others, believed such support typified the group experience.

> The feeling [of support] is reinforced all the way through the programme. When we feel that somebody does give an honest truthful account, and it's hurting to do so, then there's an immedi-ate, there's no overt, you know we don't fling our arms around each other and go all lovely, it's just a quiet subdued well done, good, you know. It really does reinforce the honesty and it's helped people to come out with things. (Finn)

A supportive group environment was therefore believed to promote cooperation and disclosure between the group members.

Of course, the effect this has on members' experiences in the group depends on the individual, as the following case studies highlight:

Quinton: A case study

During the interview stage of this research Quinton was extremely shy and nervous, an observation that was supported by comments from offenders who participated in the same group. In addition, Quinton also had acute learning difficulties. However, the group showed overwhelming support towards Quinton. As such he was encouraged to stand up in front of the group and present his work:

> [Quinton], when he first arrived he was very quiet and shy but we got him yesterday to stand up and read out the arguments for the boys . . . all he needed was a bit of coaxing which was from me, and the boys . . . and he stood up and he said it and at the end of the thing we gave him a round of applause, one for standing up and . . . actually physically doing it. Five weeks ago there was no way he'd get up, but when he got back to the table he was all chuffed up. (Euan)

> One of the boys got a bad confidence problem . . . he did well on Tuesday he got up in front of the group. He had difficulty doing it but he done it, which was a big step for him. He wouldn't have at the start of the group and we all gave him a pat on the back for doing it. (Wayne)

This, by Quinton's own account, is something he would have been 'too scared' to do without the support of the group. In addition, Quinton felt that working in a group environment had enabled him to 'stand up' for himself, whereas before he 'was shy . . . and wouldn't say a word'.

Greg: A case study

In contrast, Greg presented a macho image showing total disregard for other people's thoughts and opinions. He presented himself as a 'loner' and was happy to describe himself as 'not a people person'. The interviews with Greg were some of the most difficult interviews that I undertook. Despite agreeing to take part in the research, as soon as he came into the room he positioned himself in the chair so that he faced the wall, so that I only had a side view of his face. Although he answered the questions, he did so in monosyllables and repeatedly tapped his feet, indicating his dislike for me and/or the situation. In addition, during the interview he initially refused to discuss his offending behaviour and made it perfectly clear that he felt that the questions were pointless.

This ambivalence towards others persisted within the group. Greg failed to contribute verbally to group exercises in the early sessions, preferring instead to write everything down:

> I'm a great believer in writing things down; if I've got any problems I write them down I don't say anything I write it down. (Greg)

Indeed, according to Ben, a fellow group member, Greg's participation 'was practically nonexistent'. However, by the end of the programme Greg had contributed fully to a number of group sessions, including a role-play exercise. Similarly, shifts in behaviour were noticed during the interviews. He attributed this change in character to the fact that he began to feel supported and respected by the other group members:

> I was beginning to get to know everyone and feel secure, finally getting to the point where I could trust people because normally I don't do that. I don't trust people, I don't get on with people, I'm always angry, but towards the end I started being a bit better. (Greg)

> The course has made me as I am now. As before nobody wants to know me because I'm such a bad-tempered person so I'm doing well I think. (Greg)

The group therefore provided Greg with the opportunity to develop warm and supportive relationships within the group setting, in contrast to his confrontational macho style outside the group.

To reiterate, this section has shown that the group climate, including the facilitators' teaching style, sex, and role within the prison, can effectively encourage open expression and a sense of responsibility among the group members with regard to their current offence. However, in contrast, the rest of this chapter highlights how participants felt pressured to conform to the dominant models of sexual offending.

Pressure to conform

As Chapter 3 outlined, sex offender treatment programmes tend to incorporate multifactorial theories of sexual offending. These explanations are then incorporated into models that focus on the causes of sexual abuse that might predispose somebody towards committing a sexual offence (Allam 2001). Two predominant models were used to explain the process of sexual offending within the treatment programmes observed in this study. The first is that of Finkelhor (1984) who proposed the existence of four preconditions before sexual abuse can take place. The second is the cycle of offending, which presupposes that offenders go through a number of stages leading up to their offence (Wolf 1984, 1988; Eldridge 1998). Despite being criticized for conveying an idea that sexual offending follows a formulaic pattern, these models are simply intended as a general guide. While it is assumed that they apply to most forms of sexual offending, there are exceptions. Treatment programmes therefore, at least in theory, recognize the heterogeneous nature of sexual offending.

However, this was not substantiated by all the men interviewed in this research study. In contrast, a number of interviewees claimed that they had felt pressured to conform to the models used in treatment programmes to explain sexual offending. Indeed, Albert and Jack expressed their frustration at not being treated as individuals. Albert was convicted of murder, and Jack was convicted of an internet offence. Arguably, both men will have treatment needs over and above those seen in other sexual offenders (see Chapter 3):

> They [the facilitators] don't see you as individuals, just a group of sex offenders. (Albert)

> They've got their own boxes that you've got to fit into and I don't think that's how it works, everybody is different, that X, Y happens Z automatically happens I don't believe that. I think it differs from person to person. (Jack)

It was also generally perceived that failure to adhere to the different explanations of sexual offending had negative implications. For example, a number of participants felt that if they did not conform to the models of sexual offending behaviour they would not be considered to have reduced their risk of future offending. This was also viewed to impact on the possibility of the participants obtaining the extrinsic factors that had influenced their decision to participate in treatment (i.e. early release, enhanced privileges – see Chapter 5):

> It seems like they got their set agenda and if you don't follow that well when you finish the course you're still dangerous sort of thing. (Oliver)

> I've got a feeling that they've got an agenda, you may have been there when I was on about Big Brother and thought police . . . it was just, they kept going on that you've got to consider it abuse you've got to consider it bla bla bla. I said listen this is just thought police, if we say X number of words then we're cured and it doesn't work that way. (Jack)

This in turn may encourage group members to say what they think is expected of them, rather than what they actually believe.

'Talking the talk'

A phrase that is ubiquitous among practitioners working with sex offenders is 'talking the talk'. This generally refers to instances where group members agree with everything said by the facilitators without actually making the internal change. A number of participants interviewed in this study either claimed that they had 'talked the talk' or that members of their group had done so:

> I won't feel pressured into doing anything really, I won't take anything that way I'll just keep going, saying no sorry I can't slice the [Blame] Cake.[1] I did notice some of the lads were saying, because I was first one there, I did the first cake with candles, and then they said well, now draw another cake and slice it and I said I can't, and then they said we want you to, or we need you to. If you noticed then, the boys that went up after me they did slice the cake. So when they did slice the cake and they put the blame onto the victim or whoever it was, then they got ripped into, not ripped into as such, well why are you blaming that person? I think it was the young person wasn't it, said well I blamed that person because you said I got to blame somebody, which they did in a way, which they told me I got to, but I couldn't. (Luke)

> On the five-year plan I was saying what you want me to put on here, what you want or the truth. (Wayne)

Similarly, 'talking the talk' was claimed to have been used by group members who the participants felt were attending the programme in order to facilitate their future offending (see Chapter 5):

> You could be in a group getting off on it, listening to this and doing all the right things but he's just getting ammo for himself do you understand what I'm saying? And you never know, that's why when you come to a group it's for yourself, you've got to be wanting to do it yourself otherwise it's no use, you could be sitting there, as soon as you sit there and everyone sits there and you could be sitting there the whole time in a group saying everything, doing everything, doing the right facial expressions all that and you're just thinking I can't wait, do you understand what I'm saying, and who would know the difference, it's got to be yourself that wants to do

it and if you don't want to do it nobody's going to make you do it.
(Clive)

Interestingly, a number of men interviewed in this study assumed that
the treatment facilitators were, on the whole, oblivious to a group
member's true motivation for compliance:

> In the end that's the easiest way to go forward whether I believe it
> or not it keeps them quiet. But to me there is no point in doing that,
> that's what annoys me, you're not getting anywhere by doing that.
> Anyone can just go along with the flow it's just, it doesn't sort out
> any underlying problems, I just don't know. (Jack)

> Well if I wanted to go in there and lie my head off for nine months
> you know I could. (Edmund)

As Chapter 5 identified, this was not the case with regard to Nathanial,
who was removed from the C-SOGP partly because the group facilitators
felt he was 'talking the talk'. Nonetheless, the following accounts from
Jack highlight the difficulty in distinguishing between external conform-
ity and internal change in behaviour.

Jack: A case study

Jack was required to attend the C-SOGP as part of his sentence. Having
been convicted of downloading indecent images of children from the
internet, Jack found it hard to accept that he had done anything wrong.
His main justification centred on the fact that he did not consider the
children on the screen as victims. He therefore believed his behaviour to
be victimless (see Chapter 4). Of course, it is not true that such crimes are
ultimately victimless. In Jack's case, every picture was a real child being
sexually abused. Consequently, his 'no harm done' mindset could not be
justified. Developing victim empathy is therefore a central component of
cognitive behavioural treatment programmes (see Chapter 3).

As part of the victim empathy sessions of both the Community Sex
Offender Groupwork Programme (C-SOGP) and the prison-based Sex
Offender Treatment Programme (SOTP), group members are required to
write a letter to their victim. This letter is not to be sent to the victim, but
is used instead to reflect the group members' understanding of the
impact of their actions and also to take responsibility for them. Given the
nature of Jack's offence, he was asked to recall an image that he had
downloaded. This was described to the group and the child in the image
given a name. His victim was named Alice. Jack was then asked to write
to Alice as if she were still a child. Extract 7.1 outlines Jack's first victim
letter.

Extract 6.1: Jack's first victim letter

Dear _____

You won't know me, but I've become caught up in the abuse you suffered as a child, the result of downloading pornography from the internet. As part of my punishment I'm required to write a letter to yourself.

First off it was nothing personal, your images falling into possession were a random action rather than any deliberate choice. That may not be much comfort to you as the abuse had taken place regardless.

It may comfort you to know that I'll pay the price for the rest of my life. I've become another victim of your abuse. I've been financially hit, had my freedom restricted and my good name sullied. Hopefully you will feel better now that revenge has been exercised on your behalf.

But, then again, perhaps not and your own pain is more important than talk of revenge.

Yours faithfully,

Jack

Jack's first letter clearly showed his inability to empathize with his victim. The facilitators' and the group's comments recognized Jack's failure to accept responsibility for his actions, to understand how the victim might feel, to appreciate the reasons why a victim might not physically resist or disclose the abuse, and to accept the consequences of the abuse. Overall, the treatment facilitators concluded that Jack's letter confirmed his high-risk status. Having been challenged on these points, Jack was asked to repeat the victim letter exercise, including in it what he had learnt (if anything) from the group discussion.

Significant improvements can be seen in Jack's second victim letter. Indeed, the second letter is substantially longer than the first and is clearly well written. Extract 7.2 outlines Jack's second victim letter.

Jack's second victim letter suggests that he had accepted that he was accountable for his actions. He also appeared to have recognized the harmful effect of his abuse. Consequently, the facilitators felt that Jack had intrinsically changed his thoughts and behaviour. However, the following remarks in an interview with the researcher shed a different light, and give some insight into Jack's interpretation of both letters:

The first time I was angry and that's the one they didn't like . . . I just put it down that basically I was the victim and they didn't like that version, so I wrote another one and they seemed happy with that so . . . I could have written that in the first place but I wanted to put my point of view across first before theirs. (Jack)

Extract 6.2: Jack's second victim letter

Dear Alice,

You won't know me, and this may seem a strange letter, but do try and read on. I'm one of the bad men who have been hurting you. You won't have seen me, but I have been as bad as the men who hurt you. I am sorry that I have hurt you, but maybe that won't help you.

What I can say to help is that none of the bad things that have happened to you is your fault. You are still a good little girl, you did nothing wrong. It is all the bad men who did wrong. That won't take away the pain, but perhaps it will help you feel a little better.

I know you feel frightened and trapped, just a little girl stuck with bad grown-ups. I can tell you that I won't be hurting you again. I didn't pick on you because I wanted to hurt you, but I did hurt you and that was wrong. I also hurt other little girls, which makes me a very bad man. I promise you I won't hurt you or any other girl again. You may not believe me or may not want to believe me, all I can do is give you my word.

You mustn't keep what is happening to you a secret. The bad men must be stopped and most grown-ups are good and will help you. This might be hard for you to understand because grown-ups have done very bad things to you. They have hurt you badly, hurt your thoughts and ignored you when you scream and cry. But most grown-ups will help you to try and feel better and take the pain away. I know it will be hard for you to trust grown-ups, but please try. None of the bad things that happened to you are your fault, you must believe that.

If you have read this far you must be very angry with me and so you should be. Now use your anger to help yourself against the other bad men. I am being punished on your behalf if that helps you at all.

You may be wondering why I hurt you at all. Well, how can I explain it, I find it a 'turn-on' to watch other people have sex. This may be hard for a little girl to understand, especially as I ignored the fact that some of the people I was watching were little girls who were being hurt. I deliberately blocked the pain and pretended they were having fun. I don't expect you to understand that or forgive me, but that is the way I was thinking at the time. Of course I know now that I was behaving very badly and that no little girls should be hurt or scared just because I like watching sex. I'm afraid it is too late to save you from being hurt and I'm sorry. But it will stop

---

Extract 6.2: Jack's second victim letter (contd)

other little girls being hurt for my pleasure. That is of little comfort to you, I expect, but I cannot turn back time and save you from the hurt, as much as I would like to.

I could ask for your forgiveness, but deep down I know I don't deserve it and it would just be a way of making me feel better. I'm sure you would much rather just hit me to make yourself feel better, and so you should.

Jack

Evidently, Jack did not substantiate the facilitators' beliefs. Instead he claimed to have been pressured to change his initial victim letter to meet the expectations of the programme facilitators. Jack therefore implied that he was simply 'talking the talk' within the group:

> With any interrogation, torture, whatever you call it, you're going to break and say whatever the interrogator wants you to say. It's just human nature, you can't hold out indefinitely. (Jack)

However, this might simply reflect his reluctance to admit outwardly during the interview process to the harm caused by his offending behaviour. (Jack has been defined as a justifier in this study.) In addition, Jack's claim that his second victim letter simply reflected what the programme facilitators expected him to write, might also represent a *post hoc* justification for his change in perspective. This is arguably more symptomatic of the (ongoing) power struggle between group members and programme facilitators (this will be explored in more detail in the following chapter). Within this context, the facilitators' belief that Jack's second victim letter represented a genuine change in his ability to empathize with his victim might reflect their reluctance to accept that they can be deceived. It thus becomes extremely difficult to ascertain the extent to which Jack was motivated to change his sexual offending behaviour.

The comments made by Xandy during the interviews also highlight the difficulties in differentiating when, and to whom, the participants might be 'talking the talk'. Convicted of a violent sexual assault on a child, Xandy initially denied his offending behaviour, then, in the second interview, changed his plea and admitted to having committed a sexual offence:

Interviewer   So they think you're in denial?

Xandy   No, I've changed my mind now because I want to get it
               off my chest now, so there's a way it's changed my
               thinking.

Interviewer   So you did commit the offence?

Xandy   Yeah.

However, Xandy made it explicit throughout the interviews that he was
prepared to give the tutors 'a load of bullshit' in order to gain his desired
reward of parole:

I'll sit up and bark as long as they give me the biscuits. (Xandy)

Consequently, there remains a certain degree of cynicism with regard to
Xandy's true motive for admitting to his offence. In this instance it is
difficult to determine the extent to which Xandy has psychologically
taken responsibility for his offending behaviour.

Conclusions

There appears to be much agreement between the different groups
with respect to the participants' views of their group facilitators and
other group members. For example, the participants typically advocated the consistent use of two group facilitators, with the inclusion
of one male and one female, to enhance their willingness to engage in
treatment. This is consistent with findings presented by the Sex
Offender and Treatment and Evaluation Project (STEP) (Beech et al.
1999). It was also typical for the participants facilitated by a prison
officer to accept, over time, that the officer was not there as an
authoritarian figure. Indeed, all the participants interviewed in this
research generally felt supported, respected and listened to by all
programme facilitators and the other group members during treatment.
Consequently, the participants participating on both the C-SOGP and
the SOTP in particular, felt able to disclose their offending behaviour
within the group environment.

Arguably, the design of the BAP is also meant to encourage group
members to reflect upon the circumstances that led to their conviction.
This is particularly applicable to the total deniers in the group. For
example, as Chapter 5 highlighted, the total deniers would not have
volunteered if the programme had discussed their alleged offence or
challenged their denial. The avoidance of any discussion of the group
members' offences is adhered to throughout the BAP. In doing so, the

total deniers were given the freedom to examine circumstances and their actions around the time the offence was said to occur.

However, this chapter has also shown how extrinsic factors might also encourage group members to 'talk the talk'. It is therefore important to recognize that group members might be willing to say what they think is expected of them in order to distance themselves from their sexually abusive behaviour and/or present themselves more favourably to the criminal justice system (and within the interviews). However, the findings presented in this chapter appear to suggest that the group members' decision to be honest or 'talk the talk' is symptomatic of whether they are being challenged by peers, or are part of a tutor–offender battle (respectively). Of course, these individuals might simply have been unmotivated to change their abusive behaviour, in that they were purposely trying to deceive the programme tutors. Bearing this in mind, the following two chapters will explore the participants' accounts of what works. Chapter 8 also identifies other extrinsic factors that can undermine a group member's desire to disclose their true risk of re-offending without fear of incrimination.

Note

1 The Blame Cake is used in module 2 of the C-SOGP (Cycles and Cognitive Distortions) to help group members to identify and re-evaluate dysfunctional thinking relating to personal responsibility for offending. The exercise asks group members to divide up the Blame Cake into segments in proportion to who or what is to blame for sex offending (C-SOGP Manual 2001).

Chapter 7

Denial, identity and 'what works'

This chapter analyses the participants' accounts of 'what works' in their respective treatment programmes. This research has identified five main components to the sex offender treatment programmes used in this study, with greater or lesser emphasis on some aspects of treatment depending on the type of programme (see Chapter 3). These have been defined as dysfunctional attitudes and beliefs, victim empathy, sexual interest, lifestyle management and relapse prevention.

To reiterate, the first four components focus on cognitive areas that are believed to contribute to sexually abusive behaviour, whereas relapse prevention links the offenders' understanding of the above to being able to apply constructs and skills that are central to prevention of re-offending. Although all the men interviewed in this study had been convicted of a sexual offence, they are not a homogenous group. It is not therefore expected that the four cognitive areas of treatment will apply to everyone. This chapter aims to identify which of these components provide which individuals with some understanding of the damage they have caused, enabling them to become proficient in the relevant skills required to address their problem.

This chapter identifies any attitudinal and behavioural change in the areas listed above. In doing so it aims to provide the reader with a detailed account of whether these treatment targets can be successful in strengthening an individual's motivation not to offend in the future. Throughout this chapter, some of these components will be addressed as separate topics, while others are incorporated into broader categories.

Thirty-one offenders interviewed in this research started a treatment programme. The accounts of the participants who failed to complete treatment (for reasons other than re-offending) have already been discussed in Chapter 6. Both Keith and Luke committed further offences while participating in treatment. Their perspectives will be discussed in the following chapter.

This chapter will first explore the accounts of the men who believed that their participation in treatment would have no significant effect on whether they will offend in the future. The discussion then identifies individuals who claimed that they have benefited from participating in treatment, beginning with offenders who completed the Community Sex Offender Groupwork Programme (C-SOGP) and the prison-based Sex Offender Treatment Programme (SOTP). While all three programmes address the five domains mentioned above, there are noticeable differences in the way they are approached. Whereas the SOTP and the C-SOGP follow much the same format, the Behaviour Assessment Programme (BAP) places greater emphasis on improving the group members' ability to function in society, including issues of low self-esteem, fear of adult intimacy and inappropriate assertiveness. In addition, unlike the SOTP and the C-SOGP, the BAP does not look at specific offences. Instead, aspects that bear directly upon the individual's offence are addressed using hypothetical links with sex offenders (see Chapter 3). The perspectives of participants who completed the BAP will therefore be explored separately.

Nothing works

Two participants claimed that they did not gain anything from participating on their respective treatment programmes. Jack completed the C-SOGP and Yuval completed the BAP. Both men have been defined as justifiers in this research (see Chapter 4).

To reiterate, Jack was convicted of viewing and downloading child pornography off the internet. Despite never denying the offence, the main justification he put forward for his actions was that there were no victims. Yuval, on the other hand, was convicted of raping a woman. In contrast, he claimed that he was having an affair with his victim. For example, while he admitted to visiting the woman on the night that he was accused of rape, he emphatically denied the rape charge. He is 'not even sure if [he] penetrated her'. Consequently, neither man believed that they had done anything wrong or that their behaviour had created victims:

> I don't really think about the victim that much, because she's not a victim I'm a victim. (Yuval)

> I don't see there being any [victims]. (Jack)

Arguably, both Jack and Yuval's perceptions of treatment are more indicative of their state of denial, rather than a true reflection of the effectiveness of their respective treatment programmes.

Yuval's attempts to reassert his innocence clearly overwhelmed his perception of treatment content. As such, his account of the offence did not really change over the course of the three interviews. He therefore finished the BAP in the same state of denial as he started. In contrast, while Jack's justifications were readily apparent throughout his participation on the C-SOGP, they were by no means fixed. To illustrate this, Jack's progress through the C-SOGP will now be explored.

Jack: A case study

Arguably, Jack's lifestyle conforms to a predictable pattern of sexually offending behaviour. For example, the nature of his past employment meant that he was away a lot. He described himself as bisexual and claimed to have not been involved in a long-term relationship prior to the offence. In a similar vein, many sex offenders are reported to have limited intimacy in their lives (Seidman *et al.* 1994). Consequently, in the absence of a relationship, and while abroad, Jack admitted to using female prostitutes to fulfil his sexual gratification. He also admitted to having casual liaisons with gay men through chatlines, as well as becoming increasingly interested in diverse forms of pornography on the internet. Jack also admitted to lacking self-confidence. He was therefore ideally suited to the cognitive-behavioural treatment approach, both because of the nature of his denial and because of his background history.

Jack settled well into group treatment, and despite considerable denial there is some evidence to suggest that he did make some cognitive shifts in the areas of treatment that were particularly applicable to his offending behaviour. For example, by the end of the C-SOGP he had accepted that his actions did in fact harm people:

> I can sort of see where they are coming from, if you are harming people then it is wrong, I accept that now. (Jack)

He also recognized that 'telling [himself] that it is OK to be doing what [he was] doing [was a] cognitive distortion'. In addition, he acknowledged that he was 'bound to be [using] others'. Of course, it is not clear how far Jack is responding in a manner that he thinks will gain him approval over the course of the interviews. However, it seems doubtful that Jack was totally dismissive of the idea that he could be wrong. For example, even at the very beginning of the treatment process, Jack appeared to be open to changing his views:

Even in my case there must be case studies of people, of children that have taken a part in pornography and it's damaged them in some way, even there, there must be case studies, there must be information, even if there isn't any specific victim there must be a sort of generalized victim as it were, some people have suffered from it obviously so there will be information around . . . if you can show what they've been through, it will be far more likely to get a response. (Jack)

Similarly, Jack repeatedly questioned whether he was hiding anything:

I suppose what I am trying to hide in a way is am I some way or form sexually attracted to children. That's a horrible thing to admit to, and I wonder if that's what I'm hiding. (Jack)

I just dismissed it in the past, victims, so what, no empathy at all, they're just meaningless, and I think they are trying to push forward the fact that there are real people involved here, and that's the bit I either can't accept, *or won't accept*. (Jack)

Consequently, even if Jack was 'talking the talk', this is perhaps more symptomatic of the difficult task he faced in order to make such a cognitive shift, rather than no cognitive shift at all.

Despite this, Jack still claimed that he had not benefited from participating in treatment. As Chapter 6 argued, this might simply represent a *post hoc* justification for 'appearing' to have changed during treatment. Indeed, claiming that treatment had helped him in some way would imply that he needed help in the first place. In addition, after a number of discussions with Jack it was evident that his dissatisfaction centred on the programme's assumption that he will re-offend in the future. For example, despite being able to recognize himself on the cycle of offending, he did 'not entirely believe that it goes round again'.[1] Consequently, Jack did not believe that it was necessary to participate in treatment in order to prevent him from committing further offences:

I don't see the relevance of it. I've decided that I won't do it again so I won't. (Jack)

Evidently, the programme's attempts to challenge this generated sufficient animosity to prevent substantial treatment gains.[2]

Something works: The C-SOGP and the SOTP

In contrast, 15 participants felt that they had benefited from participating on both the SOTP and the C-SOGP. Thirteen had completed the SOTP. The chapter will now present their accounts of 'what works'.

The offending process

All of the men interviewed in this subgroup stated that they had gained a better understanding of their personal route from their motivation to the actual offence:

> I understood my behaviours and thoughts which led up to things. (Ben)

For example, both Greg and Oliver claimed that recounting the situational, cognitive and emotional determinants that had contributed to their offending was the most important part of the programme:

> Being bad-tempered, drinking all the time, whatever, that's the most important part for me, if I can understand why I got that way, how I got that way, and looking back and realized what I did, being like that you know what I mean? (Greg)

> [The most important part of the course has been] the cycle because I can see where I was going wrong, I can see the stages, I was at the poor me and the loneliness and the masturbation and all that, I could see where I was going on the cycle. (Oliver)

This draws on both Finkelhor (1984) and Wolf's (1984) models of the offence process.[3] Whereas both models were addressed in the C-SOGP, the SOTP adhered to the different stages of the offence process throughout the programme. As such, both programmes were able to increase the group members' understanding of their offences and to help them identify areas in their lives, and aspects of themselves, which needed to be modified.

Dysfunctional attitudes and beliefs

While both the SOTP and the C-SOGP presuppose that social, situational and cultural factors lead to abuse, the men interviewed in this study generally reflected upon the role that cognitive distortions played in their offence process:

> I got to recognize CDs [cognitive distortions], for instance when there is one ... how a thought process can lead to something, a lot of it I didn't think about, I just did it, but it's a process and you've got to recognize that. (Clive)

Cognitive distortions (CDs) are attitudes and beliefs that offenders use to deny, minimize and rationalize their behaviour (Murphy 1990). As such, it is generally accepted that these attitudes or schemas[4] perform a major role in precipitating and maintaining sexual offending behaviour (Salter 1988; Blumenthal *et al.* 1999). The participants in this research used a variety of CDs to rationalize their behaviour. For example, Ben was convicted of raping a woman. The CDs he used to give himself permission to commit the rape included his belief that his victim was 'up for it' and, based on the fact that he had taken drugs that evening, that he 'didn't know what [he] was doing'. In contrast, Matthew, convicted of sexually abusing a 14-year-old girl, 'talked [himself] around her age' by making out that she was a lot older than she was. However, the findings indicated that programme intervention enabled offenders to recognize cognitive distortions that they used in their offending.

For example, Finn recognized the CDs that he used to legitimize sex between an adult and a child:

> My cognitive distortions were it's not really doing them any harm, it's just a version of loving her and in actual fact I'm preparing her for adulthood, these are the sort of CDs I was using. (Finn)

Subsequently, Finn asserted that treatment had enabled him to lift a 'great big blanket from [his] eyes', thereby giving him a new way of looking at his thoughts and behaviour. During the interview stage of the research he described his CDs as 'just excuses, a load of horrible, stupid, pathetic excuses [that he used] to give [himself] permission to abuse [his] victims'. In such a way he was able to accept that his offence would have a detrimental effect on his victims (this will be explored in more detail later in this chapter).

While the men's accounts suggest that they were able to recognize their CDs, they may have been merely parroting psychological phrases with little, or no, understanding of the implications of working under such cognitive distortions. However, Finn also appreciated how easy it is for someone completely to bury their conscience in order to work under such distorted assumptions. He therefore indicated the importance of being able to recognize CDs in the future:

> I've got to recognize that I may still be operating under a cognitive distortion, I just haven't recognized them yet. (Finn)

This was echoed by a number of men interviewed in this subgroup. For example, Harry, convicted of raping a woman, acknowledged that his CDs related back to occasions when he had gone out to watch people having sexual intercourse. In these instances he would tell himself that he 'was not hurting anyone', as he was just watching from outside. This by his own account then allowed him to go 'out and do it again and again' until it progressed into rape:

> At the time of the actual offence I thought yeah nice girl, and maybe because I was at a distance you know, I was watching and I thought yeah she looks nice, and then you get into that way of thinking, you know what I mean, and before you know it, this time I was so like overcome by them thoughts . . . that everything else went out of my head . . . all I was thinking about was have sex with this nice woman. (Harry)

Consequently, Harry maintained that if the programme had not helped him to recognize the excuses that he was using 'for just what they are, excuses', he would have kept using them. As the above examples highlight, very often the men were not aware of the associated goals of using CDs. Failure to deal with them effectively might lead to a relapse.

A number of participants felt that it was also important to explore the link between early life experiences and the development of distorted beliefs, as the following quotation from Albert highlights poignantly:

> If you know that you've got an attitude towards females but you don't know where it's come from then you're always going to have that you know, so you have to know where it comes from to treat it really. (Albert)

This draws on Bowlby's (1969) attachment theory (see Chapter 3). In Bowlby's model, children are said to develop their core beliefs from their parents and the surrounding environment. These experiences then manifest into an individual style of attachment that continues throughout childhood and into adulthood. Attachment theory therefore proposes that there is a link between insecure childhood attachment (including childhood sexual abuse) and an individual's inability to achieve intimacy in adolescence and adulthood (Sawle and Kear-Cowell 2001; Smallbone and McCabe 2003). This in turn has been said to contribute to sexually abusive behaviour.

In both the C-SOGP and the SOTP the Life Timeline directly addresses the life trajectories and early experiences of the group members. This can include early sexual abuse. Three of the men in this subgroup indicated that they had been sexually abused as children. Edmund and Ivor both participated on the SOTP, whereas Oliver participated on the C-SOGP. All three participants, having disclosed their victimization to the group, were able to understand how their victimization contributed to their offending behaviour. For example, Edmund talked about being 'introduced to sex at an early age'. However, there is the danger that addressing an individual's sexual victimization, within treatment, may reinforce their sense of fatalism over later offending (Allam 2001). Consequently, both programmes ensure that the focus of such disclosures is about finding explanations and not excuses. This was generally accepted by this group of offenders, as the following quotations highlight:

> I was abused myself as a boy and perhaps if I'd opened up and told my mother, told my father, told somebody I wouldn't be sitting with you here now. I don't blame [my abuse] for me going out and abusing children, I was wrong to do that but if I had [told someone what was happening] I might not be sitting here today. I probably would not be sitting here today. (Ivor)

> Before all the games with [my uncle] I didn't even think about having sex with my sister, or sex with anybody, but then after the games with [my uncle] it started to go on from there, or worse sort of thing with my sister and then a couple of years later [with my next victim], so in a way I know it's not [my uncle's] fault but deep down I still blame him for doing it, but I know it's not his fault. (Oliver)

In addition, Ivor found that the focus of such disclosure within his respective treatment programme enhanced his empathy for his own victims:

> Because I was a victim, I should know really what victims, what my victims went through because I went through it. (Ivor)

Similarly, other negative life experiences were identified by participants that reflected upon their current attitudes and relationship styles. For example, Albert had an extremely negative attitude towards women, which evidently contributed towards his offence. Indeed, he described how he used CDs to justify calling all women 'slags':

> My cognitive distortions were ... women are just after one thing you know that type of thing. (Albert)

However, he felt that he had gained a deeper knowledge of where his attitude towards females came from having completed the Life Timeline exercise:

> At the beginning of the group you have to stand up for thirty minutes and talk about your life, all that there at the top that is everything that I was feeling, rejection, frustration, anger, resentment, all that, that is what I've carried through from the age of seven all the way through my life . . . but it was all against my mother . . . being brought up with my grandparents. But you could never say that to your mum but it was always in the back [of your mind], you know always at the back [of your mind] at the end of the day. (Albert)

In addition, Matthew felt that the Life Timeline session was 'one of the best sessions' of the C-SOGP, in that it 'allowed [him] to realize what [he'd] been bottling up'. In doing so, the Life Timeline session enabled him to identify early life experiences that contributed to the development of maladaptive coping strategies. This corresponds to the lifestyle management component of treatment and will therefore be addressed later in this chapter.

To summarize, in the majority of cases the respective treatment programmes appear to be successful in reinforcing individuals' nonacceptance of the use of cognitive distortions. However, while some distortions were addressed within treatment, others remained. This became particularly apparent in the case of Burt. Despite being able to identify his CDs, there was no real indication of any attitudinal change. For example, Burt was convicted of indecently assaulting two children, of both sexes. He was also charged with the abduction of a female child. Burt acknowledged that he used the following CDs to give himself permission to commit the indecent assaults:

> My typical [CDs] were this isn't causing any harm, this child is curious, I'm not harming them, they're laying back, they want to play the game again. (Burt).

However, throughout the interview Burt made further assertions that legitimized sex between an adult and a child. The effect that this has on his and other participants' ability to empathize with their victims will be discussed in the next section.

Victim empathy

Promoting victim empathy is a core component of both the C-SOGP and the SOTP. This section explores treatment effectiveness at reducing denial of harm to the victims.

All of the men interviewed in this subgroup felt that participating on either the C-SOGP or the SOTP had improved their ability to empathize with their victim(s). Furthermore, the majority of participants (80 per cent) felt that they had benefited the most from learning about the effects sexual abuse has on victims.

Both programmes include sessions that explore the meaning of empathy. This includes the use of written descriptions by sexual assault victims and videotaped accounts depicting the effects of sexual abuse to help the group members gain a better understanding of the concept of empathy. Ben, however, did not find the written accounts as 'emotional as watching it on screen' (Ben):

> On the screen you see the actual person saying it's happening, but on a piece of paper it could be just a story out of a book if you understand what I mean. (Ben)

Both programmes also include sessions that allow the offenders to participate in victim narratives and to write and present their victim letters to the group. In addition, the SOTP gives the group members the opportunity to act out victim-perspective role-plays. The victim role-plays and the victim letters received the most positive response from the offenders interviewed in this subgroup.

Victim role-plays

Within the victim empathy modules of the SOTP each group member is given the opportunity to act out scenarios that are relevant to both their offending behaviour and any identifiable empathy deficits. During the role-plays the group member will play either their victim or a member of their victim's family. The aim is to allow the group member to experience, at an emotional level, the feelings that their victim(s) went through at the time of the offence itself, and/or the emotions that their victim and/or their victim's family are likely to experience in the short- and long-term future after the offence. In relation to Albert, the only murderer in this sample, the role-plays were used to explore the wider ramifications of his offending behaviour. Eleven of the men who completed the SOTP felt that they had benefited from acting out their victim-perspective role-plays. This section now presents a number of the men's role-play scenarios in more detail.

Ben was convicted of raping the same woman on two separate occasions. Ben had to act out a scenario in which he had to play the role of his victim two weeks after the first rape:

> We had to go through an account, not as myself as my victim, so I had to go back four years and pretend I was my victim and actually go into a role and be my victim and get asked questions like what actually happened that night and things like that and then I'd say it from the victim's point of view, and understanding it from that side, that was hard. (Ben)

Ben was clearly able to get into the role of his victim, as the following quotation highlights:

> You close your eyes and it blocks off everything and they take you back to the actual day of the event, for me that was four years ago and it's like going back that far. (Ben)

In the role of the victim, Ben claimed that he gained good insight into how scared his victim would have been. For example, during the role-play he observed, as the victim, how his 'eyes were speaking more', and that his 'eyes were being more threatening'. In doing so it enabled him to understand the consequences of what he had done to his victim:

> [I could see] how I was acting, but that wasn't me, I was talking to myself, I was seeing it how my victim would have seen it, and it was evil. (Ben)

In addition, whereas before treatment Ben claimed that on the occasion of the second rape, the victim 'consented to half ... of the things that happened', he later acknowledged that 'because of the first time, because [he] put so much fear into [his] victim, she would have done anything, she would have bent over backwards to make sure that she didn't get hurt'. In the light of this, he appeared to take full responsibility for the offence:

> Before I even did this course and before I even spoke to you I used to believe in a way that she led me on to some of the things, that I think, it was like flaunting to me and I took it, but when I look at it now, she didn't flaunt it, she didn't do anything, she didn't tease me in any way, I asked for what I wanted and she didn't want to give it to me but I still took it, it was all down to me. (Ben)

Evidently, Ben gained a good understanding of how scared and helpless his victim would have felt as a result of the rapes during his participation in the role-play exercises.

Clive also felt that the victim empathy role-plays enabled him to understand the wider ramifications, or the ripple effect, of his offending behaviour, as the following quotation highlights:

> I had to play my victim's father in a situation when he was invited to his friend's party because his friend's daughter had passed the exam and they were celebrating but he didn't go because he was upset because that made him remember when his daughter maybe didn't pass her exams or something, so I had to play that role, so it was very frustrating not as me but as her father ... But it was an insight ... because it doesn't just affect two people it affects loads of people you know. (Clive)

This was supported by a number of participants in relation to the victim empathy modules as a whole:

> I've learnt a lot of empathy. I've realized that I've let my professional colleagues down. Until I went on this course I didn't realize the enormity of what I had done. (Andrew)

> I think I have a fair grasp of it how much I've hurt people, not just the victims as in [my actual victim], but her family which is obviously hurting, my family's hurting, these are all victims at the end of the day. (Matthew)

Similarly, Finn had a clear understanding of the amount of people who were affected by his offending:

> As far as I'm concerned I've hurt more people, I've created more victims, they talk about ripples well in my case those ripples become tidal waves because I've hurt an awful lot of people beside my victims, you know my wife went through hell because of me and my family. (Finn)

In addition, the victim empathy role-play clearly enhanced his insight into a wide range of short- and long-term effects his abuse will have had on his victims. For example, the following quotation emphasizes Finn's ability to engage at an emotional level with a broad range of feelings his victims would have experienced, such as how their trust in him would have eroded:

She was eight, so I was imagining this girl, she was my niece and here was an uncle somebody that she loved, trusted, she looked on not just as an uncle but as a friend and suddenly he changed and became this horrible person and it, it's all right thinking about it but when you can actually feel what your victim went through and imagine what your victim is feeling, when they look at you and think why's he doing this, why's he changed, why has he become this horrible person, it does literally take your breath away, it makes you look at things in a way that you never thought possible. (Finn)

Victim letters

Similarly, the victim empathy exercise provided a number of participants with further opportunity to experience vicariously thoughts and feelings regarding their specific victims. The victim letter is a hypothetical exercise, in which the group members are asked to write an apology letter to their victim(s). The writing of this is believed to reveal the level of empathy that the group member has for their victim(s) (Webster 2002). Three of the men interviewed in this subgroup spoke at length about the victim letter during the interview stage of this research. All three men, Albert, Ben and Finn, claimed that the victim letter exercise undermined any belief that the victim's experience of abuse was harmless. For example, in Ben's first victim letter, he wrote that the victim would probably hate him. He later acknowledged that 'probably is not a word that you can use', replacing it instead with 'I know you're going to hate me, I know you hate me'. Albert also showed his ability to imagine that he was his victim's parents being addressed in his letter to make sure that he was not using any justifications in the letter:

I put myself in the situation if it had been somebody in my family that died and I think that I would want to know, not all their problems in their life, but to try and know the person as they was then, you know what was actually happening, but I think it's hard to try, because to put it in a letter like that you know you can go into it but then it's all about you, you know what I'm saying, if you ever write a letter then you're putting it all about you and it's not about you at all, it's about them, you know, what they're feeling and what they've lost in their lives, so do you tell them this was happening in your life and are they going to take it as that you're trying to justify your actions? (Albert)

Finally Finn, despite finding the victim letters and the role-plays extremely painful, recognized that 'what [he] was going through is absolutely sod all compared to what [he] put [his] victims through.'

The participants in this subgroup found both the victim-perspective role-plays and the victim letter emotionally very difficult. Albert described the victim letter as a 'killer', whereas Andrew claimed that writing the victim letter made him feel terrible. In addition, the role-play exercise tended to be accompanied by emotion for a lot of the men participating in this research:

> I did a role-play where I played the victim. I was very emotional, I felt weak doing it, but after a day or two you think back on it and think that's what I put [my victims] through. (Graham)

During the role-play exercise Finn 'cried like a big girl', not because he felt sorry for himself but 'for the fact that he had put somebody he loved very much though an awful lot'. He also described how after the role-play exercise he 'felt unclean, a leper'. Evidently, Finn's recollection of the harm and pain that he has caused his victim meant that he saw himself 'for the first time as an abuser'. The danger is that both exercises might reinforce an offender's poor self-image, and in doing so encourage offenders to withdraw into defence mechanisms such as the use of denial, minimization and/or fantasy that precede offending.[5] Consequently, both the C-SOGP and the SOTP aim to enhance the group member's self-esteem before attempting victim empathy. Both programmes' effectiveness at tackling the participants' self-confidence will be discussed later in this chapter. This section will now explore the effect that an individual's remaining CDs have on their ability to empathize with their victim(s).

Cognitive distortions and victim empathy

As this chapter has already shown, CDs are used both to minimize and rationalize an individual's perception of their sexually abusive behaviour. This can effectively disavow or lead to an underestimation of the harm done to victims. For example, Clive denied that he had used a weapon during his offence.[6] Nevertheless, the victim empathy modules evidently ameliorated his ability to empathize with his victims:

> I had empathy before I went on the group, my empathy was on one level, now I think my empathy goes a bit more to different directions because I felt for my victim but I don't actually realize all the ... consequences, I'd had empathy but not as much as I do now, I realize that there are more consequences than I thought you know. (Clive)

Despite still denying the use of a weapon, Clive at least acknowledged feelings of self-blame that his victim would have felt as a result of the rape:

> I've come to realize that my victim could have imagined there was a knife . . . I didn't have a knife but her imagination could be realistic to her. I mean if you listen to someone on the streets . . . the first thing they think of is a man with a knife . . . so it's not hard for me to realize that she could have imagined that . . . or maybe she wanted to believe that because maybe at the time she felt, you know she might have even felt the guilt that maybe she thought that she led me on or something, so you understand what I'm saying, a victim can think like that, a victim can try and blame themselves. (Clive)

Clive's remaining denial might reflect his attempt to avoid self-criticism and social disapproval both throughout the interviews and within treatment. However, on the other hand it might simply reflect his attempt to present himself more favourably without actually changing his opinion regarding the facts of the offence (if of course he did have a knife).

Likewise, having completed the SOTP, Burt was evidently still working under a number of CDs (see above). The main justification put forward for his offence was that his victims were too young to know what was happening.[7] Instead, Burt maintained that his victim empathy came 'more from the fact that [his] victims might be affected in later life', and/or that they might go on to abuse others. However, a closer examination of the data suggested that Burt was unable to understand fully the long-term effects that his offending behaviour will have on his victims. For example, one of Burt's role-play scenarios explored the long-term consequences that his abuse will have on his victims from the indecent assault charge. During the role-play, his female victim, played by one of the group facilitators, finds out that he has been released from prison and runs off crying. Burt felt that his victim would not have done this, asserting instead that 'time heals'. Consequently, the victim empathy modules of the SOTP failed to undermine Burt's remaining distorted beliefs about victim harm.[8] Similarly, as Chapter 6 highlighted, arguably Jack's victim letter reflected what he thought the tutors wanted him to write rather than a true reflection of his victim empathy.

Sexual interest

Both the SOTP and the C-SOGP explore the role that deviant sexual interest plays in sexual offending. In particular, they focus on sex offenders' use of deviant sexual fantasy.[9] Group members who have indulged in deviant sexual fantasy are encouraged to disclose this information and to explore aspects of their sexual fantasies that may have contributed to their interest in actually offending (Prison Service 2000; Probation Service 2001).

Only seven men interviewed in this subgroup claimed that they had benefited from the session that focused on sexual fantasy. It is of course not known whether this represents the participants' unwillingness to disclose deviant sexual fantasy or a genuine lack of deviant interest. However, whereas Clive claimed that he had 'never had illegal thoughts or fantasies' but 'could understand how it could lead to offending', the remaining six men admitted to having had deviant sexual fantasies. In addition, the majority of men recognized the way in which fantasy can reinforce the desire to offend and thus had began to use behavioural alternatives to control their illegal sexual interests.

Both programmes present to the group a number of fantasy modification techniques for coping with, modifying or eradicating abusive sexual fantasies. It is not expected that each analogy will work for each group member, as the following cases highlight. Both Ivor and Burt acknowledged using Distraction and Refocusing (Probation Service 2001) as a technique to avoid sexual fantasy. Essentially, both Ivor and Burt found a way to distract them from continuing with a sexual fantasy:

> You pick up the paper and you see so and so rapes a young blonde girl age so and so, and I go, you know you think for a moment . . . I could have been him, or you fantasize that persons look on it, but this course now, it is gradually [reducing this], it's going down and down until you get a thought or you see something on telly instead. (Ivor)

> Instead of carrying on masturbating . . . I pick up my guitar, get involved in what I'm doing, and then the last thing on your mind is sex, that's one way of controlling it. (Burt)

In contrast, both Colin and Edmund imagined the pain that they have caused to their victim(s) to avoid or eradicate any illegal sexual fantasies. This relates to a fantasy modification technique called Covert Sensitisation (Probation Service 2001), where sex offenders imagine a highly unpleasant event in association with a deviant fantasy:

> You replace one thought with another; you know you rehearse the effect it had on the victim. You substitute your thought with something painful, image substitution, so you don't dwell on the

image that is making you aroused, you substitute this for the pain the victim felt. (Colin)

I had fantasies over, masturbation like . . . what I thought of then was a pleasurable thing today is just like a nightmare really you know. I look back now, or think about that now and there is nothing pleasurable about it, it is pain, hurt, I don't have fantasies any more. (Edmund)

Similarly, Oliver claimed to have used Covert Sensitisation as a means of coping with his illegal sexual fantasy. However, he did so quite differently. For example, during the fantasy module Oliver claimed to be scared of sharks, and therefore decided to associate any sexual fantasy he had with a shark attack:

If you start fantasizing you put things in its place, so I put a shark . . . so if I think about my [victims] or anybody else underage I close my eyes and think of a shark coming towards me. (Oliver)

However, while he was participating on the C-SOGP he saw his sister, one of his victims, for the first time since the offence. At this meeting his sister was wearing a low-cut top. Oliver admitted to 'looking at [his sister's] cleavage' and later having sexual thoughts about his victim while in the bath. This he 'knew [he] shouldn't be doing, so [he] tried the shark to see if it would work'. When it did not, he replaced the shark with walruses. This enabled him to modify his sexual fantasies, as the following quotation highlights:

I was laying in the bath thinking of my sister and then all of a sudden I thought what can I put in place of it and all of a sudden I imagined her with a walrus's body bouncing around the beach, and it did work, and behind her I could see my other [two victims], and they were bouncing behind her as walruses, just with heads on the bodies, and it worked. (Oliver)

Consequently, both the C-SOGP and the SOTP were effective at helping at least some of the men gain control of their fantasies. However, research carried out by Mckibben *et al.* (2001) on sex offenders' perceptions of the effectiveness of strategies to cope with deviant sexual fantasies suggested that the two techniques used by men in this study might have different outcomes in relation to the offenders' risk of offending in the future. Indeed, their results indicated that the distraction technique, used by Ivor and Burt, does not effectively cope with lapses.

On the other hand, covert sensitization was reported to be the most effective for coping with deviant sexual fantasies (Mckibben *et al.* 2001).

Lifestyle management

The lifestyle management component of treatment includes a wide range of areas that relate to the efficacy of an individual's social functioning.[10] For example, it addresses factors such as assertiveness problems, lack of interpersonal skills, poor self-confidence and low self-esteem, with the aim of improving a sex offender's ability to cope in life generally. These areas are integrated into both the C-SOGP and the SOTP from the outset. However, module 3 of the SOTP and module 4 of the C-SOGP explore the way sex offenders have coped with these deficits in the past, as a way of developing more effective coping strategies to be used in the future. This was believed to be an important element of treatment for the majority (13 of the men, 87 per cent) of the participants in this subgroup. Indeed, these men claimed to have developed a range of skills to increase their effectiveness at coping generally.

A number of participants recognized that they had inappropriately dealt with problems in the past, as the following quotation from Albert highlights:

> Like with me it was all my problems, the way that I dealt with them was either avoiding them or brooding on them, you know, [they were] taking over emotionally because I never dealt with it or made all the problems focused, which is as soon as a problem comes in deal with it as soon as it happens, but in the past I never did, I never dealt with it, I always took it on, so I carried it around and you'd be brooding on it for like three or four days, and you've got that building up until something comes in to take that away. So you think it's gone, but it's still there, you can't help it, so you take another problem on, and that problem then builds up, and then another comes in and that builds up, and on and on, but you've never dealt with the two problems underlying all that. (Albert)

This is consistent with Cortoni and Marshall's (1998) research, which found that sex offenders tended to choose emotion-focused strategies when faced with problems.[11] Treatment programmes therefore introduce task-oriented (problem-focused) strategies as a more effective way of coping with problematic emotions[12] (Prison Service 2000; Probation Service 2001). Indeed, all the men in this subgroup felt that they had developed more practical strategies for coping with problems. These included defining the problem and generating options for solving it:

> I think more before I do anything now. (Ben)

It's making me look at things you know what I mean, before actually doing things I've looked at why I'm going to do it. (Harry)

Similarly, Albert had learnt to deal with his problems 'there and then', which meant that he was 'not as stressed as [he] used to be'. Likewise, Greg described himself as 'a very aggressive, bad-tempered ... kind of person' who 'used to jump in feet first and ask questions later'. Having completed treatment, he claimed that he now 'actually looks at the problem first, and worked out the best way' of dealing with it. In addition, both Albert and Greg recognized that they could turn to other people for support as a way of coping with difficulties:

I know there's somebody else I can go to, when there is a problem, whereas I've always been too ashamed in the past to ask somebody else for help because I've always looked at it like people around me have got bigger problems than what I've got. (Albert)

You can go to the police, you can go to probation, it's like a support network, if you've got something, say I went out of here and started drinking again, I've got a support network to turn to if things get worse, you've got all that to do, which is quite interesting because I wouldn't turn to anybody else but myself, all my problems everything on my own, I'd keep everything inside me but now I understand that you've got a support network and people do want to help you, so that was quite interesting. (Greg)

Matthew also emphasized how the C-SOGP had helped him to open up and talk to certain people about things that he had previously bottled up:

It's like when I lost my father I've never talked to anyone about it, I actually went and spoke to my mother about it this week and that's the first time I've done that as well. (Matthew)

Finally, Finn presented an example of how the development of effective coping strategies can reduce an individual's risk of offending in the future. He clearly experienced negative emotional states. His low self-esteem can be attributed, in part, to the feelings of guilt and shame that he felt as a result of his offending. Such feelings were clearly exacerbated throughout his participation on the prison-based SOTP (see above). For example, Finn claimed that his self-esteem 'hit rock bottom' after completing the victim empathy modules. Indeed, he described returning to his cell after his victim empathy role-play and indulging in sweets and chocolates in an attempt 'to do something that [he] thought would make [him] feel better':

In fact I did indulge myself, I ate two Mars bars, two Snickers bars, no, two Mars bars, two Crunchies and a packet of pork scratchings and a banana sandwich, I had to do something because I felt so bad. (Finn)

However, Finn's overindulgence simply contributed to his negative self-image.

As this chapter has already outlined, sex offenders routinely use deviant sexual activities as a means of coping with these negative emotions (Ward and Hudson 2000; Mckibben *et al.* 2001). Despite this, the SOTP evidently succeeded in motivating Finn to find an effective, and safe, coping strategy to deal with his negative self-perception. For example, Finn started to go to the prison gym. This relates to a coping technique that relies on more positive life goals (Prison Service 2000). For example, by engaging in other tasks, in this instance keeping fit, Finn was able to distract himself from his negative emotional state. Consequently, this new task made it possible for Finn to balance his feelings of personal distress with more positive mood states, as the following quotation highlights:[13]

Now that I'm exercising ... I'm working out my frustrations plus I'm getting on with people that are at the gym with me, having a bit of a laugh and a giggle ... so I can intellectually say to myself, right OK, you know you're guilty, you know you've got this shame and it's going to be there for the rest of your life, but if you let it take over then ... that is a possible way to end up down that road to re-offending. (Finn)

Subsequently, Finn was able to recognize that he could do something about his low self-esteem, and ultimately his risk of offending in the future, not just mentally but physically.

Relapse prevention

In summary, all of the cognitive components of treatment outlined above were effective at providing some of the men interviewed in this research with some understanding of the factors that influenced their decision to offend. In doing so, a number of participants learnt how to anticipate and cope with the problem of relapse. However, the relapse prevention components of both the C-SOGP and the SOTP are designed to 'enhance maintenance of change over time and across situations' (Craissati 1998: 93). Accordingly, while relapse prevention techniques are integrated into both the C-SOGP and the SOTP from the outset, the last module of the C-SOGP and the last three modules of the SOTP look specifically at avoidance, coping and escape strategies to deal with such situations appropriately. In doing so, the relapse prevention modules act to reinforce group members' ability to recognize warning signs and risk situations that could lead to future offending. It is important to note at this point that the interviewees who participated in the C-SOGP failed to complete the programme's relapse prevention module due to its unaccredited status at the time this research was conducted (see Chapter 3). This discussion addresses the effect this might have on both Oliver and Matthew's risk of offending in the future.

All of the men who had completed either the C-SOGP or the SOTP felt that they had developed their own individual strategy for maintaining an offence-free lifestyle. In addition, it was typical for the participants to claim that they could cope with situations that can lead to relapse by pulling together concepts from the different treatment modules:

> I'm starting to pick things up that I've got to make sure I don't do again so I don't put myself in the same situation again, and as long as the course is going on and the more you're hearing other people talking in there, you're picking things up from their stuff and I'm thinking bloody hell I thought like that in a relationship, I got to keep off that, do you know what I mean? (Matthew)

> I mean to be frank what I've learned up to now as far as I'm concerned is all relapse prevention ... so for me from day one it's been relapse prevention. (Finn)

Indeed, a number of men pointed to the importance of the victim empathy modules in reinforcing their motivation not to offend in the future, as the following quotations highlight:

> We haven't actually got to relapse prevention because we're busy with empathy at the moment but to me, and I brought this up on the group, this is a part of relapse prevention, because I have got to picture her father's face in court, never mind her face, I mean her father's face and her father is not the person I actually raped do you know what I mean, this is just a person from the ripple effect, and I know I'm saying it casually now but there is more to it than that, but the look on his face is enough for me not to re-offend do you know what I mean, so the empathy is in its own right part of relapse prevention for me. (Clive)

> I feel no, I won't do it again because I'm thinking about the victims. (Oliver)

> Yes I have enough things to stop me re-offending, if I can flash back to the empathy stuff it will be enough. (Colin)

However, the participants in the SOTP also felt that they had benefited from rehearsing the skills required to achieve these goals.[14] For example, Ivor described the Future Me role-play that he completed in module 19 of the SOTP. During this role-play, his neighbour is said to ask him to look after her little girl while she takes her son to the hospital. By acting out this scenario in the group, Ivor was able to practise strategies that he would use in order to avoid, control or escape from a high-risk situation:[15]

> All of a sudden the neighbour says, 'Oh my little boy's had an accident, we've got to go to hospital, here's the little girl, can you look after her until I get back from the hospital?', and before you've had time to say no, wait, no, she's gone down the corridor and the little girl's left with you ... What would I do? I'd go right, before she goes, I'd run out to the mother and say hold on what's happening here, 'I've got to go the ambulance coming now the little boy's going to hospital', I'd say, 'Right, keep the little girl here with you a minute, I'll go back, grab my coat, come with you', I'll get in the ambulance, I'll go to the hospital and we'll watch the little girl in the hospital, or she could take the little girl to hospital with her, there's people there that could watch her like, and if she says the little girl has to stay overnight, [I'll tell her to] get in touch with a relative because there's no way I could keep the little girl overnight and if she says I don't have any I'll say she'll have to call social services and social services will have to take her overnight or something like that, just to get the situation away from me. (Ivor)

In addition, a number of interviewees commented upon having their own ACE (Avoid, Control and Escape) cards for responding to risk situations and thoughts, and managing high-risk emotions in the future:

> You leave the course with printed out ACE cards specific to your crime, your thoughts, feeling and emotions. If you are having inappropriate thoughts you use them. (Burt)

> You have ACE cards to help, one for thoughts, one for emotions and one for behaviour. They cover things like if I was in the house of a potential victim, and started to feel that I wanted to re-offend, how would I go about avoid, control, escape? (Daniel)

Accordingly, the SOTP offered the group members the opportunity for further practice of coping responses that are needed to maintain abstinence from re-offending. In contrast, neither Oliver nor Matthew had this opportunity. Whereas Matthew felt that the C-SOGP had given him 'plenty of food for thought to bring up if [he] ever [started] going down that line', Oliver felt that he needed additional help.

For example, while Oliver had successfully identified risk situations, he felt that he had not developed effective coping strategies to deal safely with such situations. Oliver acknowledged that he relied upon his wife for support. As such he felt that 'if anything happened to [his] wife, if [he] got divorced, [then he] might go back and re-offend again'. Oliver felt that he had not been offered any alternative coping strategies if this should happen:

> I'd like to know what, what is the word, what sort of aids, or whatever it's called, support is out there to help me not to re-offend, and I'd like to find some more avenues. (Oliver)

Evidently, Oliver would have benefited from the opportunity to consider practical behavioural strategies for achieving an offence-free lifestyle. This is consistent with research in this area. Indeed, research has emphasized the importance of behaviour practice in developing an offender's skill of being able to behave differently in high-risk situations (Marques *et al.* 2000).

Something works: The Behaviour Assessment Programme (BAP)

This section of the chapter evaluates the effectiveness of the BAP in helping group members to develop strategies to minimize their risk of re-offending. The analysis is based on the perceptions of nine participants who felt that they had benefited from completing the BAP.[16] This subgroup consists of four men who admitted to having offended (including individuals who minimize some, or even most, aspects of their offending). These men have been defined as acceptors in this research. The group also consists of five participants who categorically claim to be innocent (defined as total deniers). However, Xandy admitted to his offence while participating in treatment.[17] He will therefore be defined as an acceptor throughout this section. Nonetheless, the BAP is not an admittance course. Instead, it is based on the argument that group members can reduce their risk of offending without outwardly admitting to their offence. Within this context, this section identifies the different ways in which attitudinal and behavioural change can occur. In doing so, it begins by exploring the acceptors' perceptions of the BAP. The section will then examine how effective the BAP is at helping total deniers to avoid offending in the future.

Acceptors and what works

Although the BAP sets aside issues regarding the group members' specific offences, it does not avoid addressing the four cognitive components to most sex offender treatment programmes (see Chapter 3). Indeed, the majority of acceptors who completed the BAP claimed that they had benefited from looking at victim empathy, lifestyle management issues and, to a lesser extent, sexual thoughts and fantasies. In addition, the acceptors in this subgroup were able to reflect upon their own sexual offending behaviour throughout the programmes. To illustrate the effectiveness of the BAP in bringing about attitudinal change in these areas, this chapter will briefly describe one acceptor's progress through the BAP.

Euan: A case study

Euan was sentenced for three years for indecently assaulting his 14-year-old daughter. While Euan clearly admitted to the offence, he minimized his responsibility for the abuse. For example, prior to starting the BAP Euan denied that there had been any premeditation to his offending behaviour, claiming instead that it 'just happened'. Euan claimed that as he was 'afraid of the dark' he would wake from his sleep and then sexually assault his daughter:

> It started off as just standing in the doorway, just watching her sleep and it progressed to assaulting her, over a period of five to six months. (Euan)

Having completed the BAP, Euan however recognized that he went through all the stages of the offence cycle 'one by one'. For example, he admitted to having sexual fantasies about his daughter, which he then acted on. In doing so, he acknowledged that he planned the offence:

> I was actually waking myself up, not knowing why but I did, I was convincing myself that it was just something that was happening, but it was not. I'd already planned it. It was a thought that actually woke me up at four o'clock in the morning saying she's asleep, go and do it and that was it. (Euan)

Consequently, he accepted that his initial claim that he was 'afraid of the dark' was a 'justification', a 'lie' that he used to convince himself that what he was doing was not wrong.

Euan was also able to recognize further cognitive distortions that he used to repeat the abuse:

Because of the way she acted or didn't act when I was doing it, nothing was spoken, nothing was said, she never objected as such which I convinced myself was her letting me, you know so I gave myself permission which I wasn't, I found out that she had been terrified, scared or something, a million scenarios to do with it, yeah so, now I know, although she never done anything I was convincing myself that it was OK because she didn't object but all the time it could have been a thousand reasons why she didn't object. (Euan)

The fact that she didn't do anything, I perceived that as a go ahead and do it, I don't mind it as such, but in reality I can't do anything because I'm scared stiff, petrified, I can't talk, I can't move, I can't do anything. It's something that I knew but I lied to myself about. (Euan)

As such he clearly gained a better understanding of why his daughter did not scream out during the abuse. In doing so, he was able to empathize with how his victim would have felt as a result of the offence, and to understand why these feelings prevented his daughter from disclosing the offence to anyone. In addition, Euan was also able to accept the extent of harm his actions had caused, not just to his victim, but 'how it affects everyone . . . the friends, the neighbours, the town you live in and everything else like that':

I'm not dealing with it very well so her anger, hatred and loathing must be 110 times greater . . . and her mum and her sister and her brother and everybody else. I suppose I just blocked it out before and . . . wouldn't acknowledge that it was wider than it was. (Euan)

As a result, Euan claimed that he will probably 'look, think, analyse almost everything [he does] from now on' in order to prevent it from happening again. In contrast, he acknowledged that without treatment, he would 'still [have] had twisted thoughts'. Consequently, he accepted that he could have then gone through his cycle of offending and therefore 'would have definitely done something again'. However, this time he acknowledged 'it would not have been indecent assault it would have been . . . classed as rape'. Having completed the BAP, Euan claimed that he now 'knows enough to see the warning signs to avoid situations in the first place':

I know now how to avoid [situations], how to avoid acting on a feeling without thinking of the consequences or anything like that. (Euan)

Euan showed significant cognitive change in the areas that contribute to sexual offending. While this was also true of the remaining acceptors who completed the BAP,[18] they were more likely to hold on to certain distancing techniques, thereby minimizing their offending behaviour. For example, both Zack and Quinton continued to deny the extent of their offensive behaviour. Zack continued to deny that he raped one of his victims, whereas Quinton denied that he performed oral sex and digitally penetrated his victims, insisting instead that they merely sat on his chest naked. Similarly, Russell, convicted of raping a woman, continued to believe that his offending behaviour was not planned:

> I didn't really plan anything it just sort of happened, I didn't sort of spend lots of time planning it, it just happened in the one night. (Russell)

In addition, Russell attempted to neutralize his offence by showing contempt for other types of offences that are supposedly worse than his. For example, he disliked the way in which the course tutors directed questions to the group that were related to paedophilia. He also disliked the relapse prevention session in which a paedophile, who had completed the BAP, came into the group to highlight how easy it was to re-offend:

> I didn't like that at all. I don't think that should have, I shouldn't have to listen to that the way he was talking to us all was as if we were all paedophiles and I didn't like it. (Russell)

While the remaining distancing techniques may reflect the offenders' attempts to avoid self-criticism and social disapproval throughout the interview process, they may also reflect the design of the BAP. To reiterate, the BAP does not directly challenge an offender's denial. This might have resulted in the acceptors on the programme being less forthcoming about aspects that bear directly upon their offending. Consequently, the acceptors on the BAP may have been better suited to the SOTP. However, given that four of these men volunteered to participate in the SOTP having completed the BAP, this is not a major concern. In addition, Quinton agreed to continue with individual therapy, which was considered to be more appropriate given his severe learning difficulties.

Total deniers and what works

In contrast, the very fact that the BAP does not challenge an individual's denial was critical in securing the total deniers' participation and cooperation in the group. Without actually admitting to their offence, the total deniers who completed the BAP displayed increased awareness of their offending cycle, including the thoughts, beliefs, actions and behaviour that led to their abusive behaviour, as highlighted in the following case studies.

Paul claims that having participated in the BAP he was able to 'understand the justice system a bit more'. For example, he recognized that an 'adult is supposed to be in control, in charge and that a child is still a child, and hasn't got control':

> I'd say I've learnt that through the course which I would never have thought of really before, because I always thought that a child could be in control. (Paul)

Similarly, Stuart, having been convicted of indecently assaulting his niece and her friend, recognized his actions around the time of the offence could have been perceived as grooming:

> The grooming and things like that, you realize then what, perhaps they did class it as grooming even though it wasn't, you can see how other people have seen it, that's what I'm saying it makes you realize how vulnerable you are when you do things, even though I did nothing wrong, people can say well he took her on his own [I gave the sweets and money, etc.]. (Stuart)

In addition, both Thomas and Wayne felt that through their participation on the BAP they were 'slowly piecing together and seeing the chain of circumstances . . . of how [they] came to be accused' (Thomas).

The total deniers who completed the BAP all claimed that they had learnt to 'think a lot more before [they] did anything' (Paul). For example, Stuart recognized that in the future '[he] cannot give [his] niece a lift in the car, [he] cannot give them money, because people will count it as grooming'. He also recognized that he has to be more assertive and take greater responsibility in high-risk situations, as the following quotation highlights:

> I've learnt about being in control of myself, like when kids ask me, want to go somewhere in the future, [I've learnt] that I'm the adult, I'll be responsible and I won't take them. (Stuart)

Consequently, the total deniers were able to identify strategies that they would use in order to avoid, control or escape from a high-risk situation:

I think for me why I done the course is so I can prevent anything happening again, being in a situation where someone can say 'oh he done so and so'. So I've learnt a little bit to do with that, like ACE, I think it's avoid and control and escape . . . as I say that bit has sunk in. (Wayne)

I've learnt that it's best to think twice, how to avoid a situation, avoid, control, escape . . . so it's made me think twice, I've got to avoid situations, things that I wouldn't have thought of before, like I say I used to take my niece and nephew down to the beach, take them down to the beach for a day. I wouldn't do it no more because it leaves yourself vulnerable, you leave yourself open to what not, so it's going to change my behaviour. (Stuart)

Following on from this, Paul recounted a scenario that the group was presented with on the BAP in order to practise relapse prevention techniques. In this scenario there were two buses that the men could catch to work, one that left at quarter to eight in the morning and the other that left at half past eight. While the later bus meant that you could stay in bed longer, it went past a school. The aim of this exercise is for offenders to recognize Seemingly Irrelevant Decisions (SIDs). These are choices that appear superficially reasonable and unrelated to sexual offending but that actually create high-risk situations. Paul was able to recognize that it made 'a lot more sense if you take the longer journey to avoid the situation'. Whereas before he claimed that he would have taken the later bus and gone right by the school and not thought about it, having completed treatment he can be seen to have incorporated such avoidance strategies into his relapse prevention plan.

In contrast, Thomas's relapse prevention plan centred on his ability to develop more effective and positive coping strategies for dealing with his emotional deficits.[19] Research has shown that sex offenders generally report high levels of emotional loneliness and have difficulty in developing intimacy with adults (Garlick *et al.* 1996; Bumby and Hansen 1997; Fisher *et al.* 1999). This was certainly true of Thomas. Indeed, throughout the interview process Thomas admitted to having 'always had problems with relationships'. However, he felt that the BAP had helped him to recognize factors in his early childhood that may have contributed to his inability to form relationships:[20]

It was my father, I'd hit another lad with a piece of wood and as punishment he'd taken all my favourite toys and burnt them and I think I got scared he would stop loving me if I did something wrong, [consequently] I have always been nervous in getting involved in a relationship in case I make a mistake and lose their love and affection and friendship. (Thomas)

He was also able to reflect upon his own victimization throughout the course of the BAP. In doing so, he was better equipped to understand how this had contributed to his low self-esteem and fear of forming relationships:

[My own victimization left me with] the fear that I'm not good enough for them, I'm tainted goods. (Thomas)

Thomas claimed that without the BAP he would have gone on 'thinking that everyone was against [him] when [they were] not'. Accordingly, he recognized that he had to challenge his feelings of low self-esteem and develop better relationship styles.

All the total deniers who completed the BAP were able to identify a range of background problems and action choices that they made at the time of the offence to generate relapse prevention plans. Consequently, unencumbered by any attempt to reduce their culpability, the total deniers, like the acceptors participating in treatment, are also able to gain some significant insights into the factors that might lead them to offend, and hence perhaps reduce their risk of future offending.

Conclusions

Only two of the participants, Jack and Yuval, claimed that they had not gained anything from their respective treatment programmes. Arguably, both Jack and Yuval's state of denial contributed to their dissatisfaction with the C-SOGP and the BAP respectively. Both men have been defined as justifiers in this research. In contrast, the remaining participants claimed to have gained some insight into their offending process. For example, it was typical for the acceptors in this subgroup to claim that they had a better understanding of the childhood influences and experiences that had contributed to their personality. In addition, they were able to recognize factors that might have predisposed them towards committing a sexual offence, including their dysfunctional attitudes and beliefs, their lack of victim empathy, and their deviant sexual interest and/or fantasies.

The participants defined as total deniers in this study were also able to recognize events both in their childhood and directly leading up to the 'alleged offence', that might have resulted in them being charged and convicted of a sexual crime. Finally, both the acceptors and the total deniers were able to recognize personally relevant risk factors that might put them at risk of offending in the future. In so doing, the majority of men were able to articulate strategies that they would be able to use to avoid, control and escape from high-risk situations.

As outlined in Chapter 6, a number of participants felt compelled to appear as if they had changed their thoughts and behaviours while participating in treatment. Discrepancies from the men's own accounts and arguments, and, where possible, analysis of post-treatment assessment documents, have been used to help differentiate between participants who were simply 'talking the talk' from those who had intrinsically changed. It is therefore possible to conclude that all three programmes were successful at providing some of the participants with some understanding of the damage they had caused in order to become proficient in the relevant skills required to avoid future sexual abuse. However, two participants, Luke and Keith, committed further sexual offences while participating on the C-SOGP. Their circumstances will be explored in the next chapter.

Notes

1 This appears to be a problem of the design of sex offender treatment in general. Indeed, the rationale behind treatment is to alter behaviour by developing anti-offending beliefs. The assumption is, therefore, that all offenders can and will re-offend.

2 Arguably, this might also be more indicative of the power struggle between Jack and the treatment facilitators, which was highlighted in Chapter 6.

3 The elements of both models have been well documented in Chapter 3.

4 Schemas represent the offender's underlying belief system.

5 It must be acknowledged that Ward and Hudson (2000) conclude that not all sexual offending is preceded by a negative mood state.

6 Clive was convicted of the rape of a woman.

7 Burt was convicted of indecently assaulting two children, of both sexes, under the age of five, and the abduction of a female child aged eight.

8 The effect that this might have on Burt's risk of re-offending will be discussed later in this chapter.

9 The role of fantasy in offending is explored in module 5 of the C-SOGP and 6 of the SOTP.

10 This also draws on Bowlby's (1969, 1973, 1979) attachment theory, which has already been discussed in this chapter.

11 Emotion-focused strategies include emotional responses to problems such as putting yourself down, brooding or ruminating, getting upset, and fantasizing that things are different (Prison Service 2000).

12 Problem-focused coping strategies involve both cognitive and behavioural techniques to tackle the problem head-on (Prison Service 2000).

13 Chapter 4 also shows how Finn used these feeling to distance himself from those evidently less repentant than him. In the same way as going to the gym, this is also intrinsic to the way he copes with his negative self-image.

14 This relates to modules 16, 17, 18 and 19 of the SOTP.

15 Craissati (1998) defines a high-risk situation as any situation that poses a threat to perceived control and thereby increases the probability of a lapse (these relate to the early stages of the cycle of offending) or a relapse (a relapse is quite simply a return to sexually abusive behaviours).

16 Although Zack failed to complete the BAP, he only missed two sessions, one of which was a revision session. His views on programme content will therefore be included in this chapter.

17 As Chapter 6 identified, it is difficult to determine the extent to which Xandy had psychologically taken responsibility for his offending and how much he was simply 'talking the talk'.

18 It was extremely difficult to ascertain to what extent Quinton actually benefited from the BAP, given his fragile emotional state and severe learning difficulties. Nonetheless, despite at times displacing blame onto his victims, he did accept that what he did was wrong. In addition, as Chapter 6 has already shown, Quinton was able to increase his self-esteem and evidently became better equipped to deal with emotional distress as a result of participating on the BAP.

19 This relates to the lifestyle management component of the BAP.

20 This draws on Bowlby's (1973) attachment theory (see Chapter 3).

Chapter 8

Managing future risk

Chapter 5 identified a number of extrinsic factors that influenced the participants' decision to start and continue with treatment. Similarly, Chapter 6 highlighted how extrinsic factors can encourage the participants to 'talk the talk' without making any internal cognitive and/or behavioural shifts in the areas related to sexual offending. Chapter 7 also indicated instances where the men who completed treatment had not fully changed their thoughts and behaviour, despite claims that they had. The extrinsic factors are discussed in this chapter in relation to treatment goals, and in particular the ways in which they undermine the main goal of all sex offender treatment programmes: that of preventing future abuse and re-offending.

The chapter explores the accounts of the two men who re-offended while participating on the C-SOGP. The discussion first considers what (if anything) they gained from participating in treatment. It then presents their reasons for committing further sexual offences. To this end, the rest of the chapter explores all the participants' views on measures designed to manage their risk of future offending in the community.

Treatment conformity and re-offending

As Chapters 6 and 7 highlighted, it is dangerous to assume that simply because a group member appears to be motivated to change their sexual offending behaviour that they have intrinsically changed. The following quotation from Euan epitomizes this fact:

> Yes everyone does participate but whether they take on board all the information, use it, is a different matter, that's something you're

never going to know until perhaps next time they're in, and suddenly realize that they should have taken a lot more notice about what was happening, what was going on and the change you should have been going through to not to arrive back at this stage again. (Euan)

In addition, it was also acknowledged by a number of the men participating on prison-based sex offender treatment programmes that it was easy to be motivated to change their behaviour while in prison and removed from temptation:

The problem for me is if I get pissed again, when I get outside if I get tanked up again, those things might come back into my way of thinking, like well she's up for it. (Ben)

It's easy to talk about inside prison but I don't have any teenage boys around, it may be harder to put into practice. (Colin)

This corroborates the Travers (1998) view that treatment programmes are best located in the community. According to Travers (1998), whereas programmes within prison occur within a vacuum of an artificial world, offenders who continue to live in the community have to 'work out a method of doing so in a way, which is described in treatment, as being beyond suspicion' (Travers 1998: 231). However, the obvious disadvantage of community-based treatment programmes is that group members have the opportunity to sexually offend. Indeed, this was the case for two of the men, Graham and Luke, participating on a Community Sex Offender Groupwork Programme (C-SOGP). This, despite the fact that both men showed considerable change in their behaviour and attitude while attending the C-SOGP. Of course, these men might simply have been talking the talk (deceiving both the programme facilitators and the researcher). However, if the changes they showed are to be believed, their actions support the claim that motivation is not a sufficient condition for change.

Both Graham (initially convicted of indecent assault on a 17-year-old male)[1] and Luke (initially convicted of indecent assault on two female children aged ten) accepted their offending behaviour. As such, both men have been defined as acceptors in this study. Furthermore, they both articulated that they wanted to change, as the following quotation from Luke shows:

Why am I doing it? To cure myself, as we started in the beginning or to help myself, to stop myself from re-offending. (Luke)

147

Nonetheless, Graham re-offended against a 13-year-old male while attending the programme. He was subsequently convicted and sentenced to several years in prison. Luke was recalled to prison to serve the remainder of his sentence for exposing himself in a children's play area. This section examines what both men felt they had gained from participating on the C-SOGP. It is important to note that Graham joined the C-SOGP at the beginning of module 2 (Cycles and Cognitive Distortions), having previously participated in one-to-one treatment with a group facilitator. This meant that Graham was only interviewed once, and after he had re-offended. The findings presented in this chapter are predominantly based on observation from his participation on the C-SOGP, as well as comments made by the programme facilitators. This section then explores the explanations given by both men for committing further sexual offences.

Luke: A case study

Luke's first offence was against two ten-year-old girls who were regular visitors to his home. The offence involved Luke indecently exposing himself and asking the girls to masturbate him while he was in the bath. Luke also had previous convictions of indecent exposure.

While Luke clearly admitted to the offence, he initially minimized his responsibility for the abuse. Indeed, in the Induction Module of the C-SOGP group members are asked to present an 'active account' of their offence to the rest of the group. This is done by using the hot-seat technique. This is where a group member sits centre stage and undertakes a piece of work which is related to their offending behaviour. The main objectives of this exercise are to determine the form of future work that needs to be done with each group member, as well as enabling the group members to understand the pattern of their offending behaviour. However, Luke's description of his offence highlighted his inability to take responsibility for his offending behaviour. Indeed, he failed to admit that he had planned the offence, and that he had become emotionally and sexually preoccupied with the girls that he routinely invited to his house. Instead, he claimed that he was drunk and could not remember what had happened. However, almost immediately (the next day) he admitted to the group that he had been lying and described himself as having an active rather than a passive role in the offence. When asked why he had changed his account, Luke gave the following reason:

> When I first sat there, I said I blamed it on the drink, I said I can't remember what happened and I blamed it on the drink. When I went out of there at the end of the session and I thought about it in

the night, I thought, you're not helping yourself here, you told yourself that nine months ago before you were sentenced, and you know totally different, you know it was not totally to do with the drink, the drink was something it was some help but not all. So I came back in the next morning and before the group started I got up and had my say, and said look, what I said was a load of bull, I knew exactly what I'd done. And I felt a lot better for saying it. (Luke)

Consequently, Luke accepted that he had to be honest in order to help himself change his sexually abusive behaviour. As such, Luke came to recognize that he had created a highly groomed environment, to the extent that he was able to offend with some regularity and some casualness:

I suppose to me it was just automatic to me which I never even thought about, because I had done certain things and it was just something that would just come, I can't say natural because it's not natural is it, but they would just come automatically. (Luke)

Thus, it appeared that Luke had accepted full responsibility for his actions:

I can't blame anyone apart from myself. (Luke)

In addition, Luke showed considerable change in his ability to empathize with his victims for his current offence and for his previous offences of indecent exposure:

I wasn't thinking before that I was harming or hurting anyone, I didn't think that I was doing that, but now when they're talking about it, you know little things make you think, oh God I must have been harming her, that child like, you know I wouldn't even think I was like that. (Luke)

Moreover, he identified techniques that he had learnt from the C-SOGP to help reduce his risk of re-offending in the future. For example, he described how on Halloween he had turned off all the lights and shut all the curtains in his house, so children 'trick or treating' would assume that no one was home. Permanent alterations were also made to his house to prevent further offending:

I avoid things, I change things, I've changed my house around, so I can't be in a position to get into any problems like I have done before … yeah with my previous offences yeah, so I've actually altered my house around because I've got a three-storey house so instead of living in the basement where people can walk past and see in the window I live actually on the second floor and I got my main bedroom on the top floor so even if my curtains were open and I'm walking around stark naked there is no way unless people are in a helicopter, there is no way they can see in, so I've altered my house around. (Luke)

Luke also claimed that he had used 'self-talk'[2] to stop him from relapsing:

I think I did come close halfway through the programme, I went somewhere, another day, a nice day, but I got out of it … I think it was I was telling myself, what the hell are you doing here, you shouldn't be here now go. (Luke)

Nonetheless, Luke was recalled to prison to serve the remainder of his sentence after he was seen exposing himself in a children's play area by an off-duty police officer. A roll of masking tape was also found in his possession.

In the interview that took place with Luke in prison, Luke denied aspects of the event that led to him being recalled. Indeed, he can be seen to use a number of the distancing techniques outlined in Chapter 4 to distort the truth. For example, Luke claimed that he acted spontaneously, denying any premeditation:

It wasn't planning to go somewhere where children were. (Luke)

He was also reluctant to disclose in the interview that he had exposed himself:

Yes I did think of exposing myself, like I say I didn't at that stage but I am one hundred per cent sure that I would have if that police officer hadn't come there. (Luke)

Despite later admitting that he had exposed himself, and that he was in fact masturbating, he remained defiant that he was watching 'women' and not targeting children:

Luke   I shall read you what the police officer says, ahh this is the report, reason for reconviction. 'On so and so date you were at [name of place] funfair, indecently dressed with your penis hanging below the leg of your shorts,

> touching your genitals and watching the children in the fairground.'

Interviewer   And do you agree with that?

Luke   I wouldn't say my penis was *hanging* out of my shorts. Touching myself yes, I would say yes to that, because obviously as I said to you I would have been slightly aroused the way the 'women', I'll put women, obviously they say children there, but the way the women were dressed.

Following on from this, he emphatically denied that the roll of masking tape he had in his possession was to be used to restrain a child:

> The other point that I want to pick out is, 'also a concern is [Luke] was watching the children in the playground, of even greater concern is when [the police officer] looked at the contents of [Luke's] holdall he found a roll of masking tape for which [Luke] could give no satisfactory explanation', which I give the officer an explanation at the beginning, I said to him I couldn't remember how it got there and when I recalled how it got there it was given to me by a member of the group and I put it into the bag and just left it there, but taking it, they're taking it that it was well basically for use for restraining somebody which I think they've gone over the top with. (Luke)

> I know myself that I wasn't there to restrain anybody, the tape wasn't there for any reason like that whatsoever, and I can honestly say that. (Luke)

Evidently, to have admitted to taking the masking tape to restrain a child would suggest that some planning had taken place. It would also insinuate that Luke would have used physical force to gain his victim's compliance, which he was quick to deny.

The distancing techniques used by Luke relate to premeditation, the use of force (lack of consent) and the age of the victim. As Chapter 4 outlined, the majority of men interviewed identified planning (which includes sexual fantasy and masturbation) with the popular image of the sex offender. Similarly, the younger the victim is, the more serious the offence is considered. Luke can therefore be seen to distance himself from his interpretation of the popular image of a sex offender, i.e. someone who plans to abuse children and uses violence to do so. The distancing techniques are fuelled further by Luke's reluctance to regard his actions as an offence. This was clearly reinforced by the fact that he had not been arrested by the police officer. During the interview Luke articulated every excuse in his repertoire to maintain a more acceptable self-identity, as Extract 8.1 highlights.

Given Luke's state of denial, it was extremely difficult to produce any convincing explanations for his behaviour. However, on closer examination of his account, it is possible to identify two possible warning signs that he was at risk of re-offending. The first relates to a stage on Wolf's (1984) offence cycle. The cycle of offending is used in treatment to introduce the concept that an individual's behaviour is usually planned, rehearsed or has been imagined beforehand. Wolf's (1984) offence cycle charts the entry level and then all the stages an offender must go through in order to sexually abuse. The entry point is usually related to a negative self-image, feeling alone and isolated, and low frustration, tolerance and poor social adjustment. Similar factors were expressed by Luke to account for his behaviour:

> I don't want to blame it on this but I think I told you I was caring for my mother, so basically I was over there all the time but she'd been away that week, she's been to stay with my brother for a week. (Luke)

Sexual abuse is then used to compensate for these feelings. According to Wolf (1984), sexual gratification is another way of displacing more painful feelings.

During his time in treatment, Luke was able to recognize that his offending behaviour was triggered by his feelings of 'insecurity'. However, he had also claimed that the programme had not helped a lot with these problems:

> Well it hasn't helped a lot because as I say I still feel insecure about myself . . . I'm hoping that the [programme] will give me suggestions on how to go about [changing] things. (Luke)

Luke's new offence occurred before he was given the opportunity to learn new skills that might have increased his self-confidence. Indeed, Luke was recalled at the very beginning of module 3, the Relationships and Attachment Styles module of the C-SOGP. The main objective of this module is to develop group members' insights into their own intimacy deficits. The next module, Self-management and Personal Skills, might have given Luke the opportunity to learn skills to improve his feelings of inadequacy and similar destructive feelings.

The second possible warning sign was unique to Luke's previous conviction of indecent exposure. During the programme Luke disclosed to the group that he would wear running shorts when committing this offence. This was said to have been done to provide Luke with an alibi

Extract 8.1: Luke's negotiation of identities

Interviewer	OK but that day you would say you were touching yourself and getting aroused.
Luke	Yes oh yeah.
Interviewer	Do you think you were committing an offence at that point?
Luke	If somebody saw me then it would be yes, but apparently the only one that saw me was the police officer, unless somebody else saw me but then I can't understand why I wasn't arrested, this is what is getting me as well isn't it like, if the police officer was watching me for an hour he would have seen me.
Interviewer	If you had been arrested would that change how you feel now?
Luke	If I had been charged with something I had done and say somebody had come along and said that they had a witness and they said this young lady actually saw you touching yourself whatever, I would say right fair enough, but because no one saw me, only the police officer as far as I can gather of it how is it an offence, well it is an offence so I upset the police officer perhaps.
Interviewer	Is it the idea that there was no victim; can you relate it to Jack's offence?
Luke	Jack, the internet?
Interviewer	Yeah, because you're saying there was no victim.
Luke	Yeah, but there was a victim in his case.
Interviewer	But there was no one there.
Luke	Yeah but the photographs Jack was looking at were of children, I was looking at women in general.
Interviewer	Women aged 14.
Luke	Could have been 14, 15, as you know yourself a lot of 15-year-olds look a lot older so.
Interviewer	OK, so what if everyone there was over 16, would it have been an offence then?
Luke	If they had seen what I was doing yeah, but if they hadn't have seen, or if I was, just say if they were that side of the window then I was just sat here just looking at them I wouldn't class that as an offence that would be like looking

Extract 8.1: Luke's negotiation of identities (contd)

Luke *(contd)* at an adult movie in a way because they're there and I'm here and to me that's quite natural, well I would say that's quite natural, obviously a lot of psychologists and our group leaders disagree with pornographic films but to me that's something I've always done and I still don't find that an offence as such, so the people I was looking at in [place name] as I say some of them may have been under 16 but I should imagine there were an awful lot over 16, so I don't class that as an offence of looking at somebody. If like you say somebody had reported me for touching myself or whatever then yes that would be an offence which as far as I can see no one reported me, well the police officer, but no one had reported me for committing an offence only the police officer.

Interviewer So you have to be seen, what about a Peeping Tom then?

Luke That is an offence yes.

Interviewer Why?

Luke Because he's invading somebody's privacy.

Interviewer What if that person doesn't see them?

Luke Yeah but what do you class a Peeping Tom? I class a Peeping Tom as someone that has gone into changing rooms and looking.

Interviewer Yeah, say going past someone's house and watching them get undressed, watching two people having sex.

Luke Yes that's what I would class as an offence, because he puts himself out to do that.

Interviewer But he's watching and they can't see.

Luke Yeah but he's going there to watch or he's looking, he's invading someone's privacy then isn't he, but walking through [place name] high street then and looking at some ladies, I wouldn't class that as invading someone's privacy, would you?

if he was caught. For example, given the length and type of short, it would have been easy to portray any exposure as accidental. As such, Luke's running shorts were described as his 'offending uniform' while on the C-SOGP. Luke was wearing his offending uniform the day he was caught indecently exposing himself to children:

I had my, what do I call it, my 'uniform' on. (Luke)

Like I say the weather, I think that was a lot to do with it, another thing that I should have clicked on straight away because of the way I was dressed but everyone was dressed that way that day so. (Luke)

This clearly suggests that he intended to commit a sexual offence that day, despite his attempts to deny that the offence was planned.

Graham: A case study

Graham was initially convicted of indecently assaulting a 17-year-old boy. At the time that he was convicted of this offence, 18 was still the age of consent for sex between consenting males. However, Graham admitted that he thought that the boy was 'around 16' and that the act was not consensual.

Given that Graham only joined the group at the beginning of module 2 and re-offended before completing it, he only attended the C-SOGP for a short period of time. Nonetheless, Graham's contribution to the C-SOGP was generally described as consistent and relevant. For example, during this time Graham readily accepted that he was 'sexually attracted to young boys':

I do feel sexually attracted to young boys. It took a long time to admit to that . . . it actually came out on the group, and when I said it, it was like a weight lifted off my shoulder type of thing. (Graham)

He was also able to recognize the stages that had led to his offending behaviour. For example, Graham claimed that he had been feeling down prior to the offence, marking the entry point of his offending cycle:

I kind of hit rock bottom in myself and the fantasies were running through my head and the opportunity was there to re-offend. (Graham)

He also admitted to grooming his victim. Grooming can involve a long process of gaining the trust of the victim, setting up a situation where the offender will be alone with the victim. It might involve coercion or it may simply consist of ensuring that no one else is around (Allam 2001). Graham clearly groomed his victim and environment in order to ensure that he was able to abuse. It could also be argued that Graham used alcohol to overcome his own inhibitions:

As soon as I saw him [the victim] I fancied him, straight away and I knew that I wanted him, it was just want there straight away so I deliberately got him on his own, I was planning all the time, grooming him ... so I plied him with drink, fags, made him feel at ease, got him drunk enough, invited him to stay and then in the early hours of the morning I abused him ... My plan was to get him drunk so he would fall asleep so I could touch him. (Graham)

In addition, similar to Luke, Graham claimed to have used 'self-talk' to stop him from relapsing:

[The programme] started to make you realise some of the situations that I had found myself in, like stop and think sometimes, you know I'm in a dangerous situation here where I could offend and there were times, I have one particular where one of my victim's friends came up to me and offered himself to me in a sexual way ... this was while I was on the group. And it was the first time that I used stuff like self-talk to get out of a situation. (Graham)

Graham claimed that the programme had been helping him. Nonetheless Graham re-offended while participating on the C-SOGP. His second offence was, on the whole, a re-enactment of his first:

I was out of work, and I was drinking quite heavily every day. I was just rock bottom. I knew I was there and I was having these fantasies to make me feel good about myself so I knew I was on this cycle, [Graham] you've got to get off this, this is no good, and it all came to a head then that New Year's Eve and it was just *déjà vu*, everything was exactly the same. I was there, [my victim] was there, early hours of the morning again. (Graham)

Consequently, he was able to recognize patterns in his thoughts, feelings and behaviour that were similar to how he had felt and acted prior to committing his first offence. For example, as with his first offence, he claimed to be feeling down prior to committing the second offence, as well as grooming his second victim:

[Before this offence] I was quite down I mean, not long before Christmas I had tried to commit suicide this was probably more a call for help. (Graham)

[With this offence] I was grooming him; I'd got a big bottle of vodka, this kind of stuff. (Graham)

His apparent awareness of his offence cycle is accentuated further by his ability to articulate his personal route to offending using treatment vocabulary:

I wouldn't have put it that way at all. Actually working on the group then I realized the actions that I was doing, like purposely keeping him away from the other group [at the party] and just with me, so he's got to rely on me type of thing. I wouldn't have realized I was doing that but looking back on it now you realize the cycle as it's going around. (Graham)

Of course, it could be argued that Graham was merely talking the talk and parroting psychological phrases used in treatment, thus implying that he had not intrinsically learnt anything at all from his time in treatment. This might also be the case for Luke. Indeed, both men might simply have been unmotivated to change their sexually abusive behaviour. Similarly, understanding the reasons for committing a sexual offence does not necessarily equate with a motivation to stop offending in the future. However, even if this was not the case, and both men were intrinsically motivated to change, this research has identified a further extrinsic factor that might have undermined their ability to manage their risk effectively.

Disclosing risk without incrimination

The elements of the offending cycle, described by both Luke and Graham above, are intended to act as a warning sign to avoid re-offending. Indeed, the overall aim of the offence cycle is to help group members understand how and why they found it easy to overcome inhibitions to offend. While Graham clearly understood his personal route from motivation to offence, this was not enough to stop him from re-offending:

It was like I didn't have any willpower to stop, it was like an urge overtaking me to commit the offence. Because I was thinking when I went over to [my victim] you know come on now, next week you're going back to [the programme] but it didn't stop me. (Graham)

It was the case of want again, no willpower. (Graham)

It could also be argued that Luke recognized, at least to an extent, that he was on his offence cycle prior to going to a children's park and indecently exposing himself. In light of this, both men were asked whether they felt that they could have disclosed this on the C-SOGP. Neither Luke nor Graham felt that they could, but for different reasons. Luke's explanation clearly reflected his state of denial:

No because I was feeling OK, through the week I was OK because I was doing so much, like I say my parents had been away, I think they went away, it must have been the weekend of that week, I had odds and sods to do through the week and I think it was coming up to the weekend and I didn't have nothing to do, so, no I didn't feel in the stage then to speak to anybody. (Luke)

In contrast, Graham claimed that he felt uncomfortable presenting his true feelings while on the C-SOGP:

Graham   I could see myself in the sorry, poor me stage I knew I was well into that.

Interviewer   And did you feel you could say that on the group?

Graham   No I never, I would say to the group every morning, or every Tuesday morning they would say well how are you, yeah I'm fine, fine, fine, you know, and say have you had any sexy thoughts, you wouldn't say, I mean no one would say, if it was going round that way, by the time it came to me, no, no, I'd say no.

Interviewer   So you didn't feel comfortable to say that you . . .

Graham   No, not in that situation . . .

Interviewer   And do you think that if you had had spoken to someone?

Graham   Yeah especially now yeah you know. My own belief is that if I had confided in someone then yeah but I didn't so . . .

The other men interviewed in this study expressed similar views.[3] These observations challenge some of the findings outlined in Chapter 6. Chapter 6 suggested that the group process created an environment where it was safe to share common attributes, such as comparable factors in an individual's personal route from their motivation to the actual offence. In contrast, this chapter has identified the interviewees' reluctance to disclose their true risk of future offending during treatment. Consequently, while a positive group environment clearly encouraged disclosure of events that happened in their current offence, there remained barriers with regard to the expression of an individual's present and possible future feelings, thoughts and desires.

This might be attributed to the group process. For example, Forsyth (1999) has argued that groups have the capacity to 'bind members together to form a single unit'. However, logically, inclusion entails exclusion. Indeed, according to Jenkins (1996: 80), 'to define the criteria for membership of any set of objects is, at the same time, also to create a boundary'. Exclusion also influences an individual's self-esteem. Consequently, individuals strive to be included in groups and avoid exclusion to protect their own feelings of self-worth. This draws on the 'Belongingness Hypothesis', which asserts that group members will change their attitudes and beliefs to agree with the overall consensus of the group in order to prevent themselves from being excluded.

Arguably, a similar process occurred within the groups described within this study. Evidently the sharing of personal information between the groups, and the self, created a social link between the men. Thus, on the one hand, the group allowed its members to speak openly when they were being reflective. On the other hand, the group process discouraged members from disclosing characteristics that were associated with sex offenders in the present and/or future. In doing so, the group process became intrinsic to the way the group collectively coped with their negative self-image. For example, the group collectively upheld what would be the desirable ideal of treatment; that is, having participated in treatment they will no longer be at risk of future offending. Disclosing present characteristics associated with sexual offending therefore entailed revealing flaws that the group collectively attempted to distance themselves from.

Of course, the participants' reluctance to disclose their true risk of future offending might also reflect the setting of treatment within the criminal justice system. For example, a number of the participants were reluctant to reveal past offences that they had not been convicted of. Their reluctance to be completely open regarding such offences was typically associated with the fear of further punishment from the criminal justice system:

> I could reveal it [past offending behaviour that he had not been convicted for] I just don't want to do more prison sentence. (Harry)

This supports findings from Garland and Dougher (1991). They have argued that the lack of clarity about the facilitator's role in the legal or institutional system might undermine the group members' willingness to discuss their sexual offending behaviour.

The treatment manuals for the respective programmes make it clear that group members cannot be assured total confidentiality. The principle of the prison-based programmes is to inform all group members that if an offence for which they have not been convicted is disclosed, facilitators have a responsibility to pass this information on to the treatment manager, who may then decide to take further action (Denvir 2000; Kirkegaard and Northey 2000; OBPU 2000; Prison Service 2000; Sex

Offender Unit 2000; Home Office 2001b). Group members attending the C-SOGP should also be told at the beginning of the programme that 'disclosure of any offence that has not been previously reported – where there is a named or identifiable victim – will be reported to the police' (Leyland and Baim 2001: 5). Yet this does not include disclosure where an offender feels at risk of re-offending. Indeed, a goal of the treatment programmes is to establish within the group an atmosphere that is supportive of such disclosure. However, the guidance on disclosure of past offending may understandably make group members generally resistant to this course of action. It is perhaps unrealistic for an individual with a conviction of a sexual offence to disclose their true risk of offending in the future, bearing in mind the likely consequences within a criminal justice setting, and to their perception of self. Either way, the implications are the same. Failure to disclose current thoughts and feelings will ultimately affect how successful either the system or the individual (see Chapter 7) is at managing their risk in the future.

If group members are reluctant to disclose this information, it is therefore crucial that the information they do disclose is used effectively. For example, both Graham and Luke identified risk factors throughout the C-SOGP. Luke's was clearly warm weather and the opportunity to wear clothing that made it easier for him to offend. It is not that surprising that he relapsed on a hot summer's day. Similarly, Graham's first offence was committed during the Christmas holidays, a time of year which he maintained was 'a really bad time of the year for [him]'. His second offence was committed on exactly the same day, one year later. The rest of this chapter puts this kind of issue into a broader context, through an exploration of the control mechanisms in place for managing sex offenders in the community.

Effectively managing sex offenders in the community

A number of new initiatives are in place to manage the risk of sexual offending behaviour in the community. For example, the police are responsible for maintaining registers of convicted sex offenders, applying for numerous civil prevention orders (see Chapter 2) and, in consultation with the prison and probation services, for assessing and managing the risk convicted sex offenders pose. In addition, Risk Predicting and Monitoring Forms (RPM) are now being used in conjunction with community accredited programmes, enabling programme facilitators to identify and monitor risk accordingly throughout treatment. It is also typical for accredited programmes to have a programme and treatment manager (see Chapter 3) to ensure that the practical arrangements for running the programme are in place. The programme manager will also be responsible for developing links with outside agencies, including the police, social services, housing, and other local voluntary bodies. In particular, information arising from work conducted on the programme 'should be passed, as required, to the Multi-Agency Public Protection Panel (MAPPPs, as established by the Criminal Justice and Court Services Act 2000) to assist in the management of an offender' (OBPU 2000: 9).

The C-SOGP that the men in this research were participating in did not benefit from any of these initiatives due to its unaccredited status. Indeed, substantial changes took place in both the organization of the programme and the level of management support provided to the programme facilitators during the period of this research. Arguably, the more systematic approach for recording risk provided by the RPM form, and the availability of a full-time treatment and programme manager, might have helped ensure that the group members' risk was better managed. Nonetheless, all the men interviewed in this research were subject to the registration requirement outlined in the Sex Offenders Act 1997 (and subsequently re-enacted through the Sexual Offences Act 2003).

The Sex Offender Register

The Home Office has described the purpose of registration as ensuring that police have up-to-date and relevant information about the whereabouts of convicted sexual offenders. It is believed that this information will help police to identify suspects after a crime has been committed, as well as act as a form of deterrent in order to prevent future crimes (Home Office 1996). These two objectives were identified by the men interviewed in this research. For example, a number of participants recognized that the Sex Offender Register could be used to aid the investigation of sexual crimes after they had been committed:

It just means if something happens in that area they know who to go and look for or where that certain person is. (Paul)

If a crime is committed the police have to visit everyone who's done that crime in the past. (Edward)

It makes the police's job easier, because if something happens in their area, before they can do anything they look on the register and a name will come up for whatever offence and he goes off and he sees him and the man gets out of the picture straight away, or he's in the picture straight away, you know depending on which it gives the police a step ladder, you know some girl gets raped down the street, you know they have a book to go to. Oh Joe Bloggs lives down here, and he's been convicted of rape so let's go and see what he's been doing. (Euan)

Similarly, the Register's capacity to control future crime was also acknowledged, to some extent, by a number of men interviewed in this research:

Hopefully, knowing that they're on the Register, that they are known by the police, that they are known by the authorities and that if something does happen to a child then they are going to be one of the first people that are going to be examined by the police . . . I think that those people will do their best to stay on the straight and narrow. (Finn)

I think that it's needed, we need to know that we are being monitored for possible prevention. (Andrew)

However, Clive claimed that the Register would only 'bother [people] if [they were] planning to do something wrong'. As such, he implied that it would only act as a deterrent for sex offenders who wanted to re-offend. Clive used the following analogy of a pupil planning to cheat in school exams to highlight his point:

You take your exams right? Say a bloke or a woman, or whatever was standing at the top there and walking around the room, now if you're not planning on cheating . . . you are oblivious to that person, you are concentrating on your work, you want to pass, you know your work, or you've spotted a question that you don't know and you're worried about that, you're not worried about that person there. But if you've got something written [up your sleeve], then you're worried about that person, and it's the same with the Register. If you've got plans to do something that will bring their attention towards you then you've got to start worrying about it. (Clive)

Conversely, Paul claimed that 'somebody that was going to relapse wouldn't care [about the Register] and go out and re-offend'. Finn also questioned whether it would affect the 'worst case people, the people who are severe predators who will go out and snatch children'.[4] In addition, Zack argued that the register would not succeed in preventing people from offending, as he believed that most people tended to forget that they were on it.

The men interviewed in this research also identified a third objective of the Sex Offender Register. A number of participants claimed that the Register was part of the government's overall agenda to restore public confidence (see Chapter 2):

> I think that it's there as well to make the community feel more safe . . . it will give the public a peace of mind knowing that . . . the police have a list of sex offenders and paedophiles on the register. (Oliver)

Indeed, a number of men claimed that the Register was on the whole a publicity stunt used by the government to denounce sexual offending and gain political advantage. For example, both Clive and Edmund described the Register as a 'public relations exercise' (Clive):

> It's just putting it in the public eye isn't it? (Edmund)

This clearly supports the arguments presented by Garland (2001) that sex offenders operate as 'tokens in a political process'. As such, it was typical for this group of participants also to view the Register as an additional form of punishment or, as Wayne described it, 'as another form of stigma'.

Compliance

An official Home Office study, *Where Are They Now?* (Plontikoff and Woolfson 2000), suggested that the Register was 'working well', with compliance rates of 94.7 per cent on 31 August 1998. In addition, the White Paper *Protecting the Public* (Home Office 2002b) reported compliance rates of 97 per cent in 2002. Similarly, all of the men in this subgroup claimed that they would, at least initially, comply with the registration provisions. However, they did so with varying degrees of reluctance depending on their state of denial. For example, the men defined as total deniers in this research, while agreeing to comply, did so unwillingly based on their claim that they had not committed a sexual offence:

> I'm not very happy about it, but what can I do? (Stuart)

> I'm not very happy about it, but it's another one of those things that you can't really do anything about. (Thomas)

Similarly, the justifiers claimed that, although they would comply, they were not happy to do so:

> I don't think that I should be on the Register, that's not what I'm in for. (David)

> I'm looking forward to five years' time when I'm off the Register. (Keith)

Consequently, similar to the reasons presented by the participants for starting and cooperating in treatment, the majority of men in denial claimed that they would comply with the registration requirements due to external factors. For example, all the deniers recognized that failure to comply had negative implications:

> If I don't do it I will probably be sent back to prison. (Thomas)

> I was thinking, I have been thinking of when I go, of refusing to sign the Register but I thought what good will that do me, it will only mean I end up back in here like and I don't want that like. (Yuval)

The threat of additional punishment was also generally accepted by the men defined as acceptors in this study, as the following quotation from Ben highlights:

> I know that it's back into prison unless my licence is over and if an offence happens when I'm missing, I'll be in the frame for it. (Ben)

However, in contrast, it was also typical for the acceptors both to understand and accept why they had to comply with registration:

> I agree with it . . . I won't like it but it is one of those things that you have got to accept. (Andrew)

> Because I'm on the Sex Offender Register I'm going to be a sex offender for the rest of my life, I will accept that. (Zack)

While Clive accepted that the Register would become part of his life, he was adamant that it would not become the defining part of his identity:

> I look at it as although it's part of my life and I have to incorporate it into my life it's not going to define me. I'm a convicted rapist, so I have to walk with my head down all the time? I'm not allowed to speak to a woman sort of thing? No, no I can't let that happen to me because I'm still human, I'm still [Clive], I've still got a life, I'm still going to work, I'm still going to have relationships and maybe get married, I still want the same things as most people probably want,

and I can't stop and say I'm not allowed to have that now because I am still allowed to have it, and why not? (Clive)

Moreover, he claimed that if the Register jeopardized 'his right to privacy' he would reconsider whether he would comply.

Similar concerns were echoed by a number of the men interviewed in this study (regardless of their state of denial). For example, a number of the participants voiced concern that the information given to the police would be leaked to the general public:

> It's a big fright if the list ever got out of all the offenders, that is the one thing that has worried me because of stuff that has leaked out in the past in the press that is one thing that has frightened me to death. (Matthew)

> I worry about the information getting into the wrong hands, the police finding out that you live down the road from their sister, tells her and then it just spreads and before you know it's out there, out of hand, bricks and all sorts through your window. (Burt)

For this reason, Xandy claimed that while he was prepared to sign the Register during the time he was on licence, he would then disappear:

> Once I've done my five months that's it, I'm gone . . . because I can pick up passports and birth certificates, and I'm quite happy to live in a different country. I've told everybody I'm not signing it, so it's as simple as that. Whether I commit another offence for not signing it, so be it, come and get me, we'll cross that bridge when we come to it. (Xandy)

The issue of disclosure

All the men interviewed were fully aware of the public's persistent calls for community notification of the identity and the whereabouts of sex offenders following the death of Sarah Payne, coined by the media as 'Sarah's Law' (see Chapter 2). As such, the participants were asked their views on implementing Sarah's Law in the UK. Only David claimed that 'it was right that people should be aware of sex offenders in their area'. However, given that he has been defined as a justifier in this study, he did not think that this should include him. The remaining participants felt that full public disclosure would result in community vigilantism, similar to that which occurred on the Paulsgrove Estate in Portsmouth in August 2000 following the *News of the World*'s 'Name and Shame' campaign:

What happened in Portsmouth, that type of thing will happen to me. (Ben)

They want it on the internet; they want it posted up in public libraries everything. . . . if I go out [to that] I'm going to be castrated, shunned, I'm going to be a social leper. (Finn)

In addition, a number of the participants also recognized the damaging effect it would have on their families, supporting arguments presented by Edwards and Hensley (2001):

I think it can be damaging for the families of the people that are trying to get their lives back together . . . [if someone] is trying to get their lives back together, hoping and praying never to commit another offence again, and then you see a picture in the paper and it just says, 'so and so sexually abuses children', quote, unquote, and everyone sees it, what's going to happen? You'll have to move and soon there will be no place left for you to go, and you'll put your wife through all this shit and nonsense. (Euan)

As a consequence, Euan acknowledged that it might be easier to 'disappear so nobody knows where you are'. Indeed, a number of participants claimed that the implementation of a public notification law would drive offenders underground:

I would go to ground because of these situations. (Paul)

They're just going to go underground and if they go underground, there'll be nobody keeping an eye on them . . . and they'll just re-offend again. (Finn)

The views expressed by the men interviewed in this research suggest that full public access to the Register will do little towards meeting its intended objectives and may in fact exacerbate many of the problems commonly associated with sexual offending. These findings are consistent with research in this area (Brooks 1996; Tier and Coy 1997; Edwards and Hensley 2001). For example, under such laws sex offenders are likely to become ostracized from society, reinforcing many of the emotional factors that trigger offensive behaviour (Edwards and Hensley 2001). In addition, sex offenders will be denied the opportunity to seek suitable housing and employment, as well as forming appropriate and supportive adult relationships. It is not unreasonable to assume that community notification laws might further discourage an offender from disclosing their true risk of offending, and instead drive offenders underground such that neither the police nor the probation service can keep track of them. Whereas Clive felt that the latent consequences of community notification laws would prevent it from being implemented in the UK, Albert's comments show his awareness of the emergence of what Bottoms (1995) has called 'populist punitiveness':

> Because of pressures from society after Sarah Payne, society needs something done. The government wants to be voted in so they'll do it. Keep us in power, that's all that matters to them. (Albert)

Nonetheless, the government has not (yet) granted full public access to the Sex Offenders Register. Arguably, to have succumbed to public pressure would have involved the government's admission of the failure of the Register.

Conclusions

During their participation on the C-SOGP, both Luke and Keith appeared to have changed aspects of their thoughts and behaviour that had contributed to their current conviction. Both men committed further sexual crimes while attending treatment. The findings presented in this chapter suggest that this might have been prevented if both men had felt able to disclose during treatment that they were on their offending cycle. However, as this chapter has suggested, it is not unreasonable for individuals with a conviction of a sexual offence to conceal their risk of future offending, given that they felt that this would result in additional punishment. In addition, disclosing present characteristics associated with sexual offending also entailed group members revealing flaws that the group collectively attempted to distance itself from.

To some extent both factors are a result of the highly emotive response to sexual offending in today's society, due in part to the misleading portrayal of sex offenders in the popular media, in particular the tabloid press (Soothill and Walby 1991; Howe 1998; Cobley 2000; Farrell and Soothill 2001; Reiner 2002; Greer 2003). For example, with the emergence of what Bottoms has called 'populist punitiveness' (Bottoms 1995) and the emotionally charged response sexual offending increasingly generates, governments have very little option but to react with extreme punitiveness (Edwards and Hensley 2001). The Sex Offender Register (introduced under Part one of the Sex Offenders Act 1997 and revised under the Sexual Offences Act 2003), new civil prevention orders, and the latest 'grooming' legislation (introduced under the Sexual Offences Bill 2003) clearly penalize individuals for crimes that they might commit in the future. If individuals convicted of a sexual offence cannot be honest in treatment, which is supposedly supportive of such disclosure, given current sentencing laws they are unlikely to be able to ask for help when their treatment is over.

Ultimately failure to disclose this information prevents sex offenders from managing their risk effectively and thus undermines their ability to refrain from sexually abusive behaviour. For this reason it is crucial that effective mechanisms, to predict and monitor the risk posed by sexual offenders, are used to manage sex offenders in the community.

The men interviewed in this research generally agreed that the Sex Offender Register would ensure that the police have up-to-date information on the whereabouts of convicted sex offenders that could then be used for both the investigation and prevention of crime. The latter suggests that the Register might act as a deterrent. In contrast, the majority of participants felt that due to the intense stigma surrounding sexual offenders, full public access to the Register would drive sex offenders underground. Greg therefore argued that if the public had to be told their identity and whereabouts, they should also be told about how well a sex offender is doing in the community, as the following quotation highlights:

> The public should also be told that this is what he's doing, this is the progression of where he is now to what he was before. (Greg)

However, the effectiveness of this scheme would require the public to view sex offenders as a heterogeneous population, some of whom may benefit from treatment, rather than as one-dimensional beings that are incapable of change.

Notes

1 Eighteen was still the legal age of consent between men.
2 'Self-talk' requires the offender to remind themselves of the consequences that their behaviour will have, in the hope that this will prevent them from committing further offences.
3 This was not a common factor for the offenders participating on the BAP, as the programme design does not require the men to disclose their offence.
4 Arguably Clive's assertion that the Register would not bother him, and Paul and Finn's claim that the Register would not succeed in deterring the 'worst' sex offenders, can also be seen as inadvertent attempts to distance themselves from the social representation of the sex offender.

Part III
Conclusions

Chapter 9

Closing remarks

While a great deal has been written about sex offenders and their treatment, surprisingly few studies have approached the issues through an understanding of offenders' own views and perspectives of their offending behaviour and others' responses to it. This book draws on repeated in-depth interviews with 32 male sex offenders attending one of three sex offender treatment programmes, namely the prison-based Sex Offender Treatment Programme (SOTP) and the Behaviour Assessment Programme (BAP), and the Community Sex Offender Groupwork Programme (C-SOGP).

Through a rigorous and systematic analysis of the participants' accounts of their offending behaviour, and of aspects of their identity, both in their own and others' eyes, this research has developed an understanding of the social construction of the sex offender, and identified ways in which this can hinder crime-reduction strategies. In addition, by examining the participants' perceptions of their respective treatment programmes, and the impact that treatment has on their thinking (more specifically exploring their ability to manage effectively their risk of re-offending), the study has contributed to the 'what works' literature in the treatment of sexual offenders. This final chapter summarizes the key arguments raised in the research before presenting the policy dilemmas associated with effectively managing sex offenders in the future.

The social construction of the 'sex offender': Impact on identity

Sexual crime evidently dominates media headlines. As Chapter 2 identified, a number of research studies have shown the media to exaggerate both the levels of sexual crime in society and the risk of being offended against (Reiner 2002). As an example, the mass media typically focus on the threat posed by predatory paedophiles (Greer 2003). Consequently, although risk of sexual victimization is more likely to be posed by people you know, the myth of 'stranger danger' captures the popular imagination (Greer 2003). Moreover, the mass media present sex offenders as somehow distinct from the rest of the population.

The men interviewed in this research did not live in a vacuum and had access to the mass media. They were therefore eminently aware of society's indignation towards them. In fact, they felt that the public viewed all sex offenders, regardless of their crime, as the 'worst case' offenders; namely the predatory paedophile who rapes and murders young children. However, despite the mass media's portrayal of sex offenders as demonic sexual monsters, the stigma of a conviction for a sexual offence is not apparent in an individual's physical appearance. The men interviewed in this research therefore recognized that this social representation of a sex offender would become their master status (Becker 1963) if it were revealed to others. Finding ways to manage their identity therefore became a primary concern.

The men interviewed in this research attempted to conceal and/or distance themselves from the popular image of the 'sex offender' in order to protect themselves from being excluded from the rest of society (including other prisoners and members of society who do not have a conviction for a sexual offence). This was achieved in three distinct ways. Firstly, six participants 'totally denied' their offending behaviour. Total denial refers to the denial of a specified behaviour on a specified day. Secondly, four of the men attempted to 'justify' their behaviour. Here the emphasis is not on whether the offence took place but whether it can be justified. It was typical for these men to deny that their behaviour could have caused any harm. As such, they described their so-called victim(s) as culpable. In contrast, Jack, who was convicted of downloading pornographic images of children from the internet, claimed that he did not have any victims. Finally, the remaining 22 participants also used denial to 'excuse' their offending behaviour. However, unlike the total deniers and the justifiers, this subgroup of participants identified themselves as sex offenders. Consequently, they both admitted to their offending behaviour, and that their behaviour was wrong and beyond justification. These men have been defined as acceptors.

As Chapter 4 highlighted, the use of 'total denial' and 'justifications' enabled these two subgroups to protect themselves from negative perceptions typically attributed to 'sex offenders'. In contrast, despite attempting to excuse their behaviour, the acceptors in this study ultimately accepted the label of 'sex offender'. They therefore engaged in a number of distancing techniques in order to preserve a *more acceptable* identity in the eyes of others. The distancing techniques outlined in Chapter 4 represent the participants' interpretation of the worst-case offence.

Of course, an individual's ability to conceal their extended social identity depended, to some extent, on their social situation. As Chapter 4 identified, it was typical for the participants, irrespective of which category they were defined as, to conceal their conviction from those unaware of their offending behaviour (Goffman 1959). The men serving a custodial sentence were, however, unable to conceal completely their offence given that they were located either in a prison exclusively for sex offenders or on Rule 45.

Chapter 4 also concluded that, irrespective of their state of denial, the men interviewed in this research were unable to separate completely their criminal act from their overall sense of self. The 'stigma' of having been convicted of a sexual offence has therefore been represented as the men's extended social identity. In so doing, it views convicted sex offenders as individuals with multiple identities and characteristics besides the label of a sex offender. It also encapsulates the idea that the extended social identity has an existence independent of its presence in any one individual (Breakwell 2001). Arguably, denial, minimizations, excuses and the various distancing techniques outlined above were also used by the interviewees to enhance their own sense of self-worth.

The current manner in which society perceives and reacts to sexual offenders evidently has an impact on the way in which individuals convicted of a sexual offence manage their identity. The participants' desire to distance themselves from the image of a stereotypical sex offender, i.e. a predatory stranger who relentlessly victimizes women and children, also affected their *performance* in treatment and, more importantly, their ability to self-manage effectively their risk of future offending.

Identity, treatment and self-control

Over the last two decades sexual offenders have been singled out by the media and in legislation and penal policy. The overarching ideology is to incarcerate sex offenders for longer periods of time (this will be discussed in more detail later in the chapter). However, despite the harsh set of policies relating to sexual crimes (see Chapter 2) there still remains a degree of faith in relation to the rehabilitation of sexual offenders. However, treatment has moved away from the arguments of the past that claimed to be able to 'cure' offenders. Instead, today's treatment programmes are based on the assumption that offenders can learn new skills to control their behaviour. This has led to the endorsement of cognitive behavioural treatment programmes.

Within the cognitive behavioural tradition, sex offender treatment programmes view sex offenders as rational decision-makers who are capable of changing and/or controlling the thoughts, feelings and behaviours that contributed to their deviant sexual behaviour. Chapter 3 outlined the three group cognitive behavioural treatment programmes used in this study. To reiterate, these are the Sex Offender Treatment Programme (SOTP) and the Behaviour Assessment Programme (BAP), and the Community Sex Offender Groupwork Programme (C-SOGP). All three programmes focus on four major factors that contribute to sexual offending. These have been defined as dysfunctional attitudes and beliefs, empathy, deviant sexual arousal, and factors relating to poor lifestyle management and social functioning. However, the BAP does so at one step removed. Designed specifically for total deniers, the BAP does not focus on an individual group member's sexual offending behaviour. Instead, the main areas of treatment are presented in a hypothetical manner. It is then hoped that the group members will be able to make links with their own sexually abusive behaviour (assuming, of course, that they are guilty). All three programmes then explore relapse prevention techniques in order to help apply skills that are central to prevent re-offending.

This book has shown that the popular image of the sex offender can obstruct both the programme and the offender's ability to minimize the risk of future victimization. The arguments presented throughout the book will now be discussed under the following headings:

i. Treatment attendance

ii. Talking the talk

iii. Concealing risk

Treatment attendance

A sex offender's willingness to start and complete treatment has typically been used to reflect their willingness to change their sexually abusive behaviour. In addition, it is generally assumed that total deniers will be unwilling to participate in treatment programmes and therefore lack motivation to change. Indeed, the majority of total deniers in this study claimed that they would not have voluntarily participated on the prison-based SOTP. However, this was arguably more indicative of their desire to preserve an acceptable public image, rather than their lack of motivation to change.

As Chapter 5 highlighted, the main reason presented by the total deniers for not wishing to start an SOTP was based on semantics. It became evident that their reluctance to participate on an SOTP was to avoid the unwanted connotations of the term 'sex offender' in the programme title. Similarly, the total deniers would not have volunteered to start the BAP had the programme discussed their alleged offence or challenged their state of denial. Consequently, the design of the BAP enabled the total deniers to seek help legitimately while avoiding the emotional expressions of disgust, fear and contagion associated with the social construction of the sex offender. What is more, a number of the total deniers inadvertently expressed the benefit of receiving help in changing their behaviour.

The findings presented in Chapter 7 also suggest that treatment intervention with total deniers can be effective in enabling them to develop strategies to avoid relapse. All the total deniers who started the BAP showed at least some attitudinal and behavioural change in the areas that are said to contribute to sexual offending. It would therefore appear that the total deniers were able to apply what they had learnt on the BAP to their own situations. Moreover, without admitting to the offence, the majority of total deniers were able to identify strategies that they could use to avoid future offending.

Arguably, this style of treatment might have benefited David and Keith. Both men were defined as justifiers in this study, and both men failed to complete the SOTP and the C-SOGP respectively. As Chapter 5 indicated, their failure to complete treatment reflected their reluctance to admit to the harm caused by their offending behaviour. Both men left treatment with their level of risk unaltered. However, it is not expected that the Behaviour Assessment Programme's approach to treatment will work for all deniers. Indeed, Vincent's reluctance to admit that he had committed a sexual crime might have accounted for his reluctance to start the BAP.[1] Furthermore, Yuval claimed that he had not gained anything from completing the BAP. As Chapter 7 highlighted, Yuval's attempts to reassert his innocence overwhelmed his perception of treatment. Consequently, he continued to embellish his victim's actions over his own, and failed to accept that his behaviour had been abusive.[2] Nonetheless, essentially the BAP achieved its goal of engaging the majority of deniers' participation in treatment, which might prove to be effective. In terms of future policy direction, these findings suggest that treatment intervention should be matched to an individual's state of denial rather than their suitability for treatment. Arguably, it is better to try to modify (total) deniers' risk of future offending rather than not treat them at all.

Talking the talk

The participants' level of denial also had an impact on their ability to engage with treatment. This was particularly true of the men participating on the C-SOGP and the SOTP, where they were expected to discuss the events leading up to the offence, and the offence itself.

As Chapter 3 identified, the rationale behind sex offender treatment programmes is based on multifactorial theories of sexual offending. These theories have been amalgamated into models of offending behaviour. Both programmes used the two dominant models to explain the process of sexual offending. The first is that of Finkelhor (1984), who claimed that before an offence can occur four steps must be followed (see Chapter 3). The second is the cycle of offending, originally developed by Wolf (1984, 1988) and later modified by Eldridge (1998) to explain a sex offender's route from motivation to offence. As with Finkelhor's (1984) model, the cycles of offending outline preconditions that sex offenders must overcome in order not to abuse.

It is not expected that all sex offenders will conform exactly to either models of offending behaviour. Indeed, the treatment content, style and delivery of both the SOTP and the C-SOGP embrace the heterogeneous nature of sexual offending. Despite this, a number of the interviewees felt that they had been denied individuality in terms of their offending behaviour. This is consistent with criticisms that current sex offender treatment programmes are too narrow to meet the different needs of all offenders (see Chapter 3). The result was that a number of men felt pressured to 'talk the talk' and outwardly comply with the theories used in treatment to explain the offence process.

The group members might have felt pressured to appear as if they had changed their thoughts, feelings and behaviour relating to their offence, due to the demands of a process that is designed to reduce a person's offending behaviour. In addition, as Chapter 5 identified, a number of the men interviewed in this research entered treatment under some degree of coercion. For example, it was typical for the participants to identify a number of extrinsic factors that influenced their decision to start treatment. Their primary motive for starting treatment was either to comply with the conditions of their sentence, to enhance their chances of early release, and/or to gain certain incentives associated with treatment participation (or indeed to retain the ones they had). It is perhaps not unreasonable to assume that these reasons might also affect their behaviour in treatment, and, more specifically, their desire to please the programme facilitators.

It might also be the case that the participants who claimed to have talked the talk during the research were simply trying to present themselves more favourably during the interview process. For example, during the victim empathy module of the C-SOGP, Jack showed considerable insight into how his victim would have felt in the second victim letter he wrote, and the discussion that followed during treatment (see Chapter 6). However, by commenting in the interview that he had simply written, and said, what he thought the treatment tutors expected of him, he was able to present a more respectable social identity, unencumbered from any negative connotations associated with sexual offenders.

The participants' desires to distance themselves from the popular image of the sex offender might also explain the participants' accounts of what works in treatment. Only two of the participants, Jack and Yuval, claimed that they had not gained anything from their respective treatment programmes. Both men have been defined as justifiers. Arguably, both Jack and Yuval's state of denial contributed to their dissatisfaction with their respective treatment programme. In contrast, this chapter has already shown how the total deniers benefited from participating on the BAP. Similarly, the majority of acceptors interviewed in this research claimed that they had made cognitive and behavioural shifts in the areas associated with sexually abusive behaviour. However, it could be argued that the observations of the total deniers and the acceptors (who completed treatment) were also biased by their desire to conceal or distance themselves from their extended social identity. This will now be discussed in more detail.

What works?

As this research has shown, treatment programmes can provide some sex offenders with some understanding of the factors that predisposed them to commit a sexual offence in order to become proficient in the relevant skills required to prevent future victimization. However, the 23 interviewees who felt that they had benefited from participating in treatment were more likely to claim that they had benefited from exploring their cycles of offending, their use of distorted thinking, and the victim empathy and lifestyle management components of treatment. In contrast, the majority (67 per cent) of participants were unwilling to admit, or discuss, the benefits of exploring the role of deviant sexual fantasy in the offence process.[3] In addition, only seven of the eight men[4] who commented upon the sexual fantasy component of treatment actually admitted to having had deviant sexual thoughts. Arguably this discrepancy exists due to reasons of social desirability.

It is perhaps not surprising that this subgroup of participants, regardless of their state of denial, admitted to having improved their ability to cope generally in life. This relates to the lifestyle management and social functioning component of treatment. For example, the areas that are related to an individual's social functioning (which include under-assertiveness and low self-esteem) are not unique to sexual offenders. Thus the way in which the group members define themselves in this section of treatment is no different from anyone else. Consequently, the social functioning component of treatment enabled the group members to align themselves with 'normal' (Goffman 1963) members of society who do not have a conviction for a sexual offence.

Chapter 4 also identified further ways that this was achieved by the men interviewed in this research. For example, it was typical for the total deniers to assert that they were not the type of person that would commit a sexual offence, whereas the majority of justifiers and acceptors claimed that aspects of their behaviour were no different to other peoples' behavioural traits. This is consistent with the findings presented in Chapter 2, which point to the fine line between sex offenders and the average person. Arguably, this is the point. Sex offenders are ordinary people, and not the demonic creatures portrayed in the mass media. However, the fact that all sex offenders are homogenized in this way makes it necessary for individuals convicted of a sexual offence to reinforce their 'normalness'.

The victim empathy components, and the sections of treatment that explored dysfunctional attitudes and beliefs, also provided the participants with further opportunity to present themselves more favourably. However, the way this was achieved depended on the individual's state of denial. For example, by fully comprehending the distress that they had caused to their victim(s), the acceptors in this study were able to distance themselves from sex offenders who were evidently less repentant than themselves, namely the fixated perpetrator who purposely (in that they do not need to use cognitive distortion to become disinhibited in order to abuse) goes out to rape women and/or children. In addition, as Chapter 7 highlighted, while treatment was effective at challenging some of the acceptors' cognitive distortions, others remained. For example, the acceptors were more likely to claim that they had recognized a wide range of distorted attitudes and beliefs where they portrayed children as able to consent to, and not be harmed by, sexual contact with adults. Conversely, the acceptors were less likely to accept that their offending behaviour was premeditated and/or violent. Consequently, the acceptors' willingness to recognize that they had benefited from looking at factors that were directly relevant to their sexually abusive behaviour might also be confined by their desire to present themselves more favourably.

This was also the case for men in total denial, although they did so quite differently. By removing the demand that group members outwardly take responsibility for their conviction, the total deniers were able to recognize how victims of sexual abuse would feel in general, as well as a range of background problems, and action choices, that led to them being 'accused' and convicted of a sexual offence. Consequently, the design of the BAP allowed the total deniers to discuss the benefits of these components without challenging their innocence. Accordingly, as these men claimed not to have offended, their identity remained unblemished.

As this chapter has already noted, in contrast, the majority of acceptors and total deniers who claimed to have benefited from completing a treatment programme were less likely to claim that they had benefited from exploring the role of sexual fantasy in the offence process. Research has argued that an individual's sexual thoughts and fantasies will follow their sexual preference. If, for example, an individual has sexual fantasies about children, this might indicate possible deviant sexual behaviour and activities towards children. The sexual preference of a person convicted of rape is less easy to see. However, research suggests that a rapist's primary sexual interest is in violence. Individuals convicted of a sexual offence therefore face strong social pressure to deny or minimize their deviant sexual thoughts. It is possibly for this reason that the majority of participants failed to comment on the sexual fantasy component of treatment.

Concealment of risk

This book has also indicated that a number of participants were reluctant to disclose characteristics that reflected their current level of risk of future offending. Two main arguments have been presented to account for this. The first relates to the setting of treatment within the criminal justice system. For example, as this chapter has already shown, a number of extrinsic factors influenced the participants' decision to start treatment. It is not unreasonable to assume that individuals convicted of a sexual offence would conceal their risk of future offending to obtain the extrinsic factors that influenced their decision to participate in treatment in the first place. This raises the question of whether or not treatment programmes can operate effectively within a criminal justice setting. While this research would suggest that they can for some people, the extrinsic factors associated with participating in treatment, within this setting, cannot be ignored.

The second explanation signified an individual's attempt to focus attention away from their extended social identity. As Chapter 8 indicated, this is accentuated by the fact that treatment is conducted in group settings. The men interviewed in this study participated in one of six treatment groups. Each group consisted of between eight and ten members. As Chapter 8 argued, the group members typically conformed to the attitudes and beliefs that were accepted by the group as a whole in order to avoid exclusion. This meant that while it was acceptable to discuss factors relating to their current offence (and thereby express their willingness to learn from their mistakes), the group process discouraged disclosure of characteristics that were associated with sex offenders in the present and/or future. In so doing, the group members collectively attempted to distance themselves from the media profile of sex offenders as highly recidivistic and irredeemable.

Current effectiveness studies suggest that sex offender treatment programmes have an impact on the factors believed to be associated with offending, which appear to be related to a reduction in reconviction rates (Hedderman and Sugg 1996). However, it is not suggested that treatment will prevent all sex offenders from committing future sexual crimes. 'Appropriate' intervention is therefore essential in order to minimize the risk of future sexual victimization. Arguably, the relationship between treatment and legislation can best be described as a fusion of self-control and external control. The latter will now be discussed.

External control

The key sex offender legislation was outlined in Chapter 2. To reiterate, concern for protecting the public, and children in particular, from the apparent risk posed by sexual offenders has evoked both reactive and proactive legislative responses, including measures to incarcerate sex offenders for longer periods of time, and measures to control and monitor sex offenders in the community.

Current legislation is in accordance with new risk penality, which has come to dominate punishment rhetoric and practices in recent years. For example, it views sex offenders as members of a high-risk group. Consequently, through current sentencing laws the stigma of a conviction of a sexual offence has taken on renewed value (Garland 2001). Indeed, Garland (2001) has argued that current trends in sex offender management render sex offenders 'more and more abstract, more and more a projected image rather than an individual person'.

The prominence of risk management is also 'combined with a strong appeal to populist punitiveness' (Simon 1998: 456). As Chapter 2 highlighted, the current manner in which the public perceive and react to sexual crimes has a clear impact on legislation. Indeed, crime has become increasingly politicized over the last two decades, with political parties promising to reduce crime both to gain political advantage and regain the public's confidence in the criminal justice system.

Consequently, it is now broadly accepted that sex offenders require special forms of response to reduce the risk to potential victims (many of whom are among vulnerable groups in society, especially children). However, there appear to be no clear boundaries or ethical constraints with regard to how this is achieved.

An example is the new civil order contained in the Sexual Offences Act 2003 allowing for the policing of sex offenders whose conduct indicates that they still pose a serious threat to the public. The offender's conduct may be perfectly lawful but may result in criminal sanctions. Consequently, noncriminal acts are being brought into the jurisdiction of the criminal justice system, thus raising issues of human rights. Similarly, the Sex Offender Register (introduced under Part one of the Sex Offenders Act 1997 and re-enacted through the Sexual Offences Act 2003) requires convicted sex offenders to register their names and addresses with the police. Such initiatives clearly penalize individuals for crimes that they might commit in the future. While arguments about the acceptability of such penalties were prominent during the 'dangerousness debate' in the 1970s, and successfully opposed – for example, the introduction of a 'Reviewable' sentence – today's sex offender laws are 'valued precisely because of their unambiguous punitive character' (Garland 2001: 8).

Edwards and Hensley (2001) have argued that the government's need to court popularity with the public in emotive policy areas limits its ability to deal effectively with sexual crime. Given the emotionally charged response that the problem of sexual offending increasingly generates, governments have very little option but to react with extreme punitiveness. In doing so, differences between individual 'sex offenders', including their level of risk and harm, tend to become blurred, and the impression is created and reinforced that *all* sex offenders are morally and socially irredeemable. This in turn inadvertently heightens the current panic surrounding sexual offenders, triggering further demand for 'appropriate' punitive reaction from the government (Kemshall and Maguire 2003). The current demand for full public access to the Sex Offender Register, following the death of Sarah Payne, is a case in point.

Registration and community notification

The majority of men interviewed in this research generally agreed that the Sex Offender Register would help the police both to identity suspects once an offence has been perpetrated, and deter some registered sex offenders from committing further offences. However, a number of the participants were perceptive enough to recognize that the Register was also intended to curtail the public's fear of the threat posed by sexual offenders. In addition, while the majority of participants claimed that they would comply with the registration requirements, it was apparent that their decision would be reassessed if community notification laws were passed, i.e. public disclosure of their identity and their whereabouts similar to Megan's Law in the US.

The core premise of community notification laws is to enable parents to inform their children about who is dangerous and who to avoid. It is felt that this will reduce the occurrence of sexual offences because everyone will know of their past (Edwards and Hensley 2001). However, the findings presented in this research support the argument that convicted sex offenders would be less likely to register under the Sex Offenders Act 1997. This was primarily due to the current moral panic surrounding sexual crimes, and fears that convicted sex offenders and their families would become subject to vigilante attacks. To this end, a number of participants claimed that they would go 'underground' to avoid disclosure. In these circumstances it becomes extremely difficult for the criminal justice system effectively to monitor their behaviour. The implementation of community notification laws would therefore undermine the government's capacity to control future crime.

Garland (2001) has described the enactment of such laws as a process of 'acting out', whereby the government and/or state provide an instant response to a public outcry with complete disregard for the rights of those being sanctioned. Indeed, it took less than two months for Megan's Law to be passed in the US. Brooks (1996) described it as a 'quick fix solution to soothe an outraged public'. An equivalent 'quick fix' solution has not been adopted in the UK. However, within three months of the murder of Sarah Payne the government sought to pacify public concerns through the adoption of a compromise package. This includes the publication of an annual report, which includes statistical information on the number of registered sex offenders in a specified geographical area.[5] In addition, lay members have been appointed to Strategic Management Boards of Multi-Agency Public Protection Panels (MAPPPs, as established by the Criminal Justice and Court Services Act 2000) in an attempt to offset public calls for community notification (Kemshall and Maguire 2003).

Whether this information will be sufficient to allay calls for full access to the information contained in the Register is yet to be seen. However, arguably before the public will accept the information and use it effectively, they will have to abandon the perception of sex offenders as the 'alien other' (Garland 2001). This in turn will then enable the government effectively to minimize the risk of future sexual offending by enacting laws that reflect how different individuals convicted of a sexual offence might best be dealt with.

Moreover, a convicted sex offender's inability to disclose current thoughts and feelings might prevent them from seeking the help they need to refrain from sexual offending. If individuals convicted of a sexual offence cannot be honest in treatment, which is supposedly supportive of such disclosure, then they are unlikely to be able to ask for help once their sentence is over. Again this draws on Becker's (1963) concept of the Master Status, whereby the variety and diversity of an individual's character is overshadowed by their conviction for a sexual offence. The ostracism that sex offenders face as a result of deviant stereotypes (to which the media and current sentencing laws give prominence) prevents convicted sexual offenders from managing their own problems effectively. Failure to see sex offenders as individuals, with multiple identities and characteristics, therefore affects how successful the criminal justice system and/or the individual is at minimizing the risk of future offending.

Effectively managing risk: Future directions

The arguments presented in this book point to the need to educate the public that sexual offenders are not a homogenous group, and that some can benefit from treatment and refrain from sexual offending. This would mean challenging some of the oversimplified views regarding sex offenders.

Society's ability to acknowledge sex offenders as individuals who vary in insight and levels of dangerousness would mean challenging the media's image that sexual crimes are committed exclusively by strangers. The alternative is addressing the fact that most sex offences occur in the family, or are carried out by relatives or individuals who are close to the victim. However, this might further heighten the moral panic surrounding sexual crimes, creating a society in which no one trusts anyone: wives might distrust their husbands, and parents might question their parent's motives for wanting to look after their grandchildren. Furthermore, it is also plausible that the public already accept that the chance of being sexually abused by a stranger is slight, but are reluctant to conceptualize the risk of sexual victimization in domestic terms (Greer 2003). Arguably, they choose to ignore it because any alternative undermines the conventional views of the family and the home.

Arguments presented in Chapter 2 also point to society's failure to question the social construction of childhood and sexuality. In particular, how our inability to talk of children and sexuality outside the context of sexual abuse affects both our 'understanding of child sexual abuse as a "problem" and our visions of a "solution" ' (Kitzinger 1997: 166).

Evidently in today's climate, an individual's stigma of a conviction of a sexual offence places restrictions on their identity, their reintegration, and ultimately on their ability to refrain from further offending. In contrast, Maruna *et al.* (2004) have argued that desistance from future offending is only possible when an ex-offender develops a coherent pro-social identity for themselves. Consequently, the best way to manage the threat posed by sexual offenders is to include (rather than exclude) individuals convicted of a sexual offence in society (Kemshall and

Maguire 2003). Indeed, Wilson (2003) has argued that it is naïve to assume that sex offenders will stop offending if there is nothing in society for them. Instead, the fact that sex offenders are denied 'individuality' prevents them from putting all their good intentions into practice and, according to Wilson (2003), 'sets them up to fail'.

Including sex offenders in society, however, takes into account that the majority of these men will have paid their debt to society and can refrain from sexually abusive behaviour. It also acknowledges that some might need help in doing so. This argument clearly supports the underlying principle of cognitive behavioural treatment programmes, which recognize 'control' not 'cure' is the aim of treatment (Travers 1998).

The ideology is similar to the general approach taken to alcoholics: once an alcoholic always an alcoholic, once a sex offender always a sex offender. The difference is that an alcoholic is able to attend AA (Alcoholics Anonymous) meetings to get help; they are also applauded for abstaining from alcohol. In contrast, sex offenders are unable to reveal their conviction for fear of reprisals. This is not to say that sex offenders should not be held accountable for their behaviour. Nor is it trying to belittle the harm caused by sexual crimes. It is precisely because of this that it becomes essential to deal with the threat of sexual abuse in the most effective way.

Appropriate intervention in the community is essential in order to minimize the risk of future sexual crimes. Active cooperation between the police, prison and probation services through Multi-Agency Public Protection Arrangements (MAPPAs) is a step in the right direction. Similarly, Circles of Support and Accountability recognize that sex offenders' inclusion into society is an indispensable component in protecting the public (see Chapter 3). However, the effectiveness of both schemes is likely to be restricted if they are used simply as a policing mechanism and not as a means of encouraging disclosure of risk of future offending.

While early findings of the use of polygraph testing in the treatment and supervision of sex offenders (Grubin *et al.* 2004) indicate that offenders are more likely to disclose information to supervising probation officers or treatment providers, their very use might heighten the stereotype that sex offenders are proficient and practised liars. Government agencies therefore need to be realistic as to the dilemmas that sex offenders face in the community. Again, the only way this can be achieved is to let go of certain stereotypical perceptions of sex offenders. In order to achieve this, it is necessary to listen to what sex offenders have to say.

Notes

1 Vincent has been defined as a total denier in this research.
2 Yuval has been defined as a justifier in this research.
3 It is important to acknowledge that there is no proof that the participants interviewed in this research all had deviant sexual interest. This research is therefore not implying that the participants who did not disclose sexual fantasies in this research were lying and/or in denial.
4 Six men who had participated on the SOTP, one participant in the C-SOGP and one participant in the BAP claimed that they had benefited from exploring the role of sexual fantasy in their offending behaviour. However, the remaining men on the BAP felt that they had benefited from looking at sex education issues in more general terms (session 9 of the BAP).
5 This responsibility is placed upon Multi-Agency Public Protection Panels as set out in the Criminal Justice and Court Services Act 2000.

Bibliography

Adams, D.B. (1999) *Summary of State Sex Offender Registry Dissemination Procedures*. Bureau of Justice Statistics, Department of Justice, Washington, DC.

Adi, Y., Ashcroft, D., Browne, K., Beech, A., Fry-Smith, A. and Hyde, C. (2002) Clinical effectiveness and cost-consequences of selective serotonin reuptake inhibitors in the treatment of sex offenders. *Health Technol Assess* 6: 28.

Alexander, M.A. (1999) Sex Offender Treatment Efficacy Revisited. *Sexual Abuse: A Journal of Research and Treatment* 11: 101–16.

Allam, J. (2001) *Community Sex Offender Groupwork Programme (C-SOGP) Theory Manual*. National Probation Service, Sex Offender Unit (West Midlands).

Ashworth (2000) *Sentencing and Criminal Justice, Third Edition*. Butterworth, London.

Bainham, A. and Brooks-Gordon, B. (2004) Reforming the Law on Sexual Offenders. In B. Brooks-Gordon, L. Gelsthorpe, M. Johnson and A. Bainham (eds) *Sexuality Repositioned: Diversity and the Law*. Oxford, Portland, Oregon, 261–96.

Barbaree, H.E. (1991) Denial and Minimisation among Sex Offenders: Assessment and Treatment Outcome. *Forum on Corrections Research* 3: 30–33.

Beck, U. (1992) *Risk Society: Towards a New Modernism*. Sage, London.

Beck, U., Giddens, A. and Lash, S. (1994) *Reflexive Modernization: Politics, Tradition and Aesthetic in the Modern Social Order*. Polity Press, Cambridge.

Becker, H.S. (1963) *Outsiders: Studies in the Sociology of Deviance*. Free Press London, New York.

Beckett, R., Beech, A., Fisher, D. and Fordham, A.S. (1994) *Community-based treatment for sex offenders: an evaluation of seven treatment programmes*. HMSO, London.

Beech, A. and Fisher, D. (2004) Treatment of Sex Offenders in the UK in Prison and Probation Settings. In H. Kemshall and G. McIvor (eds) *Managing Sex Offender Risk*. Jessica Kingsley Publishers, London, 137–64.

Beech, A. and Fordham, A.S. (1997) Therapeutic climate of sexual offender treatment programmes. *Sexual Abuse: A Journal of Research and Treatment* 9: 219–37.

Beech, A., Erikson, M., Friendship, C. and Ditchfield, J. (2001) *A six year follow-up of men going through probation-based sex offender treatment programmes.* Home Office, Research Development and Statistics, London.

Beech, A., Fisher, D. and Beckett, R. (1999) *STEP 3: An evaluation of the Prison Service Sex Offender Treatment Programme.* Home Office, London.

Blumenthal, S., Gudjonsson, G. and Burns, J. (1999) Cognitive Distortions and Blame Attribution in Sex Offenders against Adults and Children. *Child Abuse and Neglect* 23: 129–43.

Bottoms, A. and Brownsward, R. (1983) Dangerousness and Rights. In J. Hinton (ed.) *Dangerousness: Problems of Assessment and Prediction.* Allen and Unwin, London.

Bottoms, A.E. (1977) Reflections on the Renaissance of Dangerousness. *The Howard Journal of Criminal Justice* 16: 70–96.

Bottoms, A.E. (1995) The Politics and Philosophy of Sentencing. In C. Clarkson and R. Morgan (eds) *The Politics of Sentencing.* Clarendon Press, Oxford.

Bottoms, A.E., Gelsthorpe, L.R. and Rex, S. (2001) *Community Penalties: Change and Challenges.* Willan Publishing, Cullompton, Devon.

Bowlby, J. (1969) *Attachment and Loss: Volume 1. Attachment.* Hogarth, London.

Bowlby, J. (1973) *Attachment and Loss: Vol. 2. Separation: Anxiety and Anger.* Hogarth, London.

Bowlby, J. (1979) *Attachment and Loss: Vol. 3. Loss: Sadness and Depression.* Hogarth, London.

Bradford, J. (1997) Medical Intervention in Sexual Deviance. In D.R. Laws and W. O'Donohue (eds) *Sexual Deviance: Theory, Assessment and Treatment.* Guilford Press, New York.

Breakwell, G.M. (2001) Social Representational Constraints upon Identity Processes. In K. Deaux and G. Philogene (eds) *Representations of the Social.* Blackwell Publishers, Oxford.

Brewer, M.B. (2001) Social Identities and Social Representations: A Question of Priority. In K. Deaux and G. Philogene (eds) *Representations of the Social.* Blackwell Publishers, Oxford.

Brody, S. (1976) *The Effectiveness of Sentencing.* Home Office Research Study No. 35, London, HMSO.

Brooks, A.D. (1996) Megans Law: Constitutionality and Policy. *Criminal Justice Ethics*, Winter/Spring, 55–66.

Brooks-Gordon, B., Bilby, C. and Kenworthy, T. (2004) Sexual Offenders: A Systematic Review of Psychological Treatment Interventions. In B. Brooks-Gordon, L.R. Gelsthorpe, M. Johnson and A. Bainham (eds) *Sexuality Repositioned: Diversity and the Law.* Hart Publishing, Oxford, 395–420.

Bumby, K.M. and Hansen, D.J. (1997) Intimacy deficits, fear of intimacy and loneliness among sexual offenders. *Criminal Justice and Behavior* 24: 315–31.

Burman, E. (1995) What is it? Masculinity and Femininity in Cultural Representations of Childhood. In S. Wilkinson and C. Kitzinger (eds) *Feminism and Discourse: Psychological Perspectives.* Sage Publications Ltd, London.

Burt, M.R. (1980) Cultural Myths and Supports for Rape. *Journal of Personality and Social Psychology* 38: 217–30.

Burt, M.R. (1983) Justifying Personal Violence: A Comparison of Rapists and the General Public. *Victimology: An International Journal* 8: 131–50.

Butler Committee (1975) *Report of the Committee on Mentally Abnormal Offenders.* Home Office, London.

Cameron, H. and Telfer, J. (2004) Cognitive-Behavioural Group Work: Its Application to Specific Offender Groups. *The Howard Journal* 43: 47–64.

Clarke, A., Simmonds, R. and Wydall, S. (2004) Delivering cognitive behavioural skills programmes in prison: A qualitative study. *Home Office Online Report 27/04.*

Cobley, C. (1997) Keeping Track of Sex Offenders – Part 1 of the Sex Offender Act 1997. *The Modern Law Review* 60: 690–99.

Cobley, C. (2000) *Sex Offenders: Law, Policy and Practice.* Jordans, Bristol.

Cohen, S. (2001) *States of Denial: Knowing about Atrocities and Suffering.* Polity Press, Cambridge.

Coker, J. (1987) The Probation Office and Long-Term Prisoners. In A.E. Bottoms and R. Light (eds) *Problems of Long-term Imprisonment.* Gower, Aldershot.

Cortoni, F.A. and Marshall, W.L. (1998) The Relationship Between Attachment and Coping in Sex Offenders. ATSA 17th Research and Treatment Conference. Vancouver, Canada, Oct. 1998.

Cote, S. (2000) *Approaching the Problem of Violent Crime through Community Control Trust and Empowerment: Modernity, Risk Management and Current Sex Offender Statutes.* Paper presented at the American Society of Criminology 52nd Annual Meeting, San Francisco, California.

Craissati, J. (1998) *Child Sexual Abusers: A Community Treatment Approach.* Psychology Press Ltd, Hove, East Sussex.

Crawford, C. and Conn, L. (1997) Female Sexual Abuse: Unrecognised Abuse and Ignored Victims. *Journal of the British Association for Counselling* 8: 278–80.

Denvir, G. (2000) Accredited Offending Behaviour Programmes in the Wider Regime. *Prison Service Journal* 129, 16–18.

Duveen, G. (2001) Representations, Identities, Resistance. In K. Deaux and G. Philogene (eds) *Representations of the Social.* Blackwell Publishers Ltd, Oxford, 257–70.

Edwards, W. and Hensley, C. (2001) Contextualizing Sex Offender Management Legislation and Policy: Evaluating the Problem of Latent Consequence in Community Notification Laws. *International Journal of Offender Therapy and Comparative Criminology* 45: 83–101.

Eldridge, H. (1998) *Maintaining Change: A Personal Relapse Prevention Manual.* Sage, London.

Endler, N.S. and Parker, J.D.A. (1990) Multidimensional Assessment of Coping: A Critical Evaluation. *Journal of Personality and Social Psychology* 58: 844–5.

Epstein, D. and Johnson, R. (1998) *Schooling Sexualities.* Open University Press, Buckingham.

Ericson, R.V. and Haggerty, K.D. (1997) *Policing and the Risk Society.* Oxford University Press, Oxford.

Falshaw, L., Friendship, C. and Bates, A. (2003) *Sexual offenders – measuring reconviction, re-offending and recidivism.* Home Office Research Findings No. 183, Development and Statistics Directorate, London.

Farrell, P. and Soothill, K. (2001) Television documentaries on sex offenders: The emergence of a new genre? *Police Journal* 74: 61–7.

Feeley, M. and Simon, J. (1992) The New Penology: Notes on the Emerging Strategy for Corrections. *Criminology* 30: 449–75.

Feeley, M. and Simon, J. (1994) Actuarial Justice: The Emerging New Criminal Law. In D. Nelkin (ed.) *The Futures of Criminology*. Sage, London.

Fergusson, D.M. and Mullen, P.E. (1999) Childhood Sexual Abuse: An Evidence-based Perspective. *Developmental Clinical Psychology and Psychiatry* 40.

Fernandez, Y.M. and Marshall, W.L. (2003) Victim Empathy, Social Self Esteem, and Psychopathy in Rapists. *Sexual Abuse: A Journal of Research and Treatment* 15: 11–26.

Fernandez, Y.M., Marshall, W.L., Lightbody, S. and O'Sullivan, C. (1990) The Child Molester Empathy Measure. *Sexual Abuse: A Journal of Research and Treatment* 11: 17–31.

Finkelhor, D. (1984) *Child Sexual Abuse: New Theory and Research*. Free Press, New York.

Fisher, D. and Beech, A. (2004) Adult Male Sex Offenders. In H. Kemshall and G. McIvor (eds) *Managing Sex Offender Risk*. Jessica Kingsley Publishers, London, 25–64.

Fisher, D. and Mair, G. (1998) *A Review of Classification Schemes for Sex Offenders*. Home Office, London.

Fisher, D., Beech, A.R. and Browne, K.D. (1999) Comparison of sex offenders to non-sex offenders in selected psychological measures. *Journal of Offender Therapy and Comparative Criminology* 4: 473–91.

Fisher, D., Faux, M., Eldridge, H. and Still, J. (unpublished) *Thames Valley Project: Theoretical Background to TVP Sex Offender Treatment Programme*. Thames Valley Project.

Floud, J. and Young, W.C. (1981) *Dangerousness and Criminal Justice*. Heinemann, London.

Forsyth, D.R. (1999) *Group Dynamics*. Wadsworth Publishing Company, London.

Freund, K. (1991) Reflections on the development of the phallometric method of assessing sexual preferences. *Annals of Sex Research* 4: 221–8.

Freund, K. and Blanchard, R. (1989) Phallometric diagnosis of paedophilia. *Journal of Consulting and Clinical Psychology* 57: 100–05.

Friendship, C., Mann, R. and Beech, A. (2003) *The Prison-based Sex Offender Treatment Programme – An Evaluation*. Home Office Findings 205, London.

Furniss, T. (1991) *The multi-professional handbook of child sexual abuse*. Routledge, London.

Garland, D. (1996) The limits of the sovereign state: strategies of crime control in contemporary society. *British Journal of Criminology* 36: 445–70.

Garland, D. (1997) 'Governmentality' and the problem of crime: Foucault, criminology and sociology. *Theoretical Criminology* 1: 173–214.

Garland, D. (2000) The culture of high crime societies: some pre-conditions of recent 'law and order' policies. *British Journal of Criminology* 40: 347–75.

Garland, D. (2001) *The Culture of Control: Crime and Social Order in Contemporary Society*. Oxford University Press, Oxford.

Garland, R.J. and Dougher, M.J. (1991) Motivational interventions in the treatment of sex offenders. In W.R. Miller and M.S. Rollnick (eds) *Motivational interviewing: preparing people to change addictive behaviour*. Guildford Press, New York, 303–13.

Garlick, Y., Marshall, W.L. and Thornton, D. (1996) Intimacy deficits and attribution of blame among sexual offenders. *Legal and Criminological Psychology* 1: 251–8.

Giddens, A. (1990) *The Consequences of Modernity*. Polity Press, Cambridge.

Giddens, A. (1998) Risk society: the context of British politics. In J. Franklin (ed.) *The Politics of Risk Society*. Polity Press, in association with Institute for Public Policy Research, Oxford.

Gittens, D. (1998) Childrens Sexuality: Why Do Adults Panic? In D. Gittens (ed.) *The Child in Question*. Macmillan, London, 173–201.

Goffman, E. (1959) *The Presentation of the Self in Everyday Life*. Penguin, London.

Goffman, E. (1961) *Asylums*. Anchor Books, New York.

Goffman, E. (1963) *Stigma: Notes on the Management of Spoiled Identity*. Penguin, Harmondsworth.

Greer, C. (2003) *Sex Crime and the Media: Sex Offending and the Press in a Divided Society*. Willan, Devon.

Grubin, D.H. (1998) *Sex offending against children: Understanding the risk*. Research Development Statistics.

Grubin, D.H. (2004) The Risk Assessment of Sex Offenders. In H. Kemshall and G. McIvor (eds) *Managing Sex Offender Risk*. Jessica Kingsley Publishers, London, 91–110.

Grubin, D.H., Madsen, L., Parsons, S., Sosnowski, D. and Warberg, B. (2004) A Prospective Study of the Impact of Polygraphy on High Risk Behaviours in Adult Sex Offenders. *Sexual Abuse: A Journal of Research and Treatment* 16: 209–22.

Hammersley, M. and Atkinson, P. (1995) *Ethnography: Principles in Practice*. Routledge, London and New York.

Hancock, L. and Matthews, R. (2001) Crime, Community Safety and Toleration. In R. Matthews and J. Pitts (eds) *Crime and Disorder and Community Safety: A New Agenda?* Routledge, London, 98–119.

Hanson, K. and Bussiere, M.T. (1998) Predicting Relapse: A Meta Analysis of Sexual Offender Recidivism Studies. *Journal of Consulting and Clinical Psychology* 66: 348–62.

Hanson, K. and Thornton, D. (2000) Improving Risk Assessments for Sex Offenders: A Comparison of Three Actuarial Scales. *Law and Human Behavior* 24: 119–36.

Happel, R.M. and Auffrey, J.J. (1995) Sex Offender Assessment: Interpreting the dance of denial. *American Journal of Forensic Psychology* 13: 5–22.

Hebenton, B. and Thomas, T. (1996) Tracking Sex Offenders. *Howard Journal* 35: 97–112.

Hebenton, B. and Thomas, T. (1997). *Keeping Track? Observations on Sex Offender Register in the US*. Crime Detection and Prevention Series, Paper 83 Police Research Group

Hedderman, C. and Sugg, D. (1996) *Does treating sex offenders reduce re-offending?* Research Findings No. 45. Home Office Research, Development and Statistics Directorate, London.

Hetherton, J. (1999) The Idealisation of Women: Its Role in the Minimisation of Child Sexual Abuse by Females. *Child Abuse and Neglect* 23: 161–74.

Hollin, C.R. (2001) To treat or not to treat? An historical perspective. In C.R. Hollin (ed.) *Handbook of Offender Assessment and Treatment*. John Wiley, Chichester.

Home Office (1991) *Treatment Programmes for Sex Offenders in Custody: A Strategy.* Home Office, London.

Home Office (1996) *Protecting the Public: The Governments Strategy on Crime in England and Wales.* White Paper. HMSO, London.

Home Office (2001a) *Consultation Paper on the review of part 1 of the Sex Offenders Act 1997.* HMSO, London.

Home Office (2001b) *Initial Guidance to the Police and Probation Services on Sections 67 and 68 of the Criminal Justice and Court Services Act 2000.* HMSO, London.

Home Office (2002a) *Further Guidance to the Police and Probation Services on Sections 67 and 68 of the Criminal Justice and Court Services Act 2000.* Home Office, London.

Home Office (2002b) *Protecting the Public: Strengthening Protection Against Sex Offenders and Reforming the Law on Sexual Offences.* Home Office, London.

Home Office (2003) *The MAPPA Guidance.* National Probation Directorate, London.

Hood, R., Shute, S., Feilzer, M. and Wilcox, A. (2002) *Reconviction rates of serious sex offenders and assessments of their risk.* Home Office, London.

Howard League (1985) *Unlawful Sex.* Howard League, London.

Howe, A. (1998) *Sexed Crime in the News.* The Federation Press, Sydney.

Hudson, B. (2002) Punishment and control. In M. Maguire, R. Morgan and R. Reiner (eds) *The Oxford Handbook of Criminology, Third Edition.* Oxford University Press, 233–63

Hudson, S.M. and Ward, T. (1997) Intimacy, loneliness, and attachment style in sexual offenders. *Journal of Interpersonal Violence* 12: 323–39.

Hudson, S.M. and Ward, T. (2000) Relapse Prevention: Assessment and Treatment Implications. In D.R. Laws, S.M. Hudson and T. Ward (eds) *Remaking Relapse Prevention with Sex Offenders: A Sourcebook.* Sage, Thousand Oaks, CA.

Ingersoll, S.L. and Patton, S.O. (1990) *Treating Perpetrators of Sexual Abuse.* Guilford Press, New York.

Jenkins, R. (1996) *Social Identity.* Routledge, London.

Kemshall, H. (2001) *Risk Assessment and Management of Known Sexual and Violent Offenders: A Review of Current Issues.* Home Office, London.

Kemshall, H. (2003a) The Community Management of High-Risk Offenders: A Consideration of Best Practice MAPPA. *Prison Service Journal.* March.

Kemshall, H. (2003b) *Understanding risk in criminal justice.* Open University Press, Berkshire, England.

Kemshall, H. (2004) Female Sex Offenders. In H. Kemshall and G. McIvor (eds) *Managing Sex Offender Risk.* Jessica Kingsley Publishers, London, 49–64.

Kemshall, H. and Maguire, M. (2001) Public protection, partnership and risk penality: The multi-agency risk management of sexual and violent offenders. *Punishment and Society* 3: 237–67.

Kemshall, H. and Maguire, M. (2002) Community Justice, Risk Management and the Role of Multi-Agency Public Protection Panels. *British Journal of Community Justice* 1, 11–27.

Kemshall, H. and Maguire, M. (2003) Sex Offenders, Risk Penality and the Problem of Disclosure to the Community. In A. Matravers (ed.) *Managing Sex Offenders in the Community: Context, Challenges and Responses*. Willan, Devon.

Kennedy, H.G. and Grubin, D.H. (1992) Patterns of denial in sex offenders. *Psychological Medicine* 22: 191–6.

Kenworthy, T., Adams, C.E., Bilby, C., Brooks-Gordon, B. and Fenton, M. (2004) *Psychological interventions for those who have sexually offended or at risk of offending (Cochrane Review)*. The Cochrane Library, Issue 3, John Wiley and Sons Ltd, Chichester, UK.

Kincaid, J.R. (1998) *Erotic innocence: the culture of child molesting*. Duke University Press, Durham, NC.

Kirkegaard, H. and Northey, W. (2000) The Sex Offender as Scapegoat: Vigilante Violence and a Faith Community Response. *Prison Service Journal* 132: 71–7.

Kitzinger, J. (1997) Who are you kidding? Children, power and the struggle against sexual abuse. In A. James and A. Prout (eds) *Constructing and reconstructing childhood: contemporary issues in the sociological study of childhood*. Falmer Press, London, 165–89.

Kitzinger, J. (1999) The ultimate neighbour from hell? Stranger danger and the media framing of paedophiles. In B. Franklin (ed.) *Social policy, the media and misrepresentation*. Routledge, London, 207–21.

Kitzinger, J. (2004a) *Framing Abuse: media influence and public understandings of sexual violence against children*. Pluto.

Kitzinger, J. (2004b) Media Coverage of Violence Against Women and Children. In K. Ross and C.M. Byerly (eds) *Women and the Media: International Perspectives*. Blackwell, 13–38.

Knock, K., Schlesinger, P., Boyle, R. and Magor, M. (2002) *The Police Perspectives on Sex Offender Orders: A Preliminary Review of Policy and Practice*. Policing and Reducing Crime Unit, Home Office Research, Development and Statistics Directorate.

Knopp, F.H. (1984) *Retraining adult sex offenders: methods and models*. Safer Society Press, Syracuse, NY.

Lee, K.P., Proeve, M.J., Lancaster, M., Jackson, H.J., Patterson, P. and Mullen, P.E. (1996) An evaluation and 1-year follow-up study of a community-based treatment program for sex offenders. *Australian Psychologist* 31: 147–52.

Levi, M. with Maguire, M. (2002) Violent Crime. In M. Maguire, R. Morgan and R. Reiner (eds) *The Oxford Handbook of Criminology, Third Edition*. Oxford University Press, Oxford, 795–843.

Leyland, M. and Baim, C. (2001) *Community Sex Offender Groupwork Programme Training Handouts*. C-SOGP National Training Team, West Midlands Probation Area.

Lynch, M. (2002) Paedophiles and Cyber-predators as Contaminating Forces: The Language of Disgust, Pollution, and Boundary Invasions in Federal Debates on Sex Offender Legislation. *Law and Social Inquiry – Journal of the American Bar Foundation* 27: 529–66.

Madsen, L., Parsons, S. and Grubin, D.H. (forthcoming) A preliminary study of the contribution of periodic polygraph testing to the treatment and supervision of sex offenders. *Journal of Forensic Psychiatry.*

Maguire, M. and Raynor, P. (1997) The Revival of Throughcare: Rhetoric and Reality in Automatic Conditional Release. *The British Journal of Criminology* 37.

Maguire, M. and Kemshall, H. (2004) Multi-Agency Public Protection Arrangements: Key Issues. In H. Kemshall and G. McIvor (eds) *Managing Sex Offender Risk.* Jessica Kingsley Publishers, London.

Maguire, M., Kemshall, H., Noaks, L., Sharpe, K. and Wincup, E. (2001) *Risk Management of Sexual and Violent Offenders: The Work of Public Protection Panels.* Home Office, London.

Mair, G. (1991) *What Works – Nothing or Everything? Measuring the Effectiveness of Sentences.* Research Bulletin No. 30. Home Office Research and Statistics Department, London, HMSO.

Malamuth, N. (1981) Rape Proclivity Among Males. *Journal of Social Issues* 37: 138–57.

Maletzky, B.M. (1993) Factors associated with success and failure in the behaviour and cognitive treatment of sex offenders. *Annals of Sex Research* 6: 241–58.

Mann, R. (1999) The Sex Offender Treatment Programme HM Prison Service England and Wales. In S. Hofling, D. Drewea and I. Epple-Waigel (eds) *Auftrag Prävention: Offensive gegen sexuellen Kindesmißbrauch.* Atwerb-Verlag KG, Munich.

Mann, R. and Beech, A. (2002) Cognitive Distortions, Schemas and Implicit Theories. In T. Ward, D.R. Laws and S.M. Hudson (eds) *Theoretical Issues and Controversies in Sexual Deviance.* Sage, London.

Mann, R. and Thornton, D. (1998) The Evolution of a Multisite Sexual Offender Programme. In W.L. Marshall, Y.M. Fernandez, S.M. Hudson and T. Ward (eds) *Sourcebook of Treatment Programmes for Sexual Offenders.*

Mann, R., Daniels, M. and Marshall, W.L. (2002) The Use of Role-plays in Developing Empathy. In Y.M. Fernandez (ed.) *In Their Shoes: Examining the Issue of Empathy and its Place in the Treatment of Offenders.* Wood N' Barnes Publishing, Oklahoma City, OK.

Marques, J., Nelson, C., Alarcon, J. and Day, D. (2000) Preventing Relapse in Sex Offenders: What we Learned from SOTEPS Experimental Program. In D.R. Laws, B. Hudson and T. Ward (eds) *Remaking Relapse Prevention with Sex Offenders: A Sourcebook.* Sage, Thousand Oaks, CA, 39–56.

Marshall, W.L. (1989) Intimacy, Loneliness and Sexual Offending. *Behaviour Research and Therapy* 17, 491–503.

Marshall, W.L. (1993) The treatment of sex offenders: what does the outcome data tell us? A reply to Quinsey, Harris, Rice, and Lalumiere. *Journal of Interpersonal Violence* 8: 524–30.

Marshall, W.L. (2000) Adult Sexual Offenders Against Women. In C. Hollin (ed.) *Handbook of Offender Assessment and Treatment.* Wiley, Chichester.

Marshall, W.L. and Barbaree, H.E. (1990) Outcome of Comprehensive Cognitive-Behavioural Treatment Programs. In W.L. Marshall, D.R. Laws and H.E. Barbaree (eds) *Handbook of Sexual Assault: Issues, Theories and Treatment of the Offender.* Plenum Press, New York and London, 363–87.

Marshall, W.L. and Fernandez, Y.M. (2003) Phallometric Testing with Sexual Offenders: Limits to its Value. *Clinical Psychology Review* 20: 807–28.

Marshall, W.L. and Marshall, L.E. (2000) The Origins of Sexual Offending. *Trauma, Violence and Abuse* 1: 250–63.

Marshall, W.L. and Mouldern, H. (2001) Hostility Toward Women and Victim Empathy in Rapists. *Sexual Abuse: A Journal of Research and Treatment* 13: 249–55.

Marshall, W.L., Anderson, D. and Fernandez, Y.M. (1999a) *Cognitive Behavioural Treatment with Sexual Offenders*. Wiley, Chichester.

Marshall, W.L., Champagne, F., Brown, M. and Miller, S. (1997) Empathy, Intimacy, Loneliness and Self-esteem in Nonfamilial Child Molesters. *Sexual Abuse: A Journal of Research and Treatment* 9: 321–33.

Marshall, W.L., Eccles, A. and Barbaree, H.E. (1993) A three-tiered approach to the rehabilitation of incarcerated sex offenders. *Behavioural Sciences and the Law* 11: 441–55.

Marshall, W.L., Hamilton, K. and Fernandez, Y.M. (2001a) Empathy Deficits and Cognitive Distortions in Child Molesters. *Sexual Abuse: A Journal of Research and Treatment* 13: 123–31.

Marshall, W.L., Serran, G.A. and Cortoni, F.A. (1999b) Childhood attachments and sexual abuse and their relationship to coping in child molesters. *Sexual Abuse: A Journal of Research and Treatment*.

Marshall, W.L., Serran, G.A. and Moulder, H. (2004) Effective Intervention with Sexual Offenders. In H. Kemshall and G. McIvor (eds) *Managing Sex Offender Risk*. Jessica Kingsley Publishers, London, 111–35.

Marshall, W.L., Serran, G.A. and Mouldern, H. (2002) Therapist Features in Sexual Offender Treatment: Their Reliable Identification and Influence on Behavior Change. *Clinical Psychology and Psychotherapy* 9: 395–405.

Marshall, W.L., Thornton, D., Marshall, L.E., Fernandez, Y.M. and Mann, R. (2001b) Treatment of Sexual Offenders Who Are in Categorical Denial: A Pilot Project. *Sexual Abuse: A Journal of Research and Treatment* 13: 205–15.

Martinson, R. (1974) What Works? – Questions and Answers about Prison Reform. *The Public Interest* 10: 22–54.

Maruna, S., Immarigeon, R. and LeBel, T. (2004) Ex-offender reintegration: theory and practice. In S. Maruna and R. Immarigeon (eds) *After Crime and Punishment: Pathways to offender reintegration*. Willan Publishing, Devon, 3–26.

Masson, H. (2004) Young Sex Offenders. In H. Kemshall and G. McIvor (eds) *Managing Sex Offender Risk*. Jessica Kingsley Publishers, London, 65–87.

Matthews, R. (1991) *Varieties of sex offenders – Patterns of denial*. HM Prison Service. London: HMSO.

McCarthy, J. and Stewart, A.L. (1998) Neutralisations as a Process of Graduated Desensitisation: Moral Values of Offenders. *International Journal of Offender Therapy and Comparative Criminology* 42: 278–90.

McGuire, J. (1995) *What Works: Reducing Re-Offending: Guidelines from Research and Practice*. J. Wiley, Chichester, New York.

McGuire, J. (2000) *Cognitive Behavioural Approaches: An Introduction to Theory and Research*. Home Office, London.

McGuire, J. (2002) Integrating findings from research reviews. In J. McGuire (ed.) *Offender Rehabilitation and Treatment: Effectived Practice and Policies to Reduce Re-offending*. Wiley, Chichester.

Mckibben, A., Proulx, J. and Lussier, P. (2001) Sexual Aggressors Perceptions of Effectiveness of Strategies to Cope with Negative Emotions and Deviant Sexual Fantasies. *Sexual Abuse: A Journal of Research and Treatment* 13: 257–71.

McNeil, F. (2000) Defining effective probation: frontline perspectives. *Howard Journal* 39, 382–97.

Merrington, S. and Stanley, S. (2000) Doubts about the what works initiatives. *Probation* 47: 272–5.

Mills, K. (1997) What difference do women journalists make? In P. Norris (eds) *Women, Media and Politics*. Oxford University Press, Oxford, 41–56.

MORI/*News of the World* (2000) *Naming and Shaming Poll. www.mori.com/polls/2000/nowname.shtml.*

Morolla, J. and Scully, D. (1986) Attitudes towards women, violence, and rape: A comparison of convicted rapists and other felons. *Deviant Behavior* 7: 337–55.

Murphy, W. (1990) Assessment and modification of cognitive distortions in sex offenders. In W.L. Marshall, D.R. Laws and H.E. Barbaree (eds) *Handbook of sexual assault: Issues, theories, and treatment of the offender*. Plenum Press, New York, 331–40.

Murphy, W. and Carich, M. (2001) Cognitive Distortions and Restructuring in Sexual Abuse Treatment. In M. Carich and S. Mussack (eds) *Handbook for Sexual Abuser Assessment and Treatment*. Safer Society Press, Brandon, VT.

Myhill, A. and Allen, J. (2002) *Rape and sexual assault of women: The extent and nature of the problem, Findings from the British Crime Survey*. Home Office Research Study 237, Development and Statistics Directorate, London.

OBPU (2000) *The SOTP Core Programme 'CORE 2000' Treatment Manual*. HM Prison Service, London.

O'Malley, P. (2000) Risk societies and the government of crime. In M. Brown and J. Pratt (eds) *Dangerous Offenders: Punishment and Social Order*. London Routledge.

O'Malley, P. (2001) Discontinuity, government and risk. *Theoretical Criminology* 5: 137–55.

Pattison, S. (2000) *Shame: Theory, therapy, theology*. Cambridge University Press, Cambridge.

Petersen, K. (2004) The Sexual Zone between Childhood and the Age of Majority. Claims to Sexual Freedoms Versus Protectionist Policies. In B. Brooks-Gordon, L. Gelsthorpe, M. Johnson and A. Bainham (eds) *Sexuality Repositioned: Diversity and the Law*. Oxford, Portland, Oregon, 351–72.

Petrunik, M.G. (2002) Managing Unacceptable Risk: Sex Offenders, Community Response, and Social Policy in the United States and Canada. *International Journal of Offender Therapy and Comparative Criminology* 46: 483–511.

Pietz, C.A. and Mann, J.P. (1989) Importance of having a female co-therapist in child molesters group. *Professional Psychology: Research and Practice* 20: 265–8.

Piper, C. (2000) Historical constructions of childhood innocence: removing sexuality. In E. Heinze (eds) *Of Innocence and Autonomy*. Ashgate, Dartmouth, 26–46.

Pithers, W.D. (1990) Relapse Prevention with Sexual Aggressors: A Method for Maintaining Therapeutic Gain and Enhancing External Supervision. In W.L. Marshall, D.R. Laws and H.E. Barbaree (eds) *Handbook of Sexual Assault: Issues,*

Theories and Treatment of the Offender. Plenum Press, New York and London, 343–63.

Pithers, W.D. (1994) Process evaluation of a group therapy component designed to enhance sex offenders' empathy for sexual abuse survivors. *Behaviour Research and Therapy* 32: 565–70.

Player, E. (1992) Treatment for Sex Offenders: A Cautionary Note. *Prison Service Journal* 85: 2–9.

Plontikoff, J. and Woolfson, R. (2000) *Where Are They Now? An Evaluation of Sex Offender Registration in England and Wales*. Home Office, London.

Polaschek, D. and King, L.L. (2002) Rehabilitating Rapists: Reconsidering the Issues. *Australian Psychologist* 37: 215–21.

Postman, N. (1982) *The Disappearance of Childhood*. US Vintage.

Pratt, J. (2000a) Dangerousness and modern society. In M. Brown and J. Pratt (eds) *Dangerous Offenders: Punishment and Social Order*. Routledge, London.

Pratt, J. (2000b) Emotive and ostentatious punishment: its decline and resurgence in modern society. *Punishment and Society* 2: 417–39.

Pratt, J. (2000c) The Return of the Wheelbarrow Men: Or the Arrival of Postmodern Penality? *British Journal of Criminology* 40: 127–45.

Prentky, R. (1997) Arousal Reduction in Sexual Offenders: A Review of Antiandrogen Interventions. *Sexual Abuse: A Journal of Research and Treatment* 9: 335–47.

Prison Service (2000) *The SOTP Core Programme: 'CORE 2000' Treatment Manual*. HM Prison Service, London.

Probation Service (2001) *Community Sex Offender Groupwork Programme: Manual*. National Probation Service. Sex Offender Unit.

Quaker Peace and Social Witness (2003) Circles of Support and Accountability in the Thames Valley: Interim Report November 2003. Quaker Peace and Social Witness, London.

Radzinowicz, L. and Hood, R. (1981) Dangerousness and Criminal Justice: A Few Reflections. *The Criminal Law Review* 756–61.

Raynor, R. (2000) Community Penalties: Probation, Punishment and What Works. In M. Maguire, R. Morgan and R. Reiner (eds) *The Oxford Handbook of Criminology, Third Edition*, Oxford University Press, 1168–206

Reiner, R. (2002) Media Made Criminality: The Representation of Crime in the Mass Media. In M. Maguire, R. Morgan and R. Reiner (eds) *The Oxford Handbook of Criminology, Third Edition*. Oxford University Press, Oxford, 376–418

Renolds, E. (2005) *Girls, Boys and Junior Sexualities: exploring gender and sexual relations in the primary school*. Routledge Falmer, London.

Respond Organisation (2000) *Mens Group*. Accessed via World Wide Web, 13 July 2002. *www.respond.or.uk/business/mensgroup.html*.

Rex, S., Lieb, R., Bottoms, A. and Wilson, L. (2003) Accrediting Offender Programmes: A Process-based Evaluation of the Joint Prison/Probation Services Accreditation Panel. Home Office Research Study 273.

Richardson, G., Kelly, T.P., Bhate, S.R. and Graham, F. (1997) Group differences in abuser and abuse characteristics in a British sample of sexually abusive adolescents. *Sexual Abuse: A Journal of Research and Treatment* 9: 239–57.

Rogers, R. and Dickey, R. (1991) Denial and minimisation among sex offenders: A review of competing models of deception. *Annals of Sex Research* 4: 49–63.

Rose, N. (2000) Government and Control. *British Journal of Criminology* 40: 321–39.

Ross, R.R., Fabiana, E.A. and Ewles, C.D. (1988) Reasoning and Rehabilitation. *International Journal of Offender Therapy and Comparative Criminology* 32: 29–35.

Salter, A. (1988) *Treating child sexual offenders and victims: A practical guide*. Sage, London.

Sampson, A. (1994) *Acts of Abuse*. Routledge, London.

Sarbin (1967) The Dangerous Individual: An Outcome of Social Identity Transformations. *British Journal of Criminology* 285.

Sawle, G.A. and Kear-Cowell, J. (2001) Adult Attachment Style and Paedophilia: A Developmental Perspective. *International Journal of Offender Therapy and Comparative Criminology* 45: 32–50.

Scarce, M. (2001) *Male on Male Rape: The Hidden Toll of Stigma and Shame*. Insight Books, New York.

Schlank, A.M. and Shaw, T. (1996) Treating sexual offenders who deny their guilt: A pilot study. *Sexual Abuse* 8: 17–23.

Schlank, A.M. and Shaw, T. (1997) Treating sex offenders who deny – a review. In B.K. Schwartz and H.R. Cellini (eds) *The Sex Offender: New insights, treatment innovations and legal developments*. Vol. 2, Civic Research Institute, New York.

Schopf, S. (1995) 'Megans Law': Community Notification and Constitution. *Columbia Journal of Law and Social Problems* 29: 117–49.

Scully, D. (1990) *Understanding Sexual Violence: A Study of Convicted Rapists*. Routledge, New York, London.

Scully, D. and Morolla, J. (1984) Convicted rapists' vocabularies of motive: Excuses and justifications. *Social Problems* 31: 530–44.

Segal, Z.V. and Stermac, L.E. (1984) A measure of adult sexual offenders' attitudes towards women. *International Journal of Law and Psychiatry* 7: 437–40.

Seidman, B.T., Marshall, W.L., Hudson, S.M. and Robertson, P.J. (1994) An examination of intimacy and loneliness in sex offenders. *Journal of Interpersonal Violence* 9: 518–34.

Sex Offender Unit (2000) *Community-Sex Offender Groupwork Programme: Management Manual*. West Midlands Probation Service.

Silverman, J. and Wilson, D. (2002) *Innocence Betrayed: Paedophilia, the Media and Society*. Polity Press, Cambridge.

Simon, J. (1998) Managing the Monstrous: Sex Offenders and the New Penology. *Psychology, Public Policy and Law* 4: 452–67.

Simon, J. and Feeley, M. (1995) True Crime: The New Penology and Public Discourse on Crime. In T.G. Blomberg and S. Cohen (eds) *Essays in Honor of Sheldon L. Messinger*. Aldine de Gruyter Publishing, New York, 163–9.

Smallbone, S.W. and McCabe, B. (2003) Childhood Attachment, Childhood Sexual Abuse, and Onset Masturbation Among Adult Sexual Offenders. *Sexual Abuse: A Journal of Research and Treatment* 15: 1–9.

Smiljanich, K. and Briere, J. (1996) Self reported sexual interest in children: Sex differences and psychosocial correlates in a university sample. *Violence and Victims* 11: 39–50.

Soothill, K. and Walby, S. (1991) *Sex Crimes in the News*. Routledge, London.

Soothill, K., Francis, B. and Ackerley, E. (1998) Paedophilia and Paedophiles. *New Law Journal* June 12: 882–3.

Sparks, R. (2000) Risk and blame in criminal justice controversies: British press coverage and official discourse on prison security (1993–6). In M. Brown and J. Pratt (eds) *Dangerous Offenders: Punishment and Social Order*. Routledge, London.

Stevenson, H.C., Castillo, E. and Sefarbi, R. (1989) Treatment of denial in adolescent sex offenders and their families. *Journal of Offender Counselling, Services and Rehabilitation* 14: 37–50.

Swaffer, T., Hollin, C., Beech, A., Beckett, R. and Fisher, D. (2000) An exploration of child sexual abusers sexual fantasies before and after treatment. *Sexual Abuse: A Journal of Research and Treatment* 12: 61–8.

Sykes, C.M. and Matza, D. (1957) Techniques of Neutralisation: A Theory of Delinquency. *American Sociological Review* 22: 664–70.

Sykes, G. (1958) *The Society of Captives*. Princeton University Press, Princeton, New York.

Thomas, T. (2000) *Sex Crime: Sex Offending and Society*. Willan, Devon.

Thomas, T. (2003) Sex Offender Community Notification: Experiences from America. *The Howard Journal of Criminal Justice* 42: 217–28.

Thomas, T. (2004) Sex Offender Registers and Monitoring. In H. Kemshall and G. McIvor (eds) *Managing Sex Offender Risk*. Jessica Kingsley Publishers, London, 225–48.

Thornton, D. (2002) Constructing and Testing a Framework for Dynamic Risk Assessment. *Sexual Abuse: A Journal of Research and Treatment* 14: 139–53.

Tier, R. and Coy, K. (1997) Approaches to Sexual Predators: Community Notification and Civil Commitment. *New England Journal on Criminal and Civil Confinement* 23: 405–26.

Travers, O. (1998) Treatment v. Punishment: A Case for Treating Sex Offenders in the Community. *The Irish Journal of Psychology* 19: 226–33.

Vennard, J., Hedderman, C. and Sugg, D. (1997) *Changing Offenders' Attitudes and Behaviour: What Works?* Home Office Research Findings No. 61. Home Office, London.

Walby, S. and Allen, J. (2004) Domestic violence, sexual assault and stalking: Findings from the British Crime Survey. Home Officer Research, Development and Statistics Directorate, March.

Walker, N. (1987) The Unwanted Effects of Long-Term Imprisonment. In A.E. Bottoms and R. Light (eds) *Problems of Long-Term Imprisonment*. Gower, Aldershot.

Walkerdine, V. (1997) *Daddy's girl: young girls and popular culture*. Macmillan, Basingstoke.

Ward, T. (2000) Sexual Offenders' Cognitive Distortions as Implicit Theories. *Aggression and Violent Behaviour: A Review Journal* 5: 491–507.

Ward, T. (2002) Good Lives and the Rehabilitation of Offenders: Promises and Problems. *Aggression and Violent Behaviour* 7: 513–28.

Ward, T. and Hudson, S.M. (2000) A self-regulation model of relapse prevention. In D.R. Laws, S.M. Hudson and T. Ward (eds) *Remaking Relapse Prevention with Sex Offenders*. Sage, California.

Ward, T. and Keenan, T. (1999) Child Molesters' Implicit Theories. *Journal of Interpersonal Violence* 14: 821–38.

Ward, T., Hudson, S.M., Johnson, L. and Marshall, W.L. (1997a) Cognitive distortions in sex offenders: an integrative review. *Clinical Psychology Review* 17: 479–507.

Ward, T., Hudson, S.M. and McCormack, J. (1997b) Attachment Style, Intimacy Deficits, and Sexual Offending. In B.K. Schwartz and H.R. Cellini (eds) *The Sex Offender: New Insights, Treatment Innovations, and Legal Developments*, Volume II, Civic Research Institute, Kingston, NJ.

Webster, S.D. (2002) Assessing Victim Empathy in Sexual Offenders Using the Victim Empathy Letter Task. *Sexual Abuse: A Journal of Research and Treatment* 14: 281–300.

West, D. (2000a) Paedophilia: Plague or Panic? *The Journal of Forensic Psychiatry* 11: 511–31.

West, D. (2000b) The sex crime situation: Deterioration more apparent than real? *European Journal in Criminal Policy and Research* 8: 399–422.

Wilson, D. (2003) But When Does the Punishment End? The Released Offender in the Community. Paper presented at Kent Criminal Justice Centre, Gate Fever: Preparing for Release from Prison, Friday 12 September 2003, Kent University.

Wolf, S.C. (1984) A model of sexual aggression/addiction. *Journal of Social Work and Human Sexuality* 7: 131–48.

Wolf, S.C. (1988) Assessment and treatment of sex offenders in the community setting. In L.E. Walker *et al.* (eds) *Handbook on sexual abuse of children: Assessment and treatment issues.* Springer Publishing Co., New York, 365–83.

Wykes, M. (2002) *Evil beast meets dangerous stranger: mediating masculinities in news about violent crime.* Paper presented at British Society of Criminology Conference, Keele.

Yalom, I. (1975) *The Theory and Practice of Group Psychotherapy, Second Edition.* Basic Books, New York.

Young, J. (2001) Identity, Community and Social Exclusion. In R. Matthews and J. Pitts (eds) *Crime and Disorder and Community Safety: A New Agenda?* Routledge, London, 26–53.

Young, J. (2002) Crime and Social Exclusion. In M. Maguire, R. Morgan and R. Reiner (eds) *The Oxford Handbook of Criminology, Third Edition.* Oxford University Press, Oxford, 457–90.

Young, J. (2003) Winning the fight against crime? New Labour, populism and lost opportunities. In R. Matthews and J. Young (eds) *The new politics of crime and punishment.* Willan, Cullompton, Devon, 33–47.

Young, J. (2004) Crime and the Dialectics of Inclusion/Exclusion. *British Journal of Criminology* 44: 550–61.

Young, J. and Matthews, R. (2003) New Labour, Crime Control and Social Exclusion. In R. Matthews and J. Young (eds) *The new politics of crime and punishment.* Willan, Cullompton, Devon, 1–32.

Index